Evidence for transformative policymaking

Manchester University Press

Evidence for transformative policymaking

Statistics, microsimulation and public opinion to achieve change

COMMON SENSE
POLICY GROUP

Manchester University Press

Published by Manchester University Press
Oxford Road, Manchester, M13 9PL

www.manchesteruniversitypress.co.uk

British Library Cataloguing-in-Publication Data
A catalogue record for this book is available from the British Library

ISBN 978 1 8070 7512 5 paperback

First published 2027

EU authorised representative for GPSR:
Easy Access System Europe, Mustamäe tee 50, 10621 Tallinn, Estonia
gpsr.requests@easproject.com

Typeset
by Deanta Global Publishing Services, Chennai, India

Contents

Glossary

Absolute Income Hypothesis The theory that health outcomes are positively influenced by an individual's absolute level of income, showing a concave relationship where additional income has diminishing returns on health improvements.

Absolute Poverty A poverty measure based on a fixed income threshold, adjusted for inflation over time, rather than one that moves with median incomes in the current period.

Additional Rate The highest rate of income tax in the UK, currently 45 per cent, applied to income above £125,140 per year, targeting the wealthiest taxpayers.

Adversarial Co-Production A method adapted from adversarial collaboration in behavioural science, involving working with opponents of evidence-based policies to develop persuasive narratives and arguments for policy implementation.

Artifacts Self-contained pieces of content (code, documents, visualisations) created in computational environments like Jupyter notebooks that can be referenced, updated and shared throughout analysis work.

Atkinson Index An inequality measure that incorporates society's aversion to inequality, allowing the analyst to adjust the measure based on normative judgements about how much weight to give to inequality at different points in the distribution.

Austerity A set of economic policies aimed at reducing government budget deficits through spending cuts and/or tax increases, particularly prominent in the UK from 2010 onwards.

Average Marginal Component Effects (AMCEs) Statistical estimates from conjoint experiments that measure the average effect on choice probability when an attribute is at a specific level compared to a reference level, while averaging across all other attributes.

Average Tax Rate The proportion of total income paid in tax, calculated as total tax divided by total income, important for all-or-nothing decisions like choosing where to live.

Balanced Panel A longitudinal dataset where the same individuals have data recorded for all time periods (waves) being analysed, providing complete histories but potentially introducing selection bias.

Basic Income A largely unconditional, secure, regular payment to all permanent residents to support basic needs regardless of employment status or income, also known as Universal Basic Income.

Basic Rate The standard rate of income tax in the UK (currently 20 per cent) applied to taxable income between the personal allowance and the higher rate threshold.

Before Housing Costs An income measure that includes housing costs in disposable income, used alongside After Housing Costs measures in UK poverty statistics to reflect different perspectives on living standards.

Behavioural Insights Team Also known as the 'Nudge Unit', a UK government organisation established to apply behavioural economics principles to public policy, though evidence for its effectiveness has been questioned.

Benefit Cap A UK policy limiting the total amount of benefits working-age households can receive, with different caps for single people and couples/families, introduced in 2013.

Benefit Unit A single adult or adult couple, together with any dependent children, used as the assessment unit for means-tested benefits in the UK welfare system.

Between Component In a within-between statistical model, the coefficient representing the effect of an individual's average income compared to the population average, capturing permanent income differences and objective inequality.

Bootstrapping A statistical method for estimating uncertainty by repeatedly re-running calculations with slightly different sample datasets, useful when no simple formula exists for calculating confidence intervals.

Budget Constraint A graphical representation showing the relationship between gross income (before taxes) and net income (after taxes and benefits), illustrating the trade-offs individuals face when making economic decisions.

Caseload The number of people or households receiving a particular benefit, important for administrative planning but distinct from the total cost of the benefit programme.

Chain of Custody The documented sequence of processes from data collection to analysis to publication, ensuring all steps are verifiable, reproducible and transparently recorded.

Child Benefit A UK benefit paid per child to families, currently £24 per week for the first child and £15.90 for subsequent children, subject to means testing for very high earners.

Classification of Functions of Government (COFOG) The United Nations standard classification system for government spending, used to categorise public expenditure by function (health, education, defence, etc.).

Confidence Interval The range within which a parameter estimate would fall in 95 per cent of repeated samples from the same population, reflecting the uncertainty due to sampling variability.

Conjoint Analysis A survey-based technique for eliciting preferences by repeatedly asking respondents to choose between pairs of options that vary across multiple attributes, allowing estimation of the relative importance of different features.

Consumption The use of goods and services by households, sometimes preferred over income as a welfare measure as it may better reflect permanent income and living standards.

Corporation Tax A tax on company profits, the incidence of which may ultimately fall on workers through lower wages, shareholders through reduced dividends or on consumers through higher prices.

Cost-of-Living Crisis A period of rapidly rising prices for essential goods and services relative to income growth, particularly affecting low-income households, prominent in the UK from 2021 onwards.

Covariate A variable in a study that is neither the main independent variable nor the outcome, but may influence the results, such as age or gender in health studies.

Cross-Sectional Study An observational study where all variables are collected simultaneously at one point in time, comparing between people rather than tracking changes within individuals over time.

Dalton's Principle The principle that measures of poverty or inequality should never improve when money is transferred from a poorer person to a richer person (upward transfer).

Data Matching A statistical technique for combining information from different datasets by identifying similar records based on common characteristics, used when direct linkage is not possible.

Data Wrangling The process of cleaning, transforming and preparing raw data for analysis, including tasks like renaming variables, handling missing values and reshaping datasets.

Decile One-tenth of a population when ranked by a particular variable (typically income), with the first decile representing the poorest 10 per cent and the tenth decile the richest 10 per cent.

Deep Poverty Poverty significantly below the standard poverty line, often measured as income below 40 per cent or 50 per cent of median income, indicating severe material deprivation.

Dependent Variable The outcome variable in a study that researchers hypothesise is influenced by independent variables, what is being explained or predicted.

Deservingness Heuristic The tendency for people to want to see welfare resources restricted to recipients they perceive as deserving, based on criteria such as need, control over circumstances or contribution to society.

Descriptive Statistics Summary measures that describe the basic features of data, including means, medians, standard deviations and frequency distributions.

Destitution An extreme form of poverty where individuals lack basic necessities for survival, such as adequate food, heating or shelter, often measured by inability to afford essentials rather than just low income.

Differential Weighting The use of different grossing factors for different population subgroups to correct for response bias in survey data, ensuring the weighted sample matches known population totals.

Directed Acyclic Graph (DAG) A diagram using boxes and arrows to represent hypothesised causal relationships between variables, with arrows showing the direction of influence, used to clarify assumptions in observational studies.

Disregard In means-tested benefits, an amount of income that is ignored when calculating benefit entitlement, allowing recipients to keep some earnings without full benefit withdrawal.

Distributional Analysis The assessment of how policy changes affect different groups in the population, typically examining impacts across income deciles or by demographic characteristics.

Dynamic Modelling Microsimulation that allows for behavioural changes in response to policy reforms, such as changes in labour supply or consumption patterns, as opposed to static modelling.

Effect Modifier A variable that changes the strength or direction of the relationship between an independent and dependent variable, also known as a moderator (e.g. sex modifying the effect of income on health).

Employment and Support Allowance (ESA) A UK benefit for people unable to work due to illness or disability, being gradually replaced by the limited capability for work element of Universal Credit.

Engel Curve A graphical relationship showing how household expenditure on a particular good varies with total household expenditure or income, originally studied by Ernst Engel in the nineteenth century.

Equivalence Scale A scale that adjusts household income to account for different household sizes and compositions, recognising that larger households may be more efficient than smaller ones.

Equivalised Income Household income divided by an equivalence scale to produce a measure of average wellbeing per household member, accounting for economies of scale and different needs.

Estimator A value calculated from sample data (typically denoted with Latin letters) used to estimate an unknown population parameter (typically denoted with Greek letters).

Evidence-Based Policy (EBP) Policy decisions grounded in rigorous research and empirical evidence rather than ideology, intuition or political expediency alone.

Experimental Study A study where researchers manipulate at least one independent variable (through random assignment) to establish causal effects on dependent variables.

Family Resources Survey (FRS) A large annual UK survey providing detailed information about the incomes and living circumstances of households, used as the primary dataset for many tax-benefit microsimulation models.

Financial Distress A state of economic hardship characterised by a difficulty in meeting basic expenses, lack of uncommitted income and vulnerability to financial shocks.

Fiscal Neutrality A policy design principle suggesting that, unless there are clear arguments otherwise, the fiscal system should alter economic behaviour as little as possible, or that revenue changes should be balanced by spending changes.

Fixed Effects Model A statistical model that controls for all time-invariant characteristics of individuals by examining only within-person changes, eliminating bias from unobserved heterogeneity.

Formal Incidence The first-round effect of a tax or benefit change on those directly affected, before considering behavioural responses or pass-through effects to others.

Foster–Greer–Thorbecke Measure A sophisticated poverty measure, also known as the Poverty Severity Index, that squares proportional poverty gaps before summing them, giving more weight to the very poor and satisfying Dalton's Principle.

Fuel Poverty A condition where households cannot afford to adequately heat their homes, often defined in terms of needing to spend a high proportion of income on energy or being unable to maintain adequate temperatures.

Generalised Anxiety Disorder-7 (GAD-7) A seven-item questionnaire used to screen for and measure the severity of generalised anxiety disorder, commonly used in population health research.

Gini Coefficient A widely used measure of inequality ranging from 0 (perfect equality) to 1 (perfect inequality), calculated as the area between the Lorenz curve and the line of perfect equality.

Gross Income Total income before taxes and other deductions are applied, including earnings, benefits, pensions and investment income.

Grossing Factor The multiplier applied to sample data to estimate population totals, typically the inverse of the sample frequency, adjusted for differential response bias.

Grossing Up The process of multiplying sample survey data by appropriate weights to produce estimates for the entire population.

Headcount Poverty Measure The simplest poverty measure, counting the number or proportion of people with incomes below a defined poverty line.

Higher Rate The UK income tax rate (currently 40 per cent) applied to taxable income between the higher rate threshold (£50,270) and the additional rate threshold (£125,140).

Household One person living alone or a group of people (not necessarily related) living at the same address who share cooking facilities and common living areas.

Household Representative Person (HRP) The person with the highest income in a household, or the eldest if there is no non-benefit income, used as a reference point in household analysis.

Households Below Average Income (HBAI) The UK's official poverty measure, defined as 60 per cent of median equivalised household income, available in both Before Housing Costs and After Housing Costs versions.

Housing Benefit A means-tested UK benefit to help with rent costs, being gradually replaced by the housing element of Universal Credit.

Inter-Governmental Tax-Benefit Microsimulation Model (IGOTM) HM Treasury's microsimulation model for analysing distributional impacts of tax and welfare policies, implemented in SAS.

Imputation The process of estimating or assigning values for missing data, such as imputing wealth data onto the FRS from the Wealth and Assets Survey.

Income Effect In labour supply analysis, the effect whereby higher wages increase income, potentially allowing people to work less while maintaining their standard of living.

Income Inequality Hypothesis The theory that income inequalities affect the health and wellbeing of nearly all members of a society, not just those at the bottom of the distribution.

Income Support A legacy UK benefit providing a minimum income for those not required to seek work, now largely replaced by Universal Credit.

Independent Variable A variable manipulated or controlled in an experimental study to test its effect on dependent variables, or a predictor variable in observational studies.

Inferential Statistics Statistical methods for drawing conclusions about populations from sample data, including hypothesis testing and parameter estimation with confidence intervals.

Instrumental Variable A variable that has a strong causal effect on an independent variable of interest without fully determining it, used in quasi-experimental studies to make causal inferences.

In-Work Benefit A benefit designed to boost incomes of people who work at least a certain number of hours but have low earnings, such as Working Tax Credit or the working element of Universal Credit.

Jobseeker's Allowance (JSA) A UK benefit for people who are unemployed and actively seeking work, gradually being replaced by Universal Credit, with conditionality requiring job search activities.

Jupyter Notebook An open-source web application that allows creation and sharing of documents containing live code, equations, visualisations and narrative text, commonly used for data science and statistical analysis.

Labour Supply The amount of work (usually measured in hours) that individuals are willing and able to provide at different wage rates, influenced by the tax and benefit system.

Legacy Benefits The six pre-Universal Credit means-tested benefits and Tax Credits being gradually replaced: Working Tax Credit, Child Tax Credit, Income Support, income-based JSA, income-based ESA and Housing Benefit.

Left-Behind Communities Areas that have experienced long-term economic decline, typically former industrial regions with high unemployment, low investment and poor social outcomes.

Levelling Up A UK government policy agenda (2019–24) aimed at reducing regional inequalities by improving infrastructure, economic opportunities and living standards in less prosperous areas.

Living Costs and Food Survey (LCFS) A UK household survey concentrating on recording household expenditure, used to model indirect taxes and provide weights for inflation measures.

Longitudinal Study A study that measures the same individuals at multiple points in time, allowing analysis of how changes in one variable relate to changes in another within individuals.

Lorenz Curve A graphical representation of income or wealth distribution, plotting cumulative population share against cumulative income share, used to visualise inequality.

MacArthur Ladder A measure of subjective socioeconomic status where respondents place themselves on a ten-rung ladder representing their perceived position in society, capturing subjective inequality beyond objective income measures.

Marginal Effective Tax Rate (METR) The rate at which an individual's net income changes when they earn an additional £1, combining effects of tax increases and benefit withdrawals from multiple sources.

Marginal Tax Rate The rate of tax paid on the next £1 earned, the key measure for understanding how taxes distort economic decisions at the margin.

Means Testing The practice of restricting benefit eligibility or payment levels based on the income or wealth of recipients, typically withdrawing benefits as income rises.

Median The middle value in a distribution when all values are arranged in order, such that half the population has values above it and half below, less sensitive to extreme values than the mean.

Mediating Variable A variable that lies on the causal pathway between a predictor and an outcome, helping to explain the mechanism through which the predictor affects the outcome.

Microsimulation A method of simulating policy impacts using individual-level datasets combined with computer programs to perform large numbers of calculations, enabling analysis of distributional effects and costs.

Minimum Income Guarantee A benefit system that tops up household income to a specified minimum level, with benefits withdrawn pound-for-pound as income rises, also called a minimum income benefit.

Minimum Income Standard (MIS) The income needed by different household types to reach a socially acceptable living standard, determined through public consultation and expert input.

Modified OECD Scale A standard equivalence scale giving a weight of 1.0 to the first adult, 0.5 to additional adults, and 0.3 to each child aged thirteen or under.

Moderator Variable A variable that affects the strength or direction of the relationship between an independent and dependent variable, also known as an effect modifier.

Modular A design principle for code or analysis where different sections can operate independently after running a common setup ('head'), improving reproducibility and ease of modification.

Narratives Structured stories used in policy communication that include a protagonist, antagonist, description of context and interests, and culturally particular examples to persuade audiences.

National Insurance Contributions (NICs) UK payroll taxes paid by employees and employers (and self-employed individuals) on earned income, nominally funding State Pensions and other contributory benefits.

National Living Wage The UK statutory minimum wage for workers aged twenty-one and over (previously twenty-five and over), higher than the National Minimum Wage for younger workers, introduced in 2016.

Neoliberalism An economic and political ideology emphasising free markets, reduced government intervention, deregulation and privatisation, dominant in UK policy from the 1980s onwards.

Net Income Income after taxes have been deducted and benefits added, representing the actual resources available for household consumption.

Non-Take-Up The phenomenon where eligible individuals or households do not claim benefits they are entitled to, often due to stigma, complexity or low value relative to claiming costs.

Nudging A behavioural economics approach that uses subtle environmental cues to influence people's choices without restricting options or significantly changing economic incentives.

Null Hypothesis The default assumption in statistical testing that there is no relationship or effect, which is either rejected or not rejected based on the data.

Observational Study A study containing only measured variables where the researcher observes existing phenomena without manipulation, able to establish associations but not definitively prove causation.

Outcome Variable The variable a researcher hypothesises will be influenced by predictors or independent variables – what the study aims to explain.

Overton Window The range of policies deemed acceptable or feasible to the public at a given time, often used to describe constraints on policy proposals.

p-Value The probability of observing data as extreme as that found, assuming the null hypothesis is true, not the probability that the null hypothesis is true.

Palma Index An inequality measure calculated as the ratio of the income share of the richest 10 per cent to the poorest 40 per cent, offering a simple interpretation but violating Dalton's Principle.

Panel Data Longitudinal data following the same individuals over time, allowing analysis of within-person changes while controlling for time-invariant individual characteristics.

Parameter An underlying value that controls a phenomenon being studied, typically unknown and represented by Greek letters, which researchers attempt to estimate from data.

PASOKification The electoral decline of social democratic parties that fail to offer transformative policies, named after the collapse of Greece's PASOK party, describing a hypothetical downward spiral.

Pension Credit The main means-tested benefit for UK pensioners over State Pension age, comprising a Guarantee Credit (minimum income) and Savings Credit component.

Permacrisis A term describing the extended period of instability and crisis across multiple domains (economic, health, environmental) characterising the 2020s.

Personal Allowance The amount of income an individual can receive before paying income tax, currently £12,570 per year in the UK (though being gradually withdrawn for very high earners).

Patient Health Questionnaire-8 (PHQ-8) An eight-item questionnaire used to screen for and measure the severity of depression, commonly used in population health research.

Policy Entrepreneur An individual or organisation that actively promotes policy ideas, developing both evidence and persuasive narratives to shift the policy agenda and move ideas 'lying around' into implementation.

Poverty Gap A poverty measure summing how far below the poverty line each poor person falls, representing the minimum amount needed to eliminate poverty with perfect targeting.

Poverty Trap A situation where individuals face very high marginal effective tax rates (sometimes exceeding 100 per cent), meaning that earning more money leaves them little or no better off, discouraging work.

Predictor Variable A variable hypothesised to influence an outcome in observational studies, corresponding to independent variables in experimental research.

Progressive Taxation System A tax system where the average tax rate rises with income, so higher earners pay a larger proportion of their income in tax than lower earners.

Public Expenditure Statistical Analyses (PESA) HM Treasury's annual publication providing detailed breakdowns of UK government spending by function and country, used in distributional analysis of public services.

Public Policy Preference Calculator (TriplePC) An integrated microsimulation model combining economic impacts, health outcomes and public preferences to assess policy options, developed by the Common Sense Policy Group.

Quality-Adjusted Life Years (QALYs) A standardised measure combining quantity and quality of life, where one QALY represents one year in perfect health, used in health economics to compare interventions.

Quasi-Experimental Study A study where an independent variable varies in a way that resembles random assignment but was not actually manipulated by the researcher, falling between observational and experimental designs.

Random Assignment The process of randomly allocating participants to different experimental conditions, ensuring groups differ only by chance and enabling causal inference.

Randomised Control Trial (RCT) An experimental study using random assignment to determine which participants receive different interventions, considered the gold standard for establishing causality.

Rational Choice A paradigm assuming actors develop preferences by evaluating arguments according to the quality of evidence presented, contrasted with narrative-based persuasion.

Red Wall Constituencies Traditionally Labour-voting constituencies in the North of England, Midlands and Wales that shifted to Conservative in the 2019 UK election, characterised by post-industrial decline and concerns about 'being left behind'.

Regressive Describing a tax or policy where the burden falls more heavily (as a proportion of income) on poorer households than richer ones, increasing inequality.

Relative Poverty A poverty measure defined relative to contemporary living standards, such as the UK's 60 per cent of median income, which moves up or down as median incomes change.

Replacement Rate The ratio between net income when working (typically at forty hours per week) and net income when not working, intended to measure work incentives.

Reproducibility The principle that scientific work should be completely transparent and repeatable by other researchers, requiring detailed documentation of methods, data and analysis code.

Repository A website (like GitHub or OSF) where researchers store and share raw data, code and documentation to enable reproducibility and verification of their work.

Response Bias Systematic differences between survey respondents and non-respondents, requiring correction through differential weighting to ensure the sample represents the population.

ROSSI Index A measure of inflation used for uprating some benefits, based on the Retail Prices Index but calculated differently.

Sample Frame The complete list of all units (households, addresses, etc.) from which a sample is drawn, such as all UK addresses for household surveys.

Sample Frequency The proportion of the population included in a sample, such as one in five thousand households, inversely related to the grossing factor.

Sampling Variability The random variation in estimates that occurs because only a sample rather than the entire population is observed, a main source of uncertainty in parameter estimates.

Scotben An open-source microsimulation model of Scotland's tax and benefit system written in Julia, adapted to create Great Britain-wide models.

Short Form 12 (SF-12) A widely used twelve-item survey assessing health-related quality of life, generating Physical Component Summary (PCS-12) and Mental Component Summary (MCS-12) scores.

SF-6D A preference-based health measure derived from SF-12 (or SF-36) that produces utility values for calculating QALYs, developed for economic evaluation in healthcare.

Social Determinants of Health The economic and social conditions that influence individual and population health, including income, education, employment, housing and social support.

Standard Deviation A measure of variability showing how much individual values typically differ from the mean, with about 68 per cent of values falling within one standard deviation of the mean in normal distributions.

Standard Error A measure of uncertainty in a parameter estimate, representing the average degree by which the estimate is likely to differ from the true population value.

State Pension The UK's main non-means-tested benefit for people over State Pension age (currently sixty-six), based on National Insurance contribution records, with different rates for pre-2016 and post-2016 retirees.

Static Microsimulation Tax-benefit modelling that assumes no behavioural responses to policy changes, calculating first-round effects on incomes and revenues without considering induced changes in behaviour.

Statistical Model A set of assumptions about the data-generating process in a population, used to estimate parameters and make inferences from sample data.

Statistical Power The ability to detect true effects or differences between groups, which increases with sample size but at a diminishing rate.

Statistical Significance When a statistical test suggests the probability of observing results as extreme as those found, assuming the null hypothesis is true, falls below a critical threshold (typically 5 per cent).

Stratified Sampling A sampling method where the population is divided into subgroups (strata) and samples are drawn from each, often more efficient than simple random sampling.

Subjective Social Status An individual's perception of their position in the social hierarchy, often measured using the MacArthur ladder, which may differ from objective socioeconomic indicators.

Substitution Effect In labour supply analysis, the effect whereby higher wages make leisure more expensive, encouraging people to work more to maximise income.

Taper Rate The rate at which a means-tested benefit is withdrawn as earnings increase, such as the 55 per cent taper rate for Universal Credit, functioning as an effective marginal tax rate.

Tax-Benefit Model A microsimulation model that calculates the impact of tax and welfare policies on individuals and households, requiring survey data, calculation algorithms, policy parameters and results presentation.

Tax Credit The cash value of a tax allowance, calculated as the allowance multiplied by the marginal tax rate, representing the amount an individual benefits from not paying tax on that portion of income.

Tax-Transfer Model (TTM) Microsimulation model for analysing distributional impacts of tax and welfare reforms, an example of which is the Landman TTM for the UK, which was originally developed in 2009.

Taxable Income Total income minus the personal allowance and other deductions, the amount on which income tax is actually charged.

Theil Index An inequality measure that can be decomposed to show contributions from different groups (e.g. regions) to overall inequality, distinguishing between-group and within-group components.

Trickle-Down Economics The theory that reducing taxes on the wealthy stimulates economic activity that incrementally benefits all strata of society, dominant in UK policy since the 1980s.

Triple Lock A UK policy guaranteeing the State Pension rises each year by the highest of earnings growth, price inflation (CPI), or 2.5 per cent, ensuring real-terms increases.

Two-Child Limit A UK policy restricting the child element of Universal Credit and Child Tax Credit to a maximum of two children born after April 2017, with some exceptions.

Unbalanced Panel A longitudinal dataset where individuals have data for different numbers of time periods, including all with at least two observations, larger but potentially less comparable than balanced panels.

Understanding Society Household Longitudinal Study (UKHLS) The UK Household Longitudinal Study, a panel survey tracking approximately forty thousand households annually to provide data on socioeconomic, demographic and health outcomes over time.

Universal Basic Income See Basic Income – a largely unconditional, regular payment to all permanent residents regardless of employment status or income.

Universal Credit The UK's main means-tested benefit for working-age people, gradually replacing six legacy benefits and Tax Credits with a single monthly payment, featuring a taper rate and work allowances.

Uprating The process of adjusting historical income, rent or consumption data forward to current prices and wage levels to account for inflation and economic growth.

Value Added Tax (VAT) A consumption tax levied on most goods and services in the UK at a standard rate of 20 per cent, with various exemptions and zero-rated categories including most food and children's clothing.

Wealth and Assets Survey (WAS) A UK survey containing detailed information on household wealth, including the value of property, pension funds, savings and other assets.

Wealth Tax A tax on the value of assets owned (property, investments, savings), proposed as a progressive funding mechanism, with various design challenges around valuation and payment timing.

Willingness to Pay In health economics, the monetary value society places on a QALY or other health outcome, used to assess whether interventions represent good value for money.

Within Component In a within-between statistical model, the coefficient representing the effect of deviations in an individual's income from their own average over time, capturing temporary income shocks.

Within-Between Model A statistical model that simultaneously estimates effects of individual-level changes over time (within) and differences between individuals' averages (between), combining strengths of fixed and random effects models.

Work Allowance In Universal Credit, the amount of earnings a claimant can receive before the taper rate begins reducing their benefit, higher for those with housing costs or limited capability for work.

Working Tax Credit A now-legacy UK in-work benefit for low-income working households, gradually being replaced by Universal Credit, featuring means testing and taper rates.

Years of Life Gained A measure of mortality impact calculated by estimating increases in life expectancy resulting from an intervention, derived from QALY gains using age- and sex-specific multipliers.

Figures and tables

Figures

Tables

Authors

All authors are drawn from within the Common Sense Policy Group, Northumbria University.
http://commonsensepolicygroup.com/
https://www.northumbria.ac.uk/

The Common Sense Policy Group comprises academics, policymakers, third sector leaders, community representatives, media figures and people with lived experience. We are all committed to creating a fair, equal and inclusive Britain through developing and influencing redistributive policy that addresses the inequality and exclusion that has come to define our nation. We present consensus on feasible, affordable and overwhelmingly popular evidence-based policies that can form the basis for a programme for progressive Government.

The author group for this book is as follows:

Elliott Johnson, Professor of Public Policy (elliott.johnson@northumbria.ac.uk)
https://www.northumbria.ac.uk/about-us/our-staff/j/elliott-johnson/

Graham Stark, Senior Research Fellow in Public Policy (graham.stark@northumbria.ac.uk)
https://www.northumbria.ac.uk/about-us/our-staff/s/graham-stark/

Howard Reed, Professor (Practice) in Public Policy (howard.reed@northumbria.ac.uk)
https://www.northumbria.ac.uk/about-us/our-staff/r/howard-reed/

Anna Thew, Senior Research Fellow in Public Policy (anna.thew@northumbria.ac.uk)
https://www.northumbria.ac.uk/about-us/our-staff/t/anna-thew/

Daniel Nettle, Professor in Community Wellbeing (daniel.nettle@northum bria.ac.uk)
https://www.northumbria.ac.uk/about-us/our-staff/n/daniel-nettle/

Matthew Johnson, Professor of Public Policy (matthew.johnson@northum bria.ac.uk)
https://www.northumbria.ac.uk/about-us/our-staff/j/matthew-johnson/

Suggested citation

Common Sense Policy Group (2026) *Evidence for Transformative Policymaking: Statistics, Microsimulation and Public Opinion to Achieve Change*, Manchester: Manchester University Press. DOI: https://doi.org/10.7765/9781807075132

Permissions

Material within this book has been reproduced with the permission of copyright holders from the following publications:

Common Sense Policy Group (2024) *Spend to Save Britain: A Common Sense Approach to the Budget.* Newcastle: Northumbria University. https://doi.org/10.17605/OSF.IO/3N524. Creative Commons Attribution 4.0 License.

Johnson, E. A., Hardill, I., Johnson, M. T. & Nettle, D. (2023) 'Breaking the Overton Window: On the Need for Adversarial Co-Production', *Evidence & Policy*, 20(3): 393–405. https://doi.org/10.1332/17442648Y2023D000000005. Licence date: 18 August 2025; PLSclear Ref No: 108734.

Johnson, M. T., Johnson, E. A., Reed, H. & Nettle, D. (2022) 'Can the "Downward Spiral" of Material Conditions, Mental Health and Faith in Government be Stopped? Evidence from Surveys in "Red Wall" Constituencies', *British Journal of Politics & International Relations*, 26(1): 131–148. https://doi.org/10.1177/13691481221146886. Creative Commons Attribution 4.0 License.

Nettle, D. (2026) *From Questions to Knowledge* (online), https://daniel-nettle-from-questions-to-knowledge.share.connect.posit.cloud/. Creative Commons Attribution 4.0 License.

Nettle, D., Chrisp, J., Johnson, E. A. & Johnson, M. T. (2025) 'What do British People Want from a Welfare System? Conjoint Survey Evidence on Generosity, Conditionality, Funding, and Outcomes', *Poverty and Public Policy*, 17(2): e70018. https://doi.org/10.1002/pop4.70018. Creative Commons Attribution 4.0 License.

Reed, H., Johnson, E. A., Stark, G., Nettle, D., Pickett, K. E. & Johnson, M. T. (2024) 'Estimating the Effects of Basic Income Schemes on Mental and Physical Health among Adults Aged 18 and Above in the UK: A

Microsimulation Study', *PLOS Ment Health*, 1(7): e0000206. https://doi.org/10.1371/journal.pmen.0000206. Creative Commons Attribution 4.0 License.

Reed, H., Johnson, M. T., Lansley, S., Johnson, E. A., Stark, G. & Pickett, K. E. (2023) 'Universal Basic Income Is Affordable and Feasible: Evidence from UK Economic Microsimulation Modelling', *Journal of Poverty and Social Justice*, 31(1): 146–162. https://doi.org/10.1332/175982721X16702368352393. Licence date: 11 November 2025; PLSclear Ref No: 108735.

Stark, G., Johnson, E. A., Reed, H., Nettle, D. & Johnson, M. T. (2024 in press) 'The Public Policy Preference Calculator (TriplePC): Developing a Comprehensive Welfare Policy Microsimulation', *International Journal of Microsimulation*. Creative Commons Attribution 4.0 License.

1

Introduction

1.1 The challenge

How do we 'fix' societies such as Britain? This is the question of our age and the topic of this book and associated coding resources. Answering this question often seems impossible. Age-old assumptions that hard work leads to property ownership, stable family relationships and success can no longer be relied upon. British public services are poorly resourced compared to other countries and our infrastructure is either a collection of white elephants – megaprojects scaled back to the point of irrelevance (*The Guardian*, 2023) – or failing private provision of essential goods (*Financial Times*, 2024). The central facet of this challenge is the capacity of the state to secure tax yields large enough to fund large-scale reform and then to spend that money in a way that makes an immediate difference to people's lives.

We have to understand that our broken country still remains in better shape than it was at the end of the Second World War, when the modern UK welfare state began. The Labour Government that charted a path through that era of crisis used public investment on a grand scale to re-secure British society, informed significantly by Lord Beveridge's plan (Hardill, Johnson and Johnson, 2025). If it could do it then, it can do it again now. We need that scale of public investment urgently. Our assets have been stripped and communities destroyed as if by war. But our public debt is 40 per cent of what it was in 1945, so there is no reason why fiscal reform and, say, a National Investment Bank cannot once again take bold action. As in 1945, there are no cheap means of resolving crisis.

The NHS – the UK's most expensive public health policy, introduced at Britain's lowest ebb – is a key example of how properly funded universal services transform lives. Having the doctor's bill taken away permanently was a psychological change perhaps unprecedented in human history. Likewise, having a reliable, affordable and integrated public transport system would transform how people move and improve productivity – a business-friendly end to which the government is already committed.

As the Common Sense Policy Group, we have presented a Beveridge-style programme for renewing the UK's social provision in *Act Now: A Vision for a Better Future and a New Social Contract* (Common Sense Policy Group, 2024a). This presents a whole-of-government approach to rebuilding Britain. HM Treasury is integral to this plan, tasked with improving health, education, employment and myriad other outcomes by financing radical reform to social security policy via the introduction of Basic Income – a largely unconditional payment to all citizens that is progressively recouped via higher tax yields on wealthier residents – along with various other reforms across the key areas of domestic policy.

There is *prima facie* reason to believe that a progressive package of tax-benefit policy would change individual behaviour and rebuild society by increasing the quantity, security and predictability of resources (Howard *et al.*, 2024; Common Sense Policy Group, 2025a). But there are serious economic questions that can only be answered through much more detailed analysis:

- What is the cost of introducing potentially transformative policies?
- What is the potential tax yield from reforms that may trigger various attempts at avoidance?
- What are the impacts of reforms on productivity and growth that might reduce or increase yields or needs for further investment?

Often, however, these questions produce answers that then lead to further political questions:

- Even if a policy is economically affordable and beneficial, what does the public think about it?
- Can a specific political party implement the policy without suffering grave electoral consequences?

It is these questions that often occupy policymakers to distraction. Many are the potentially sound economic policies that have been rejected out of hand by politicians who are either ideologically opposed or believe that they will suffer politically from their implementation.

It is because of this that any coherent training in economic policy necessarily requires core concern for public opinion both as it stands and how it might stand through interventions in public discourse. This latter point is important insofar as there is often an assumption, that lacks any coherent evidence, that the public's position on policy is fixed and value-based. Any number of recent political events demonstrate that the opposite is true: a large proportion of people are liable to change their positions on policy in response to argument. Brexit very quickly went from an outlying position to a position supported by a majority of voters as Britain's economic climate declined and migration increased. The notion that it is impossible to persuade the public to support policies that actually improve their lives is bizarre and highly ideological.

1.2 What policymaking needs innovation

Understanding of this is uneven in books and textbook-like material. Policymaking is the process through which governments are seen to identify problems, develop solutions and implement decisions that affect society. Howlett, Ramesh and Perl (2009) describe it as a complex activity involving multiple actors, institutions and stages that transform societal concerns into authoritative government action. Traditional textbooks on policy analysis often employ a cyclical framework dividing policymaking into distinct stages. Dunn (2018) identifies these as the following: agenda setting (recognising problems requiring government attention), policy formulation (developing alternative solutions), decision making (selecting preferred options), implementation (putting policies into practice) and evaluation (assessing outcomes and effectiveness) (Sabatier and Jenkins-Smith, 1993). Classical models assume policymakers conduct comprehensive rational analysis, systematically comparing all alternatives against clear objectives (Weimer and Vining, 2017). Indeed, contemporary coverage often emphasises the importance of evidence-based policymaking and rigorous evaluation of policy options. Bardach and Patashnik (2019) provide practical frameworks for policy analysis, including problem definition, criteria specification, alternative generation and outcome projection. For our purposes, and in the present context, these accounts need to be treated with caution.

Some accounts stress contextual constraints on policymaking rationality. Simon's (1957) concept of bounded rationality – cited extensively by Cairney (2020) – recognises that cognitive limitations, time pressures and incomplete information force policymakers to 'satisfice' rather than optimise. This seems justified, given that policymaking involves diverse participants working under increasing pressure. Hill and Hupe (2014) emphasise that bureaucrats, elected officials, interest groups, think tanks, media and citizens all shape policy outcomes through various mechanisms. However, Cairney (2016) cautions that evidence competes with ideology, interests and institutional factors in shaping decisions. This explains why some issues reach government agendas while others languish despite apparent urgency.

The advocacy coalition framework developed by Sabatier and Weible (2014) suggests that coalitions of actors sharing core beliefs compete over extended periods to influence policy subsystems. Institutional structures profoundly constrain and enable policy choices. Peters (2019) demonstrates how constitutional arrangements, legislative procedures and administrative traditions create path dependencies that make certain policies easier or harder to adopt. It is in this context that Lindblom's (1959) policymaking as 'muddling through' has some credence, highlighting preferences for incremental adjustments to existing policies rather than rational comprehensive planning. This incrementalism reflects political constraints and risk aversion, creating socially critical inequalities and preventing necessary reforms (Smith and Larimer, 2017).

This is an existential challenge for progressive policymakers insofar as their inability or refusal to make transformative change renders them hapless – the most damning characteristic any elected official can hold. This is particularly true given mounting challenges of mitigating poverty, inequality and insecurity within an international context of constraints on national autonomy, ineffectiveness of conventional solutions, polarisation impeding compromise and rapid technological change outpacing regulatory capacity (Head and Alford, 2015). We believe that these developments demand adaptive and enhanced evidence-based approaches focused on a relatively narrow set of policymaking tools (cf. Howlett, 2011) – tax-benefit policy – and narrative devices to advance change. This position aligns somewhat with Kingdon's (2011) multiple streams framework, where problems, policies and politics flow independently until critical moments – 'policy windows' – allow entrepreneurs to couple these streams and drive change.

We are in such a period, and progressive policymakers are the only ones capable of dealing structurally with the crises that have been exacerbated by successive regressive responses that render any notion of rational policy analysis and evaluation (Vedung, 2017) moribund.

1.3 A common sense need for critical interdisciplinarity

This book is an attempt to enable colleagues with some knowledge of using data in policy research to develop the data science and data management capacities to begin to develop evidence bases for policies. In this regard, the evidence base that matters is a comprehensive one encompassing the cost, impact and returns on investment from policies as well as assessment of, and means of engaging with, public opinion. The evidence such work produces necessarily includes strictly quantitative as well as forms of qualitative data.

The skills required to develop, curate and present those data may seem unhelpfully diffuse. However, this perception may often be due to the way in which data are treated paradigmatically and, in effect, ideologically. There is often hysterical dismissal of the value of forms of data on the basis of beliefs surrounding, for example, a) the importance of not treating humans as animals, meaning that quantitative approaches aligned with positivism are viewed as bad because they assume that people have limited agency and are constrained by external stimuli; or b) the need to reject people's qualitative articulation of ideas on the basis that they have limited correspondence to an objective reality independent of participants' consciousness (Johnson, 2013, pp. 13–41).

We reject such hysteria. We are, in essence, positivists. We believe that humans are animals and are subject to external stimuli and that the purpose of policy is to shape those stimuli to produce better outcomes that matter to humans, including health, wellbeing, relationships and learning (Degerman *et al.*, 2024). There is a clear evidence base to suggest that achieving such outcomes requires a commitment to increasing the quantity, security and predictability of resources and that this is best achieved by the production of more equal societies (Common Sense Policy Group, 2025a). Unequal societies are always insecure, regardless of any increase in net resources overall. This is because competition between individuals and groups becomes more existential – those with fewer resources have to engage in zero-sum competition with those around them, and the wealthy become acutely aware of the precarity of their position and engage directly in political processes and movements to protect their domination.

If you believe that humans are not subject to basic laws of nature, that everything is socially constructed and that there is no such thing as an objective reality, we encourage you to conduct a basic six thousand to eight thousand-word autoethnographic study on the effects of your not drinking for a month and reporting back 'rich textual analysis' of the experience. We look forward to reading your description of the meaning of dehydration and its entirely non-causal consequences for health. The fact that there is such a deficit in quantitative skills within social science is both a cause and consequence of the domination of these views which only appear even vaguely sensible within the narrowest social contexts of social science, arts and humanities departments. Colleagues seeking funding for quantitative studies often run aground on referee demands for qualitative elements that add nothing of actual value, but which are seen as essential cultural commitments.

This is not to say that qualitative research does not have value in a policy-making context. It clearly does. It is just that qualitative research unhinged from any concern for the broader reality within which we exist is basically unhelpful and often very harmful. One of the reasons for the ineffectiveness of the Keir Starmer-led Government has been its deference to focus groups and other quasi-ethnographic forms of research that take people's positions at face value and as having a fixed and abstract content independent of broader underpinning concerns. Focus groups that are configured in such a way as to give loud-mouthed participants the capacity to dominate discussion necessarily produce outlying positions that are adopted at government's peril. Ethnographic studies of people's positions on immigration that conclude that working-class people are basically racist, independently of concern for the resource-based pressures imposed on their communities over the past four decades, necessarily lead to bizarre and ineffectual identity-based responses – more flag waving and no attempts at addressing people's broader concerns about, say, poor pay for specific occupations (Johnson, Johnson and Winlow, 2025).

The qualitative shift over the past few decades, alongside undue policymaker credulity regarding quantitative data produced by proponents of neoliberalism, means that, in social science, we are now no better off than we were in, say, 1975. Indeed, in some respects, we are very much worse off. Assumptions that reducing poverty and inequality are good things for society have been replaced by positions that exacerbate harm: poverty stimulates economic activity by removing a comfortable safety net; inequality contributes to better economic decision making by those with the wealth to exercise judgement within the market. Advocates of neoliberal economic reform have been successful policy entrepreneurs, presenting quantitative studies that present evidence of pathways to growth, but generally growth at a lower level than via post-war Keynesian methods.

Those apparently opposed to neoliberal reform have focused on qualitative studies that focus on the need for being nicer/removing stigma and including people in low-level policy implementation, often actively dismissing the value of using quantitative evidence to present alternative economic pathways ('this treats people like animals') and failing to engage in anything approaching transformative policymaking as a consequence (Johnson *et al.*, 2024). Moreover, there are seldom qualitative data on how people's positions might change were different ideas and approaches presented to them. This is understandable. For decades, we have been told to assume that people's identities are fixed, are attached to their cultural backgrounds and directly inform their unchanging policy positions. It is odd, though reflective of the rejection of humans-as-animals, to assume that people are wholly determined by culture while rejecting any possibility of socioeconomic determinism. It is consistent with traditional liberal and indeed neoliberal accounts that hold that equality consists in upholding state neutrality between conceptions of the good.

The consequence of the neoliberal consensus has been, ironically, that research which fetishises individual agency has contributed to widespread assumptions that political agency to introduce change is both politically impossible and ethically wrong. Formal commitment to neutrality between ways of life (Hayek, 1979, 2012; Kukathas, 2003) means, for example, that promoting specific outcomes in health and wellbeing by funding prevention measures and institutions through taxation is coercive since it treats individuals as means to the ends of others (Degerman *et al.*, 2024). That position has justified the wholesale rolling back of the state from engagement in the provision and mitigation of what are known as social determinants of health and wellbeing, crime and many other outcomes. These social determinants include wealth, housing, food, education and employment. On the neoliberal account, engineering social determinants is impermissible because it undermines state neutrality concerning conceptions of the good and thereby undermines equality between citizens. It is then coercive insofar as it involves restricting choice and taxing citizens – on pain of imprisonment – to fund interventions.

The neoliberal commitment to neutrality has created a series of public crises for governments. In terms of health, there has been a significant increase in lifestyle conditions since the deregulation of society in the late 1970s. Neoliberals generally regard these as matters of conscience to be addressed in non-interventionist avenues. The most prominent of these has been the libertarian paternalist approach of 'nudging' that draws on behavioural scientific understandings of choice to attempt to improve outcomes in health, wealth and happiness without requiring the state to roll forward in mitigating social determinants (Thaler and Sunstein, 2008). Nudging was presented as a system for using salient behavioural cues to guide people toward making healthier and less harmful choices. The simple problem is that it has been highly ineffective at delivering any substantive improvements, and policymaker investment in it has detracted from more effectual approaches that require higher levels of up-front investment (Maier *et al.*, 2022; Degerman *et al.*, 2024).

This book and associated resources aim to enable those interested in research on policy to examine in detail the evidence base for policy and to overcome these substantive challenges in orthodoxy. These resources enable the development of skills required to integrate quantitative evidence on economics, health economics, health and public opinion, to be supported by clearly designed and contextually valuable qualitative evidence on argument. That latter element is crucial: neoliberal policy entrepreneurs have been successful precisely because they have developed arguments to shape understanding of what have often been highly problematic data.

1.4 Who is this book for and what is it intended to do?

In what follows, we intend to support unique, cutting-edge skills development in applied methods for policymaking. It is the main underpinning resource for the postgraduate course, '[u]nderstanding and addressing social challenges through applied statistical methods, data science and creative microsimulation', which is run by the Common Sense Policy Group at Northumbria University (Common Sense Policy Group, 2025b). This book will enable you to explore the key concepts and methods within the course, but also support your learning outside of it, if you:

- Have an interest in advanced quantitative methods and data science.
- Want to be able to code and microsimulate as part of your work.
- Wish to develop the capacity to engage in applied analysis of policy.

The book is designed for those with some prior quantitative knowledge who wish to develop advanced capabilities in applied policy analysis. By engaging with the material and activities, you will develop the capacity to understand and explain statistical methods, conduct sophisticated coding and microsimulation and deploy evidence coherently in policymaking contexts. You do not need to agree with the specific policies discussed – Basic Income, progressive taxation, education reform – to gain essential skills in evidence-based policy development.

The book builds on examples of online delivery elsewhere (Edelman, Sanders and Leiserson, 2024), along with models and methods developed by the Common Sense Policy Group to provide you with a unique experience in using statistical evidence to inform policymaking. This applied element is particularly important given the abstract and highly theoretical nature of much teaching in quantitative methods.

The concepts, theories and examples are of relevance to a range of social scientific subject areas, including economics, sociology, social policy, politics, international relations, geography, criminology, education, law, environmental planning, management, psychology and sport and society.

1.5 A chapter-by-chapter outline

In Chapter 2, we set out the core foundational requirements of research development. We begin by talking about research design itself, focusing on concerns around research questions before moving on to more quantitative foci regarding reproducibility of studies, identification of and controlling for variables, development of prediction and explanation, basic details of descriptive statistics, statistical significance and finally inference and confidence intervals.

Chapter 2 establishes foundational principles for conducting rigorous quantitative analysis in evidence-based policymaking. We emphasise that effective policy research requires identifying appropriate data sources. The chapter distinguishes between prediction – forecasting future scenarios – and explanation: testing theories about why social phenomena exist. We explore the crucial concepts of inference and uncertainty, explaining how sampling variability and model uncertainty affect our ability to make causal claims from observational data. The chapter introduces three main research designs: observational studies that establish associations; experimental studies with random assignment that prove causation; and quasi-experimental studies that approximate experimental conditions. We examine statistical significance critically, emphasising that effect sizes and confidence intervals provide far richer policy-relevant information than p-values alone. Finally, we stress that rigorous technical analysis must be complemented by clear communication through effective visualisations and honest acknowledgement of limitations. This enables development of very basic quantitative studies.

Chapter 3 introduces basic data scientific principles through practical examples, setting out general coding principles applicable to any platform. We explore large-sample datasets – particularly the Family Resources Survey (FRS); Living Costs and Food Survey; Understanding Society; and Wealth and Assets Survey – explaining their specialised purposes and overlapping content. The chapter addresses synthetic data generation as a solution to privacy constraints and examines the mechanics of grossing up sample data to population estimates. We discuss differential weighting to correct for response bias, and introduce bootstrapping as a method for quantifying uncertainty when simple formulas do not exist. The chapter confronts practical problems including under-reporting of sensitive information like high incomes and alcohol consumption, and acknowledges how survey questions may not perfectly align with policy modelling requirements. Throughout, we emphasise that while the technocratic approach to deeply personal issues like poverty may seem distasteful, systematic frameworks prove essential for evidence-based policymaking.

Chapter 4 explores fundamental concepts for measuring poverty, inequality and fiscal incentives. We begin by examining how individuals organise into households and how equivalence scales – particularly the Modified OECD Scale – help account for economies of scale and differing needs across household sizes and compositions. The chapter investigates how poverty can be operationalised through poverty lines, distinguishing between absolute measures (fixed thresholds adjusted for inflation) and relative measures (tied to median income). Beyond simple headcount measures, we explore sophisticated approaches like the poverty gap and Foster–Greer–Thorbecke index that satisfy Dalton's Principle by properly weighting the depth and severity of poverty. Our examination of inequality introduces the Lorenz curve and Gini coefficient as standard tools, alongside alternative measures like the Theil, Atkinson and the Palma indices. We address practical challenges facing policy analysts: choosing between income and consumption measures involves difficult trade-offs regarding housing costs and durable goods; multi-dimensional wellbeing indices offer broader perspectives but sacrifice analytical precision; and the distinction between formal and effective tax incidence reminds us that policy impacts may differ from initial intentions. Finally, we consider how efficiency concerns and market neutrality shape tax-benefit design, while acknowledging that deliberate departures from neutrality may be justified to address market failures or achieve distributional objectives.

Chapter 5 provides practical instruction for building your own tax-benefit microsimulation model using Python. We work through creating increasingly sophisticated models populated with synthetic datasets, enabling hands-on experience with the mechanics of fiscal policy analysis. The chapter examines the structure of tax-benefit models, explaining how they calculate liabilities and entitlements for sample households and aggregate results to estimate population-level impacts. We confront the inevitable limitations: models calculate entitlements rather than actual receipts, requiring corrections for benefit non-take-up; they typically assume no behavioural responses (static rather than dynamic modelling); and they focus on formal rather than effective incidence. The chapter discusses how to validate models through both bottom-up testing of individual calculations and top-down comparison with aggregate statistics. We explore appropriate tools for different tasks – from pencil-and-paper graphics to statistical packages, databases and high-level programming languages. Throughout, we emphasise that while perfect models remain impossible, models addressing important questions with reasonable precision and transparent assumptions provide genuinely useful policy design tools.

Chapter 6 traces the development of tax-benefit microsimulation in the UK from the 1980s emergence of IGOTM and TAXBEN through to contemporary applications analysing austerity's impacts. We examine how the Landman Economics tax-transfer model (TTM) revealed that cumulative policy changes during the 2010s – totalling over £26 billion in social security cuts by 2020/2021 – had overwhelmingly regressive effects across the income distribution. The chapter demonstrates sophisticated distributional analysis broken down by income deciles and protected characteristics like disability, ethnicity and number of children, showing how different policy types (direct taxes, indirect taxes, benefits, Universal Credit) have vastly different distributional impacts. We explore how microsimulation extends beyond traditional tax-benefit analysis to forecast future poverty levels by reweighting and uprating data to match official projections, and to analyse public services spending cuts using service usage patterns from multiple datasets. The chapter discusses critical survey data considerations including sample size limitations that constrain analysis of small subgroups, missing variables in publicly available datasets, and difficulties modelling geographically specific or sanction-based policies. We conclude by examining strengths (rigorous quantitative analysis, granular breakdowns by multiple characteristics, transparency enabling replication) and weaknesses (static assumptions, sample size constraints, data limitations) while emphasising that open-source development substantially increases microsimulation's potential for informing evidence-based policy.

Chapter 7 demonstrates advanced microsimulation capabilities through modelling Basic Income schemes and their health impacts. We begin with static distributional modelling of three Basic Income variants ranging from a modest 'starter' scheme to full Minimum Income Standard (MIS) payments, showing how revenue-neutral packages combining Basic Income with income tax increases produce dramatically progressive distributional effects – reducing child poverty from 29 per cent to potentially as low as 4 per cent while substantially decreasing inequality. The chapter then extends to dynamic modelling of health impacts, using Understanding Society panel data in within-between statistical models to establish relationships between income and both mental and physical health. We explain how the 'between' component captures permanent income differences and subjective inequality effects most relevant for permanent policy changes like Basic Income. The analysis reveals that even the modest starter scheme could prevent over 124,000 cases of depression annually, while the most generous scheme could prevent over one million cases and generate £19.65 billion in quality-adjusted life years valued at NICE's £30,000 per QALY threshold. We discuss health economic measures including QALYs, years of life gained and NHS cost savings that could fund tens of thousands of additional nurses. The chapter emphasises how this integrated economic-health modelling addresses critical gaps in previous research, providing policymakers with comprehensive evidence that Basic Income represents not just an affordable anti-poverty measure but a major public health intervention with substantial returns on investment.

Chapter 8 introduces the Public Policy Preference Calculator (TriplePC), an integrated model combining economic microsimulation, health impact assessment and public opinion analysis to evaluate policy feasibility comprehensively. We begin by examining the social feasibility challenge: why do lower-income voters increasingly support right-wing parties advocating policies that worsen inequality? The chapter presents conjoint analysis methodology, explaining how this survey technique reveals public preferences by forcing trade-offs between competing policy features – payment generosity, tax rates, funding mechanisms and outcomes like poverty reduction and health improvements. Our findings from eight hundred British respondents demonstrate that people strongly value poverty reduction and would accept substantially higher income tax rates (even 50 per cent/70 per cent/80 per cent across basic/higher/additional bands) if accompanied by dramatic poverty decreases. Preferences for wealth taxes, carbon taxes and corporation taxes over government borrowing reveal public willingness to fund generous welfare through progressive taxation. The chapter explains how we model health outcomes by converting SF-12 scores to quality-adjusted life years, and how TriplePC's web interface enables users to instantly see how different policy combinations affect economic outcomes, health impacts and electoral popularity. We discuss important lessons about coordinating conjoint surveys with microsimulation capabilities from the outset, defining appropriate baselines for comparison, and presenting diverse outputs coherently. The chapter concludes that contrary to Westminster assumptions, evidence shows the British public far more favourable to redistributive government action than politicians believe.

Chapter 9 presents adversarial co-production as a paradigm shift in evidence-based policymaking, moving beyond treating public preferences as fixed toward actively engaging policy opponents to develop persuasive narratives. We explain how this methodology adapts adversarial collaboration from behavioural science, recognising that reasoning functions primarily through dialogue and persuasion. The three-stage process begins with screening to identify firm opponents of progressive policies, continues with those opponents co-producing narratives emphasising material benefits through relatable protagonists and concrete examples, and concludes with large-sample testing of narrative persuasiveness. Example education reform narratives organised around absolute gains, relative gains, security and economic benefit demonstrate the approach. Our findings show statistically significant increases in support among initial opponents, with education reform opponents increasing support by 4.04 points. Analysis reveals that lower socioeconomic status and poorer health – precisely characteristics of those who would benefit most – predict both higher baseline support and greater responsiveness to narratives. The chapter addresses the political challenge: people with low perceived control want redistribution to increase security, yet lack faith in government's capacity to deliver, while opponents exploit anxiety by framing change as threatening chaos. We argue that progressive politicians must recognise voters seek control and predictability, which redistributive policies can provide when properly framed, and should fund through wealth taxation and productive investment narratives rather than fiscal neutrality. The chapter confronts the risk of engaging extremists, explaining how qualitative feedback mitigates narrative distortion while emphasising that alienating potential beneficiaries poses the greater danger.

Adversarial co-production offers essential tools for persuading electorates to support transformative measures addressing our permacrisis.

This book builds progressively from foundational quantitative methods through increasingly sophisticated microsimulation techniques to public opinion integration and narrative persuasion. Throughout, we emphasise that producing rigorous evidence requires not just technical proficiency but also understanding how to communicate findings effectively to different stakeholders and how to deploy narratives that shift the Overton Window.

This is necessarily, then, a diffuse, interdisciplinary book. It sets out an approach to evidence-based policymaking that looks different to the kinds of approaches we might assume exist. The reality is, though, that without this interdisciplinarity and concern for argument, evidence is unlikely to inform policy in any meaningful way. We need to remember that both the post-war and neoliberal consensuses have been grounded on a mix of quantitative evidence and thoroughgoing, highly embedded argument.

1.6 Uncertainty, framing and bias in evidence for transformative policymaking

The interdisciplinary approach advanced in this book necessarily confronts a challenge that is seldom acknowledged in traditional accounts of either microsimulation or public opinion research: the pervasive role of uncertainty, framing and bias in shaping the evidence base upon which policy decisions are made. The tools we develop here – economic microsimulation, health impact modelling, conjoint analysis and adversarial co-production – are powerful, but their outputs are only as reliable as our capacity to understand and communicate the limitations inherent in each. Failure to do so risks reproducing exactly the kind of policy-based evidence-making that has characterised the neoliberal era.

Pudney and Sutherland's (1994) analysis of the role of sampling error in UK models showed that tax-benefit microsimulation models produce estimates that are subject to multiple, compounding sources of uncertainty (Pudney and Sutherland, 1994). Their work showed that while baseline simulations are reasonably accurate at the aggregate level, widely used measures of the effects of policy changes may be imprecise estimates of population effects. This imprecision arises because microsimulation compounds uncertainties from sampling variability, data limitations, model specification and the necessarily static assumptions about behavioural responses that characterise most applied models (Immervoll and O'Donoghue, 2008).

Each of these sources of uncertainty interacts with choices made by modellers that are, in effect, framing decisions. The selection of a base dataset, the method of uprating historical incomes, the treatment of benefit non-take-up, the choice of equivalence scale and the decision to model formal rather than effective incidence all shape outputs in ways that may not be immediately apparent to consumers of the evidence. As we discuss in Chapters 5 and 6, these are not arbitrary decisions – they reflect considered judgements about how best to represent a complex fiscal system – but they are decisions nonetheless, and different choices can produce materially different results. This is particularly salient when modelling hypothetical policies, such as Basic Income, where there is no existing system against which to validate estimates and where the scale of proposed changes may exceed the range within which static assumptions hold (Reed *et al.*, 2023).

These modelling choices constitute a form of what Chong and Druckman (2007) term 'emphasis framing': by foregrounding certain features of a policy, such as its cost, distributional impact and effect on poverty headcounts versus depth of poverty, modellers inevitably shape the interpretation of results (Chong and Druckman, 2007). The choice to present distributional effects by income decile rather than by disability status, for example, or to report headline poverty rates rather than Foster–Greer–Thorbecke severity indices (which we discuss in Chapter 4), has real consequences for how policymakers and the public understand the implications of reform. As we argue throughout this book, transparency about these choices is essential for maintaining credibility and enabling independent verification. This requires provision of open-source code, detailed documentation of assumptions and honest acknowledgement of what models cannot do (Portes and Reed, 2018a).

Moreover, uncertainty in microsimulation is not merely a technical problem to be resolved through better data or more sophisticated algorithms. It is an irreducible feature of modelling complex social systems. As Chapter 5 discusses, the aspiration to build a model that fully captures behavioural responses, effective tax incidence, intra-household distribution and multidimensional wellbeing may produce something so laden with assumptions as to be less, not more, useful than a transparent static model with acknowledged limitations. The critical challenge is not to eliminate uncertainty but to communicate it honestly, so that policymakers can make informed decisions about the weight to place on different findings.

The integration of public opinion evidence into policymaking raises a parallel set of challenges in survey design and analysis. The literature on framing effects in public opinion research demonstrates that apparently minor variations in question wording, ordering and context can produce substantial differences in measured attitudes (Jacoby, 2000; Druckman, 2001; Chong and Druckman, 2007). These effects are particularly pronounced in welfare policy, in which decades of research have shown that support for government spending varies markedly depending on whether questions reference 'welfare' or 'assistance to the poor' (Rasinski, 1989), whether costs are made salient alongside benefits (Bremer and Bürgisser, 2022b) and whether recipients are characterised as deserving or undeserving (Nelson and Kinder, 1996).

This vulnerability to framing poses a fundamental problem for evidence-based policymaking. If measured public preferences are substantially artefacts of how questions are posed, then basing policy on those preferences risks circularity: policymakers frame questions in ways that confirm their priors, producing 'evidence' of public opposition to reforms they have already decided not to pursue. This is precisely the dynamic we identify with regard to the current Labour Government's reliance on focus groups and polling that takes expressed preferences at face value without testing their sensitivity to alternative framings or additional information. The normative implications of framing effects depend critically on whether frames provide genuinely useful considerations or merely exploit cognitive biases (Druckman, 2001).

The conjoint methodology we employ in Chapter 8 represents one response to this challenge. By forcing respondents to make trade-offs between multiple policy attributes simultaneously, conjoint analysis partially overcomes the problem of measuring support for individual features in isolation (Hainmueller, Hopkins and Yamamoto, 2014; Bansak *et al.*, 2023). The randomisation of attribute levels across many choice tasks means that features that are correlated in reality, such as tax rates and poverty outcomes, are rendered orthogonal, enabling identification of their independent effects on preference. This represents a significant methodological advance over traditional polling, which typically presents policies as take-it-or-leave-it propositions without requiring respondents to confront the trade-offs inherent in all fiscal reform.

However, conjoint analysis is not immune to framing effects. The selection of attributes and levels itself constitutes a framing decision: what is included shapes what can be measured, and what is excluded is rendered invisible. As we discuss in Chapter 8, the coordination between conjoint design and microsimulation capability is essential precisely because poorly specified attribute levels, such as an ambiguous 'tax on wealth', create interpretive uncertainty that propagates through the integrated model. Sample composition also matters. The over-representation of Labour voters and under-representation of Conservative voters in our conjoint sample required careful consideration, including re-estimation with electoral weighting, to ensure that findings were not artefacts of sample bias (Nettle *et al.*, 2025b).

Adversarial co-production, set out in Chapter 9, addresses framing from a different angle entirely. Rather than attempting to minimise framing effects through methodological design, it explicitly harnesses the power of narrative framing to shift preferences. This approach is grounded in the recognition that all policy communication involves framing and that the relevant question is not whether to frame but how to do so in ways that are honest, evidence-based and responsive to the genuine material interests of audiences. By engaging firm opponents in narrative development, adversarial co-production ensures that the frames deployed are those most likely to resonate with sceptical audiences, precisely because they have been developed by people who share those audiences' concerns. This represents a fundamentally different relationship to framing than that which characterises both traditional polling and conventional policy communication – one that treats persuasion as a legitimate and necessary component of democratic evidence-based policymaking rather than a distortion to be eliminated.

Taken together, these considerations underscore a central theme of this book: that producing rigorous evidence for transformative policy requires not only technical proficiency in microsimulation and survey methods but also critical reflexivity about the choices, assumptions and framings that shape what that evidence shows and how it is received. The tools we develop here are designed to make those choices transparent and to equip readers to interrogate them, whether in their own work or in the work of others.

1.7 Bracketing the British context: data infrastructure for transformative policymaking in Europe and the United States

This book focuses on the UK context, drawing primarily on British datasets, models and policy challenges. This focus is deliberate: the UK's tax-benefit system, its particular constellation of crises and the specific political dynamics surrounding progressive reform in 'left-behind' constituencies demand contextually grounded analysis. However, the methods and principles we develop are applicable far beyond Britain. Comparable data infrastructure exists across Europe and North America that enables, and in some cases surpasses, the kinds of integrated economic, health and public opinion analysis we demonstrate here. Situating our approach within this broader landscape is important both for readers working in other jurisdictions and for understanding how comparative evidence can strengthen the case for transformative domestic policy.

The most direct international comparator to the UK models discussed in Chapters 5 to 8 is EUROMOD, the European Union's tax-benefit microsimulation model, now maintained by the European Commission's Joint Research Centre (Sutherland and Figari, 2013). EUROMOD covers all twenty-seven EU member states using a common modelling framework applied to harmonised microdata drawn primarily from the European Union Statistics on Income and Living Conditions (EU-SILC). EU-SILC, coordinated by Eurostat, collects detailed cross-sectional and longitudinal data on income, poverty, social exclusion and living conditions across participating countries, providing the kind of rich household-level information that the FRS provides for the UK (Eurostat, 2023). EUROMOD's particular strength lies in cross-national comparability: because all country systems are coded within a common framework using standardised modelling conventions, it is possible to examine how a policy introduced successfully in one jurisdiction might work in another, or to assess how a common reform would have different distributional effects across different national contexts (Immervoll and O'Donoghue, 2008). This comparative capacity is something that purely national models, including our own, cannot replicate. The European Health Interview Survey (EHIS), meanwhile, provides comparable health data across EU member states, enabling the kind of income-to-health modelling we conduct in Chapter 7 to be extended to a European frame (Eurostat, 2024).

In the United States, the data landscape for fiscal microsimulation is shaped by a distinctive institutional architecture in which tax and spending programmes are generally modelled separately. The primary economic datasets include the Current Population Survey (CPS), conducted jointly by the US Census Bureau and the Bureau of Labor Statistics, which provides detailed information on income, employment and demographic characteristics for approximately sixty thousand households annually (US Census Bureau, 2024). For longitudinal analysis comparable to our use of Understanding Society, the Panel Study of Income Dynamics (PSID), running continuously since 1968, tracks families and their descendants across generations, providing the longest-running nationally representative household panel in the world (Institute for Social Research, 2024). The Survey of Income and Program Participation (SIPP) provides additional longitudinal data focused specifically on the dynamics of income, programme participation and household composition (US Census Bureau, 2023). These datasets underpin several major microsimulation models, including the Urban-Brookings Tax Policy Center model, the Congressional Budget Office's distributional analyses, HM Treasury's US counterpart at the Office of Tax Analysis and the NBER's TAXSIM model, which calculates federal and state income tax liabilities from individual characteristics (Feenberg and Coutts, 1993; Rohaly, Carasso and Saleem, 2005). The Institute on Taxation and Economic Policy (ITEP) model is notable for its capacity to analyse tax incidence disaggregated by race and ethnicity at the state level – a capability that has no direct UK equivalent, but which illustrates how microsimulation can be adapted to address nationally specific dimensions of inequality (Institute on Taxation and Economic Policy, 2024).

The health modelling we conduct in Chapter 7, linking income changes to mental and physical health outcomes via SF-12 scores and quality-adjusted life years, depends on panel data that combine detailed income and validated health measures within the same individuals over time. Comparable resources exist internationally. In Europe, the Survey of Health, Ageing and Retirement in Europe (SHARE) covers individuals aged fifty and over across twenty-eight European countries and Israel, collecting panel data on health, socioeconomic status and social networks that have been used extensively for health-economic modelling (Börsch-Supan *et al.*, 2013). For younger populations and broader health coverage, the German Socio-Economic Panel (SOEP) provides annual longitudinal data on approximately thirty thousand individuals, including SF-12 health measures closely comparable to those in Understanding Society (Goebel *et al.*, 2019).

In the United States, the Medical Expenditure Panel Survey (MEPS) provides nationally representative data on health status, healthcare utilisation and expenditures for approximately thirty-five thousand individuals annually, with a two-year panel component (Agency for Healthcare Research and Quality, 2024). The Behavioral Risk Factor Surveillance System (BRFSS), the world's largest continuously conducted health survey, collects state-level data on health-related risk behaviours, chronic conditions and use of preventive services from over four hundred thousand adults annually, enabling the kind of geographically disaggregated health analysis that sample size constraints prevent in most UK surveys (Centers for Disease Control and Prevention, 2024). For longitudinal income-health relationships specifically, the Health and Retirement Study (HRS) tracks approximately twenty thousand Americans over the age of fifty biennially, providing rich data on health transitions, economic resources and family structure that have been used for microsimulation of retirement and health policy (Sonnega *et al.*, 2014). The integration of health and economic data within a single longitudinal framework, the approach we take in Chapter 7 using Understanding Society and the Landman TTM, remains comparatively unusual internationally. Much health microsimulation models the economic effects of health rather than the reverse, meaning that assumptions of causality are often problematic (Schofield *et al.*, 2017). Our approach, in which economic microsimulation drives health predictions via empirically estimated income-health relationships, represents a methodological contribution that could be replicated using these international datasets.

The conjoint and adversarial co-production approaches we outline in Chapters 8 and 9 for assessing and shifting public preferences on welfare policy draw on bespoke survey data. However, they build on a substantial international infrastructure of public opinion research. The European Social Survey (ESS), conducted biennially across more than thirty countries since 2002, provides cross-nationally comparable data on social attitudes, including welfare preferences, trust in institutions and subjective wellbeing (European Social Survey, 2024). The International Social Survey Programme (ISSP) has collected data on attitudes to government, social inequality and the role of the state since 1985, enabling longitudinal analysis of how welfare preferences evolve in response to changing economic conditions (ISSP, 2024). The World Values Survey and European Values Study, which Bartram (2022) uses in his analysis of inequality and life satisfaction cited in Chapter 8, provide the broadest comparative frame for understanding how economic conditions shape social and political attitudes across both high- and low-income countries (Bartram, 2022).

In the United States, the General Social Survey (GSS), running since 1972, provides the longest continuous series of attitudinal data on government spending, inequality and social policy (Smith *et al.*, 2024), while the American National Election Studies (ANES) have tracked political attitudes and voting behaviour since 1948. The Pew Research Center's global surveys provide regular, comparable data on attitudes to welfare, redistribution and inequality across dozens of countries. These resources collectively demonstrate that the kinds of preference data we generate through conjoint analysis could be produced comparatively, enabling assessment of whether the strong redistributive preferences we identify among British respondents are replicated in other high-inequality democracies facing comparable political challenges.

The existence of this international data infrastructure has two implications for the approach we develop. First, the methods we outline are transferable. Readers working with EU-SILC and EUROMOD, with the CPS and TAXSIM, or with SHARE and SOEP can apply the same analytical framework to their own national contexts. Second, comparative evidence strengthens the domestic case for reform. Demonstrating that Basic Income is affordable in the UK is important; demonstrating that comparable schemes have been modelled as feasible across multiple European countries using a common framework (Martinelli, 2020) makes the case considerably harder to dismiss as national eccentricity. We return to this comparative dimension where relevant throughout the chapters that follow, but the primary focus remains firmly on developing the applied skills and comprehensive evidence base needed to influence British policymaking in the present period of crisis.

We hope this book enables you to produce the kinds of comprehensive, integrated evidence that can genuinely influence policy outcomes and contribute to rebuilding Britain through transformative change.

2

An introduction to using quantitative data in evidence-based policy research

Key foci

- Distinguishing between prediction and explanation as analytical purposes.
- Understanding inference, uncertainty and the relationship between sampling variability and causal claims.
- Comparing observational, experimental and quasi-experimental study designs.
- Emphasising effect sizes and confidence intervals over statistical significance alone.

2.1 Introduction

To answer research questions, we have to:

- **Identify** the most appropriate data with the greatest potential to develop an evidence base for policy decisions. Some of the most reliable data already exist in large-scale survey-based datasets, such as the Census, the Labour Force Survey (LFS) and Understanding Society: the UK Household Longitudinal Study (UKHLS).
- **Use** the data to generate reliable inferences and predictions that can inform policy decisions. This requires transparent and replicable methods. This is where models come in – they allow us to make inferences and predictions beyond the data to which we currently have access.
- **Communicate** our findings clearly and transparently, so that policy-makers can understand what the evidence shows and what its limitations are.

This chapter covers the fundamental concepts needed to use quantitative data in evidence-based policy making. It explains how to identify appropriate data sources, formulate clear research questions and distinguish between prediction and explanation as different purposes of analysis. The chapter introduces statistical models as tools for making inferences and emphasises the importance of transparency and clear communication in policy research.

2.2 Research questions and data sources

For our purposes, the point of social science is to observe a social challenge and to develop and apply approaches to understand and address them. The issues we investigate range radically in scale, from global phenomena around the relationship between inequality and health to the impact of specific economic phenomena around types of work and household stability, to very narrow phenomena within specific geographic spaces.

To address a social challenge, we need to gather relevant data to assert and test causal relationships and quantify those relationships, effects or outcomes. This moves us from observation to evidence and policy recommendation.

The choice of data source depends on the challenge examined. If we are examining neighbourhood-level health disparities, we might need census data and mortality registrations. For phenomena around gig economy work and financial stability, we could turn to the labour force surveys, tax records or even digital platform data. In theory, we could collect our own primary data, but in practice, many of the data needed to produce evidence-based policy already exist in large-scale datasets such as the Census, the Labour Force Survey (LFS) and Understanding Society.

Official data sources are widely accepted in policy research because they are systematically collected using standardised methodologies and undergo rigorous quality assurance processes (Office for Statistics Regulation, 2024). These data sets are publicly available and produced by official institutions, making them particularly suitable for evidence-based policy making. Examples include the Office for National Statistics (ONS) and government departments such as the Department for Work and Pensions (DWP).

You can explore official statistics through portals like ONS (http://www.ons.gov.uk/), Nomis (http://www.nomisweb.co.uk/) and the UK Government statistics website (http://www.gov.uk/search-for-statistics). Academic researchers can also access data through the UK Data Service (http://www.ukdataservice.ac.uk/). Researchers can also submit Freedom of Information requests for non-public data or establish partnerships with organisations that hold proprietary datasets. Whichever route you take, it is essential to review licensing terms and comply with data protection regulations (UK GDPR and Data Protection Act 2018) (UK Government, 2018).

2.3 Prediction and explanation

Over the past fifty years, there has been a tendency to reject the distinction between reality and human consciousness and hold that social phenomena are socially constructed. The 'qualitative turn' represented a growing belief that social science should be concerned with understanding meaning and rejecting any notion that human beings are subject to the same laws of nature as other animal species. We reject this as fetishistic nonsense. We are positivists who believe that there is a reality independent of human consciousness (e.g. the Earth is round even when people think that it is flat), that humans are subject to the same laws of nature as other animal species (e.g. humans cannot survive without homeostasis) and that predictions can be made on this basis (e.g. people who cannot afford food cannot survive) (Bryant, 1985; Howell, 2013).

Policymaking depends upon basic positivist assumptions. It is not the case that policy is implemented without some prediction about how it will affect human beings. It is the case that many predictions of impacts are simply wrong. The reasons for their being wrong are that theories of human motivation or behaviour are often highly ideological insofar as they promote the specific interests of specific individuals. This is true of neoliberal reform more broadly, which is shaped by a deontological commitment to reducing sources of government involvement in people's lives and which makes a series of assumptions regarding the social impact of increasing inequality and reducing social security that are simply evidence-free (Degerman *et al.*, 2024).

It is generally the case that researchers have some underlying series of theoretical assumptions that are drawn from people's lived experience as well as their reading of their fields (M. T. Johnson *et al.*, 2025). This needs to be acknowledged, as does the capacity of research to misidentify relationships as a consequence. However, it is not the case that evidence for policymaking can be developed without inference and prediction.

Prediction means using current data to forecast future scenarios or estimate outcomes we have not yet observed (Sohil, Sohali and Shabbir, 2022). Policymakers are by definition faced with predictive questions like 'how many more hospital beds will the NHS need by 2030?' or 'what would the state of the public finances be if we introduced a Basic Income?'

Predictive models help policymakers make informed decisions by providing empirical forecasts. Prediction requires a *model*, a function or set of functions linking measurable variables to predicted values. Simple models like linear regression are transparent and interpretable. It is easy to see what variables are included in the model and how they are used. For example, we might build a model to predict how many primary school places will be needed in

2030. The model might include variables such as current birth rates, number of children currently aged zero to four and historical enrolment rates, similar to the approach used by the Department for Education in their national pupil projections (Department of Education, 2025). This transparency is valuable in policymaking contexts in which decisions need to be justified politically.

There are many types of statistical models, from simple ones such as linear regression to more complex machine learning models that can use hundreds of variables in combinations discovered algorithmically. Examples of more complex approaches underpin those behind large language models, such as ChatGPT, that use millions of texts as data. These approaches are really good at predicting the next word in a sentence, but they operate as 'black boxes', making it difficult to explain how any particular prediction was generated (Rudin, 2019).

Explanation focuses on understanding relationships and testing theories about why social phenomena exist. Here we are not primarily concerned with forecasting, but with determining whether our theoretical understanding is supported by evidence. We might want to test our theory with a hypothesis. The difference between these two concepts is important. A theory provides a comprehensive framework of explanation whereas a hypothesis offers a more specific, testable expectation about patterns in data (William Lawrence, 2014). Testing theories and hypotheses is more of a basic scientific desire than an applied science one.

For example, we might theorise that smaller class sizes improve educational outcomes. We can then derive a hypothesis that students in small classes of twenty or fewer will achieve higher test scores than students in larger classes when other factors, such as socioeconomic background, are held constant. To test this hypothesis, we fit a statistical model in which class size is an explanatory variable (Dustmann, Rajah and van Soest, 2003). If our hypothesis is correct, this model should explain differences in test scores better than a model that does not include the class size variable. This is called statistical explanation.

2.4 Inference and uncertainty

Official datasets, such as the Labour Force Survey, collect observational data in a representative sample of the population. This allows us to make inferences about the broader population. For example, if we observe that areas with higher unemployment have worse mental health outcomes, inference helps us estimate whether this relationship reflects a genuine connection between unemployment and mental health, whether it might be explained by other factors or whether it is simply due to chance.

In policy research, there are two key variables within datasets. Measured variables are observed as they are. This is true of, for example, household income or employment status. Manipulated variables result from an intervention, such as assigning households to receive a cash transfer. Observational studies typically involve measured variables, whereas experimental studies such as randomised controlled trials use manipulated variables (Picardi and Masick, 2014).

Variables may be correlated, insofar as when one variable increases, another increases or decreases. Causal inference is the statistical approach to determining whether a causal relationship exists between these variables (Morgan and Winship, 2015). Causal inference is important for evidence-based policy as it moves beyond correlation to estimate the true impact of a social phenomenon. This is essential for policy research because policymakers need to understand not just what is happening, but why it is happening. For example, if we want to reduce unemployment and its associated mental health impacts, we need to understand what factors are driving unemployment in the first place.

When using observational data for causal inference, uncertainty is particularly important because it helps us express how likely it is that one phenomenon causes another. We might assume that the phenomena that we are studying are driven causally by some underlying parameters. For example, when studying poverty, we might assume there is a parameter that determines the proportion of working households below the poverty line. Because this parameter is unobservable, we cannot know its exact value. We only observe the outcome (whether a household is below the poverty line), not the counterfactual state (what would happen if circumstances were different). To approximate the true parameter, we use the data we have to construct an estimator, a calculated value based on observed data that serves as our best guess of the underlying causal effect (Rubin, 2025).

In observational data, we face two sources of uncertainty that affect our parameter estimator: sampling uncertainty and model uncertainty. Sampling uncertainty (or sampling variability) affects the parameter estimator because we only observe a sample rather than the entire population. When the sample is small, this variability is large, meaning that our estimator could differ substantively from the true parameter. As the sample size increases, sampling variability decreases and the uncertainty becomes much smaller (Corbetta, 2003). Model uncertainty occurs because we might not have correctly identified or measured all the confounding factors, other variables that could explain the observed relationship. This requires careful research design and statistical methods that account for confounding factors (Chatfield, 1995).

To ensure that our estimator reflects the true underlying parameter as closely as possible, we rely on random sampling. This gives each observation an equal chance of selection, reducing bias and allowing us to apply statistical inference to estimate uncertainty. Random sampling also helps to balance out potential confounding variables across groups, making it more likely that any observed effects are due to the variable of interest rather than other factors. In practice, however, many large datasets use structured sampling methods such as stratified or cluster sampling designed to ensure their samples are representative of the UK population. This means researchers often adjust for how the sample was collected. Even with these adjustments, we cannot be certain that we have identified and measured all relevant confounders. This is why transparent reporting of which variables were controlled for, what assumptions were made and what limitations remain, is essential for parameter estimators and interpreting causal claims from observational data.

We reflect uncertainty in our parameter estimates in two key ways: the *standard error* and the *95 per cent confidence interval*. The standard error tells us how far on average our estimate is likely to be from the true value. It depends on our sample size and how much variability exists in the population. The confidence interval is closely related. It shows the range within which we would expect 95 per cent of our estimates to fall if we repeated our sampling. We calculate it as our estimate plus or minus 1.96 times the standard error (Corbetta, 2003). The 95 per cent level is the most common conventional way to express 'the range of values likely to come up in our estimation'.

Both the standard error and the 95 per cent confidence interval are related to the square root of the sample size and reduce as sample size increases. This means that by doubling a sample, for example from 50 to 100 participants, uncertainty is reduced more than by increasing the number of participants from 100 to 150. This creates a practical trade-off. A larger sample increases *statistical power* to discriminate between different values of parameters, but it does so at a declining rate. Eventually, the cost of gathering more data outweighs the marginal gain in precision, making further data collection inefficient (Office for National Statistics, no date).

2.5 Types of study in social science and public policy

Research design shapes the type of evidence produced. There are three main types of research study design: observational, experimental and quasi-experimental.

2.5.1 Observational studies

Observational studies contain only measured variables. They are sometimes also known as correlational studies. In policy research, these studies might use large datasets such as Understanding Society or the Census to examine how different phenomena relate to one another. Examples include studies of job satisfaction, educational attainment and earnings, and access to green space and mental wellbeing.

Observational studies are essential for policy research. They are often the only practical means of studying certain phenomena and they can establish associations between variables. However, they cannot tell us definitively what causes what (Kang, 2013). For example, if we find that people with higher incomes have higher life satisfaction, we cannot be sure that income causes satisfaction. It might be that happier people earn more, or that something else, such as education or family background, leads to both higher income and greater satisfaction.

If there is an association between variables X and Y in an observational study, it could be because: (a) X causes Y; (b) Y causes X; or (c) some third variable affects both X and Y. Researchers attempt to address option (c) by controlling for potential confounding variables, measuring other factors that might explain the relationship and adjusting for them statistically.

However, this approach has inherent limitations. There may always be unmeasured confounders that were not available in the dataset or that researchers did not consider. Additionally, controlling for too many variables can bias the results or make them harder to interpret (Hernan and Robins, 2024).

Observational studies can be *cross-sectional* or *longitudinal*. Cross-sectional studies collect all variables at a single point in time. An example would be surveying people about their income and life satisfaction on a particular date. The association of interest is whether a person's income in, say, July 2024 is statistically related to their life satisfaction in July 2024. This involves explicitly comparing between people with different incomes.

Longitudinal studies track the same individuals over time. An example is Understanding Society, which follows the same households across multiple years. Researchers can identify how a *change* in one variable relates to a *change* in the other. For example, it is possible to examine whether people whose incomes increased from 2023 to 2024 also became more satisfied with life from 2023 to 2024. This helps rule out some causal possibilities. For example, people's childhood background or sex will not normally have changed from 2023 to 2024, so these factors could not explain why the change in income and the change in life satisfaction would be related. However, even longitudinal studies cannot identify causality in the way that experiments can, because there is always the possibility that something else changed that caused the change in both income and life satisfaction.

In observational studies, there is generally some idea of which variables might influence others. The potential causes are called predictor, independent or explanatory variables and the things being influenced are called outcome or dependent variables. In our example, income is the predictor variable and life satisfaction the outcome variable, even though we acknowledge the relationship might work the other way around. There might also be variables that sit between predictors and outcomes. These are called mediators. For example, higher income might lead to more life satisfaction *because* it enables more travel. Here, travel mediates the relationship between income and life satisfaction.

Most studies in social science and public policy are observational. This means that a degree of caution is required when inferring causality and predicting what will happen if we intervene to affect what we identify as the independent variable. An example here might concern a finding that people who use food banks have worse health outcomes than those who do not. Does this mean that food banks harm health? There are reasons to suggest that this is probably not an accurate inference. People using food banks face poverty, insecure housing and chronic stress. These are factors that are known to drive poor health (M. T. Johnson *et al.*, 2022a; E. A. Johnson *et al.*, 2023a). Food banks are a response to these problems. A policy to close food banks is unlikely to improve health independently of any other measure to increase access to food. Indeed, it would likely contribute to worse outcomes by removing a source of food for a significant number of people. The likely causal drivers in the relationship are poverty and insecurity, not food bank use, though food bank use may or may not serve as a mediator in some way. It may be that food banks provide low-quality food, consumption of which may have a causal effect on health, but the counterfactual – of starvation – is likely worse.

Similarly, observational data show that recipients of the flu vaccine are more likely to be recorded as having contracted flu than people who do not receive the vaccine. This is not because the flu vaccine increases vulnerability to infection but, rather, because high-risk people, including the elderly, those with compromised immune systems and those who work in healthcare, are most likely to receive vaccination and then to be diagnosed formally with flu. Experimental studies show that the flu vaccine reduces the risk of getting flu, so the true causal effect runs opposite to the observational pattern. This is why medical research, and increasingly, public policy research, relies on experimental studies to establish causation.

It is critical, therefore, that analysis of observational data is contextualised within broader analytical frameworks shaped by knowledge of causal relationships from other forms of study.

2.5.2 Experimental studies

Experimental studies are considered the gold standard for establishing causation because they involve deliberate manipulation and random assignment.

In an experiment, researchers randomly assign participants to different conditions. Because of random assignment, any systematic differences in outcomes between groups can be attributed to the intervention rather than to pre-existing differences between participants. For example, in a vaccine trial, participants are randomly assigned to receive either the true vaccine or an inert placebo. If the vaccine group has lower disease rates, it is possible to infer this is due to the vaccine's effect, not because the two groups differed in other significant ways. This is why randomised controlled trials (RCTs) provide the strongest evidence for causal effects.

However, experimental studies are often impractical or unethical in policy research. We cannot randomly assign people to poverty or unemployment to study their effects. This is why most policy research relies on observational data, though experimental evidence is used when feasible, as in evaluating pilot programmes or policy interventions.

Experiments often contain covariates. These are variables that are neither the intervention nor the outcome. These are characteristics that researchers can measure, but not manipulate, such as the participants' sex or age. Sometimes covariates can affect the dependent variable but have nothing to do with the study question. For example, women might get flu more often than men for reasons that are due to sex-based biological differences. The key is ensuring groups do not differ systematically in terms of these covariates. Random assignment usually balances groups, though researchers can also deliberately balance them by ensuring each group has equal gender splits. In experimental studies, it is usually best to let random assignment and any balancing do the work rather than adding statistical controls in your analysis.

Sometimes researchers are interested in how covariates affect outcomes. These become moderator variables or effect modifiers. For example, the research question might be: 'is the flu vaccine more effective for women than for men?' Here, sex is central to the question. Instead of estimating the vaccine's average effect, its effect is compared between groups. In this case, the covariate must be included in statistical analysis, usually as an interaction with the intervention.

2.5.3 Quasi-experimental studies

Quasi-experimental studies occur when circumstances create variation that resembles an experiment, even though researchers did not deliberately manipulate conditions. For example, if a policy is rolled out in some regions, but not others due to practical constraints, researchers can compare outcomes between regions, approximating experimental conditions.

The key requirements are that a) groups experiencing different conditions must not be systematically different from one another; and b) individuals must not have self-selected into different conditions. The closer a quasi-experiment resembles a true experiment with random assignment, the stronger the causal inferences we can draw. Quasi-experimental designs can provide valuable evidence when true experiments are not feasible, though researchers must work carefully to establish that the groups are genuinely comparable.

An example of a quasi-experiment is the Changing Cost of Living Study, which examined the effects of the 2022–23 cost-of-living crisis on a range of mental and physical health outcomes (Nettle, 2024; Nettle *et al.*, 2024).

2.6 Statistical significance

Regardless of whether we use observational, experimental or quasi-experimental data, we need statistical models to make sense of our findings. A statistical model is a structured way of representing the relationships between variables in our data. Models allow us to estimate effects, quantify uncertainty around those estimates and test whether observed patterns are likely to reflect genuine relationships rather than random chance.

A statistical test evaluates whether we have sufficient evidence to conclude that a relationship exists. The null hypothesis is the starting assumption. Unless there is evidence to the contrary, we should assume no link between any pair of variables. Statistical tests are procedures for asking whether we should believe the null hypothesis, or whether data support the view that the null hypothesis is not true and that there is some causal link between the two variables. This is called *rejecting* the null hypothesis, and a result that rejects the null hypothesis is described as *statistically significant*.

Statistical tests often produce a *p-value*. This is used to assess whether an observed relationship is unlikely to be due to chance alone. When the p-value falls below the conventional threshold (typically 0.05), researchers describe the result as *statistically significant* and reject the null hypothesis – the assumption that there is no effect.

P-values are often misunderstood. The p-value does not tell us the probability that the null hypothesis is true given the data. Rather, the p-value actually reflects the probability of observing data this extreme if the null hypothesis were true. Statistical significance from p-values provides useful information about whether an effect likely exists. However, for policy interventions, understanding the magnitude and direction of effects matters most.

Parameter estimates (effect sizes) and their precision provide a more complete picture than p-values alone. Parameter estimation and statistical testing are closely connected. If a parameter estimate is close to zero, or if zero falls within the confidence interval around an estimate, then a statistical test will fail to reject the null hypothesis. This means that there is insufficient evidence that an effect exists. However, confidence intervals provide much richer information than a simple significant/non-significant decision.

A confidence interval shows the range of plausible values for the effect size. For example, if we estimate that an employment programme increases job placement rates by 12 percentage points with a 95 per cent confidence interval of 8 per cent to 16 per cent, this tells us that while 12 per cent is our best estimate, the true effect likely falls somewhere between 8 per cent and 16 per cent. This is far more useful for policy decisions than simply knowing '$p < 0.05$'. Even at the lower bound of 8 per cent, the programme shows a meaningful impact. Confidence intervals help policymakers to understand both the most likely effect size and the uncertainty around that estimate.

There are several important considerations beyond statistical significance to consider when developing evidence-based policy:

- **Effect sizes are independent of sample size; p-values are not.** In a very small sample, almost no effects will be 'significant' because estimates lack precision. In a very large sample, almost everything will be significant because even tiny effects can be detected reliably. This means a p-value alone does not tell you which associations are important or meaningful. The effect size, by contrast, reveals the magnitude of impact regardless of sample size. A large sample improves the precision of the effect size estimate, but the size itself remains interpretable and comparable across studies.
- **Policy questions require knowing effect magnitude and direction, not just existence.** When evaluating an employment training programme, the relevant question is not 'does this programme have any effect at all?', but rather 'by how much does this programme improve employment rates?' A programme might show a statistically significant effect ($p < 0.05$) of increasing employment by 0.5 percentage points. This may technically be 'real', but potentially too small to justify costs. Only by examining effect sizes can we compare different interventions, conduct cost-benefit analyses and make informed resource allocation decisions. Policy questions are fundamentally about magnitude and direction, not simply about whether an effect exists.
- **Multiple testing can produce misleading significant results.** With a threshold of $p = 0.05$, one in twenty statistical tests will appear 'significant' by chance alone, even when no real effect exists. In policy research

using complex datasets with many variables, dozens of potential relationships could be tested. Finding a few 'significant' results among many tests is not particularly meaningful. This is why evidence from pre-registered predictions, where hypotheses are specified before data are analysed, is more reliable than exploratory findings where researchers test many relationships and report whichever ones happen to be significant.

2.7 Representing results

Getting the technical analysis right is essential, but for research to inform policy, it is essential to communicate findings clearly in order for policymakers to understand what the evidence shows, how it was generated and what its limitations are. There are various key considerations.

Effective communication depends upon effective use of appropriate chart types (line graphs, bar charts, scatter plots) and clear titles, labels and context, since these represent the direction and scale of relationships much more clearly to audiences than text alone.

What is obvious to a researcher analysing data may be completely unclear to someone without technical training. Policymakers need to understand research findings quickly, but statistical results are often difficult to interpret. Graphs, charts and tables make complex data accessible by presenting key findings visually.

Good visualisations provide:

Clarity: They make complex data digestible, helping decision-makers grasp key findings quickly and get a realistic sense of what the evidence shows.

Pattern recognition: Visual representations reveal trends and relationships that might not be immediately obvious from the raw numbers, enabling policymakers to spot important patterns at a glance.

Impact and engagement: While the raw data provides the evidence, visual graphs and charts strengthen persuasive power because they are easier to understand and harder to ignore.

Alongside this, it is important to display uncertainty with confidence intervals or error bars and express honesty about limitations. Honesty about limitations can actually increase confidence in the analysis overall.

Producing rigorous research is necessary but not sufficient. Research influences decisions when it reaches the right people in the right format at the right time. This means building relationships with policy teams, understanding their priorities and presenting evidence in formats that fit their decision-making processes. The goal is not just to produce good research but also to ensure it makes a difference. We return to this in Chapter 6.

2.8 Conclusion

This chapter has established the fundamental principles for conducting rigorous quantitative analysis in evidence-based policymaking. We began by emphasising that effective policy research requires identifying appropriate data sources, formulating clear research questions and distinguishing between prediction and explanation as distinct analytical purposes. Official datasets like the Census, Labour Force Survey and Understanding Society provide systematically collected, quality-assured data that forms the foundation for reliable policy analysis.

Understanding the relationship between inference and uncertainty proves essential for interpreting research findings appropriately. We explored how sampling uncertainty and model uncertainty affect parameter estimates, and why transparent reporting of assumptions, controlled variables and controlled limitations remain crucial for credible causal claims. The distinction between measured and manipulated variables illuminates why different study designs – observational, experimental and quasi-experimental – provide varying strengths of evidence for causal relationships.

Statistical significance, while useful, cannot substitute for understanding effect sizes, their direction and their practical magnitude. A statistically significant finding may be too small to justify policy intervention costs, while confidence intervals provide far richer information about plausible effect ranges than p-values alone. The multiple testing problem reminds us that exploratory findings require cautious interpretation compared to pre-registered hypotheses.

Finally, we emphasised that rigorous technical analysis must be complemented by clear communication. Effective visualisations, honest acknowledgement of limitations and of presentation formats suited to policymakers' decision-making processes ensure research actually influences policy outcomes. The goal transcends producing methodologically sound analysis. It requires ensuring that evidence reaches decision-makers in accessible formats that facilitate informed choices about interventions affecting people's lives.

Quantitative methods are essential tools for evidence-based policy making, but their value depends on rigorous application and clear communication. This chapter has shown how identifying appropriate data, careful research design and appropriate statistical methods for making inferences about the broader population can produce reliable evidence to inform policy decisions. Understanding the distinction between prediction and explanation, correlation and causation, bias and uncertainty, as well as recognising the strengths and limitations of different study designs and communicating findings accessibly, is critical.

3

Dealing with datasets

Key foci

- Exploring major UK datasets (FRS, LCFS, Understanding Society, WAS) and their specialised purposes.
- Understanding grossing up, differential weighting and bootstrapping for uncertainty estimation.
- Addressing synthetic data generation as a solution to privacy constraints.
- Confronting practical limitations including under-reporting and response bias.

3.1 Introduction

There are various recent headlines that point towards radically contrasting policy positions by parties relying on comparable data:

- Facing a funding shortfall, UK Chancellor Reeves contemplates adding a penny to income tax rates (Islam, 2025);
- The Chancellor is also reported to be contemplating ending the policy of limiting most state benefit payments to the first two children in a family (Parker, 2025);
- The Green Party proposes a Wealth Tax of 1 per cent annually on assets above £10 million and of 2 per cent on assets above £1 billion (The Green Party, 2025);
- At their annual conference, the populist Reform Party proposes large cuts in personal income tax (Vincent, 2025).

How can we analyse what is going on with these statements? How can we understand the reasoning behind the decisions that were made in each case?

We need to think systematically about questions like these. What these headlines have in common is that they are concerned with the impact on our diverse society of broad government policies – on Social Security, wage setting or the taxation of wealth, income and spending. We need to always keep this diversity in mind: microsimulation is a way of confronting what may seem on paper a good, simple idea with the reality of a society with rich and poor, able and disabled, young and old, conventional nuclear families and those living in very different arrangements. But the very complexity of a modern society makes it all the more important that we have a few organising principles to guide us – it is no use just holding our hands up and saying 'it is all very complicated', even if it is.

Broadly, we can group the questions we might want to ask about our policy changes into two:

1. Policy changes inevitably produce gainers and losers: some people might be better off, and some worse off, and we want to summarise those changes in an intelligible way. This leads us to the study of measures such as poverty and inequality; when we come to do some modelling, we will also consider some more prosaic measures such as counts of gainers and losers disaggregated in various ways, aggregate costings and the like.
2. Our policy changes may alter the way the economy works in some way – for example, an income tax cut might make people work more (or perhaps less), or a tax on plastic bags might lead people to use less of them. Some of these effects may be beneficial and part of the intention of the change; others may be harmful and unintentional. A useful organising idea here is *fiscal neutrality* – if we start from the broad premise that a market economy is reasonably efficient, then we should design our fiscal system so as to alter the behaviour of the economy as little as possible, unless there is some clear argument why we should do otherwise.

Much of the art of policy analysis and policy design lies in balancing these two aspects. For example, redistributing income while maintaining incentives to work, or raising taxes on some harmful goods without hurting the poorest and most vulnerable.

The distributional and incentive analysis of policy changes, and the art of balancing them, are huge and technical subjects that go well beyond this course, but we aim to equip you with many of the key ideas and give you a flavour of where more advanced treatments might take you. It is possible to get remarkably far with a few simple measures.

A note on our language is necessary. This section is quite jargon-heavy and covers a lot of technical issues. None of it is especially difficult, but it does mean that we will be approaching questions about very personal concepts, like poverty, whether it is worth working or whether people are being treated fairly, in a relatively detached, technocratic way. Many people find this detachment distasteful. The detachment of many researchers in this field from the problems they are modelling can be a problem, but we hope to show that there are things that a technocratic, data-driven approach can be of use to those with strong personal commitments, whatever those commitments might be.

In this chapter, we will take you through many of the concepts needed to interpret the outputs of a tax-benefit microsimulation model. Here the emphasis is on how things can be measured in practice. This will enable you to read reports produced using microsimulation techniques, and understand the concepts and something of the mechanics of how they were produced, as well as having a feel for their limitations (Savage, Callan and Walsh, 2015; De Agostini and Hudson, 2019);

This will enable understanding of how:

- You might construct packages of measures that meet some policy objectives;
- How objectives may need to be traded off, the pros and cons of different types of large-sample datasets;
- And how these large datasets are used in microsimulation, including data weighting and uprating.

3.2 Some concepts

Economics is about people – about how people behave, and whether we can make people better or worse off in some sense. But there are a lot of people – sixty-nine million in the UK (Office for National Statistics, 2025b) – and every one of the people is different. In principle we could just list the effects of some tax change on all sixty-nine million people, but without some organising principles it would be impossible to make sense of the results. If we are going to get anywhere here, we need some abstractions.

As such, we will start by briefly revisiting the summary statistics in Chapter 2 – means, medians, totals and some simple charts. In subsequent sections we will then briefly discuss poverty and inequality – these everyday words have distinct technical meanings. Mostly we will be talking about people's incomes, but before we get on to the model, we will briefly double back and discuss what the conceptthat we are trying to summarise should be: should it be people's income, wealth or consumption, or should we go directly for some measure of happiness? Do we need to account for different living arrangements?

3.3 Summary statistics

Figure 3.1 is a picture of one measure of the UK income distribution, as a bar chart.

This comes from the Department for Work and Pensions (DWP) Households Below Average Income (HBAI) data series (Department for Work and Pensions (DWP), 2025).

This shows distribution an official UK measure of income for the financial year 2023/2024. In the UK, financial years normally run from 6 April to 5 April the next year, but from 1 April to 31 March for Government Accounting.

The income measure is 'Equivalised Net Household Income, Before Housing Costs'. In the sections that follow we will discuss in some detail what you should take each of those words to mean, and consider some other possible measures. But for now, it is best to think of it as 'UK income'.

The chart uses data from the FRS (Department for Work and Pensions, 2024a), a large annual survey that provides detailed information about the incomes and living circumstances of households and families in the UK. The microsimulation model used later in this section also uses the FRS. The FRS is one of several large UK surveys. We will further discuss large sample surveys below and let you explore the FRS using our tax-benefit model.

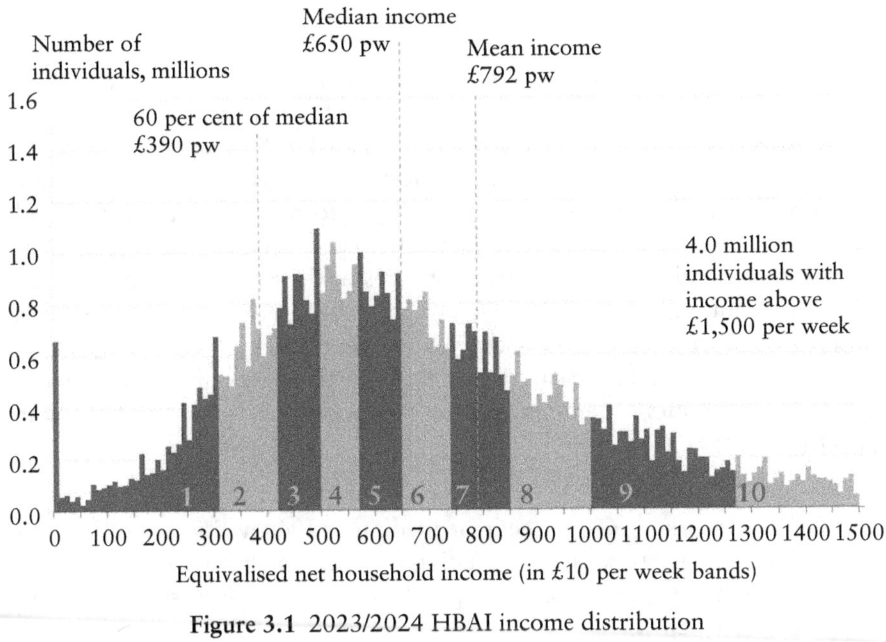

Figure 3.1 2023/2024 HBAI income distribution

There is a lot of useful material in this graph. Income in £ per week is on the X-axis, in £10 bands, and an estimate of the number of people in each band is on the Y-axis.

The chart is a little misleading in that it stops at £1,500 per week (pw). In reality, there are people with incomes higher than that – literally off-the-scale – so the full graph stretches far to the right. It is likely that the chart is truncated at £1,500 because very high incomes are hard to measure and because the high incomes are very high (on a linear scale) and including everything up to (e.g.) £10,000 per week would make the main body of the graph very small.

It is useful to be able to summarise this data in various ways. The mean and median are useful:

- The mean income is £792.
- The median is £650: half the population is richer than the median, and half poorer.

Note how the mean income is nearly £150 higher than the median. This is because there are a large number of relatively small incomes (around where the graph peaks), but a few very large ones out to the right (incomes are 'skewed right'). The large incomes pull the mean up away from the median. Right-skewed data like this are very common in economics – they include not only income but the size of companies, national incomes of countries, the distribution of wealth and consumption.

3.4 What does 'average' mean?

The insensitivity to changes at the very top is why the median is often preferred to the mean in economic discussions. Very high incomes are hard to measure in sample surveys because it is hard to persuade very rich people to participate, because those rich people who do participate may understate their income, and because the circumstances of the rich can be too complex to fit easily into a standard survey, and so recorded top incomes are uncertain and tend to jump around from year to year (Burkhauser *et al.*, 2017).

When you hear a discussion about how some change affects an 'average person', you should remember that an average person could well be comparatively rich.

A couple of other points of note in that graph.

1. The line marked '60 per cent of median (£304 pw)' is the official UK poverty line – 60 per centof median income for that year (note the use of median over mean, for the reasons we have just discussed). We return to poverty below.

2. The chart is shaded into deciles. The dark area on the left labelled '1' contains the poorest tenth of the population, the lighter area labelled '2' to the left of that is the next poorest tenth and so on. Chopping the population up like into progressively richer chunks is a simple but very useful trick. For example, you can see that the mean is halfway up the seventh decile, so about 65 per cent of people have an income less than the mean, and that the poverty line is just below the start of the third decile, so about 18 per cent of people are in poverty, on this measure. We are talking about people's income rather loosely here – obviously there are many millions of people (children, stay-at-home carers and so on) who have no income of their own at all. What we mean instead is something like the averaged income of the household to which they belong. We will be using deciles a lot in what follows.

Often, when we are trying to understand complex data like this one, the best place to start is by drawing pictures of it. The HBAI chart above is a particularly rich one, with, as we have seen, lots of different facets, and we will come to a few other standard charts as we go on.

3.5 Large sample datasets

As we have mentioned, the modelling and analysis we will be doing here mostly uses data from the UK FRS. The FRS is one of several large household survey datasets for the UK. Each dataset has its own speciality, for example:

- The Wealth and Assets Survey (WAS) (Office for National Statistics, 2018, p. 5) – this contains very detailed information on household wealth – the value of houses, pension funds, savings and the like;
- Living Costs and Food Survey (LCFS) (Office For National Statistics and Department For Environment, 2020) – this concentrates on recording household expenditure. One of the LCFS's main uses is providing the weights used in compiling the various measures of inflation, including the Consumer Price Index and Retail Price Index.
- Understanding Society (Understanding Society, 2024) – this tracks a sample of people each year, recording their health, incomes and social attitudes.
- English Longitudinal Survey of Ageing (ELSA) (ELSA, 2019) – like Understanding Society, this tracks a sample of elderly people over time, with specialised questions on health, social care and the like.

There is a good deal of overlap between all of them – all need the same basic demographic information – people's ages, gender, employment status and so on, and all ask at least some basic information on income and wealth, though the FRS goes into much more detail on incomes and WAS on wealth. All of them have been used in various specialised microsimulation models.

By the standards of modern 'Big Data', our datasets are relatively small – a few thousand households – rather than the millions of observations available to the likes of Google or Facebook; but they more than compensate for this in the richness, accuracy and detail of what is recorded. For example, the FRS is the largest of these datasets; in 2023/2024 it contained data on 28,590 adults and 7,658 children living in 17,754 households.

All these major surveys are collected face-to-face using trained interviewers. The LCFS also leaves diaries with people in which they can record their spending; other surveys use diaries to record, for example, trips to work or school. This is expensive, but necessary given the very complex material collected. All except ELSA are surveys of households – they skip, for example, rough sleepers, people in care homes, barracks, prisons and the like. (ELSA follows people to care homes.) They all aim to be representative samples of UK households (ELSA is England only), usually by picking addresses randomly from complete lists of all UK addresses. We discuss exceptions to this below. The list of everything that could be sampled is known as the *sample frame*, and the proportion of addresses picked is known as the *sample frequency*: if we pick one household in every five thousand, the sample frequency is 1/5000 = 0.0002.

The FRS, WAS and LCFS are *cross-section* surveys – each year a new set of households is surveyed. Understanding Society and ELSA are *longitudinal* surveys, where the same people are re-interviewed each year. Longitudinal surveys have advantages. For example, in the econometric modelling you came across earlier, there is always the worry that the variation in the thing that needs to be explained (the 'dependent variable') is because of things that cannot be observed in your dataset, such as tastes, attitudes and the like ('unobserved heterogeneity' in the jargon). It is often possible to exploit the structure of a panel dataset to eliminate this heterogeneity, and so to focus in on just systematic influences. However, this power comes at a cost. It is much more expensive to gather a longitudinal dataset than a cross-section of the same size. With a longitudinal dataset, if one of your subjects decides to go to live in the other end of the country, you have to send your interviewer after them. With cross-sections, it is usually good enough to pick streets or blocks of flats at random and then interview a bunch of people in that street – 'stratified sampling' rather than 'random sampling'. Also, since it is very important to keep people in the longitudinal survey for as long as possible, there is a tendency not to ask the kinds of burdensome questions about incomes, spending or wealth that the cross-sectional surveys might get away with once.

Mostly, our surveys ask questions about the household in a given month or week, with a few questions about how the household has been faring in the longer term. With longitudinal data, of course, we can look back at previous years to get a picture of how things have evolved over time.

3.6 Synthetic data

The large datasets we have been discussing canvas real 'units of observation': people, households, companies, farms, as the case may be. As such, to ensure privacy, these datasets are released under quite restrictive conditions: we cannot distribute an actual FRS dataset as a consequence. Artificial Intelligence can help here, by allowing us to generate synthetic data, which have the same structure and broad content as a real dataset. The data used in this and the next chapter are synthetic data created using programmes from the MIT Synthetic Data Vault (Synthetic Data Vault, 2022). Another popular synthetic data programme is SynthPop (Nowok, 2016). This is a rapidly developing field, some way from maturity. Presently, the algorithms are very good at generating variables with the same broad characteristics as true data (the distribution of wages for example) but less good at the finicky details that microsimulation needs – who is married to whom in a household, for example. And the algorithms struggle with large numbers of variables. As such, the dataset with which you will experiment is necessarily a bit simpler than actual datasets and is possibly a bit wonky round the edges.

3.7 Grossing up and non-response

If a sample survey is truly representative of the population, we can multiply up the observations in the data by a constant to get population estimates. If we see, say, 200 people in the survey with a certain disability, and the sample frequency is 1/2,000, our best estimate is that there are 400,000 (2,000×200) such people in the country. In microsimulation, this step is known as *grossing up*, and the number we are multiplying our sample by (2,000 in this example) is known as the *grossing factor*.

However, our surveys are voluntary. Unlike the Census, no one can be compelled to participate in the FRS or LCFS, and indeed only about 50 per cent of those approached agree to. Participation in the Family Expenditure Survey, the predecessor to these surveys, was over 80 per cent in the early 1960s, but participation has declined steadily ever since (Meyer, Mok and Sullivan, 2015). If non-participation was random, this would not pose much of a problem, but in reality, some types of household are much less likely to participate – those with high incomes, or sick or disabled members, for example. In microsimulation jargon, this is *response bias*. A way around this is *differential weighting*. If, because of response bias, a dataset sampled 1 in every 100 working-aged adults, but 1 in 200 pensioners, we could simply gross up each working-aged person by 100, but each pensioner by 200, and that would give us the correct total for each group. For this to work, of course, we need some external source of information on what the actual number of pensioners and working-age adults should be; information like this typically comes from the Census (which should include everybody) or other official sources such as tax returns or the electoral roll. In practice things are more complicated than this, because there is response bias in multiple dimensions – not just by age, but also income, health, location and other characteristics. Methods exist that can calculate weights that will allow a dataset to be grossed up so as to give correct totals for multiple sets of targets (Creedy, 2003). The models you will be exploring in subsequent chapters use such weights.

3.8 Dealing with uncertainty

If we re-ran our sampling procedure, randomly picking different households, we would likely get a slightly different number for our estimate of disabled people. As such, we cannot be certain that four hundred thousand is the true number. We can use statistical theory to quantify the uncertainty around our estimate. We are not able to discuss the mechanics of this in detail here, but, broadly, the larger the sample and the smaller the amount of variation in our dataset, the more confidence we can have in our estimate (Department for Work and Pensions, 2014). The uncertainty is often expressed using 'confidence intervals' (sometimes called the 'margin of error' in popular discussions). Confidence intervals have a slightly unintuitive interpretation: roughly, the confidence interval is the range that, if we re-ran our sampling many times, the observed value would fall in in 95 per cent of the samples. For simple cases like this, where we want the uncertainty surrounding an estimate, there are usually nice formulas we can apply. But a microsimulation model might need information from dozens of variables (for wages, hours of work and so on), and there might be other sources of uncertainty such as how people's behaviour responds to tax changes. In these cases, there may be no simple formula that we can use to calculate our confidence intervals. Instead, we often estimate uncertainty using *bootstrapping*. Bootstrapping involves running our calculations many times, each with a slightly different sample dataset, and perhaps also with different assumptions about behavioural responses. You can simulate a different sample by deleting a few observations randomly on each run. The little simulation below shows a simple simulation of bootstrapping a sample dataset.

3.9 Other problems with large datasets

There are other difficulties we should briefly mention:

Firstly, some people might be reluctant to answer some embarrassing questions. When grossed up, the LCFS records spending on smoking and drinking that are of about half the level suggested from official tax statistics (Pugh, 2023). This is *under-reporting*. There may be other reasons for the survey estimates being too low; for example, a lot of smoking and drinking may be by non-households, such as tourists, and so outside the sample frame. Particularly important for our purposes is possible under-reporting of high incomes. In most official estimates of poverty and inequality, such as the HBAI estimates we discussed earlier, the incomes reported by the very richest people in the FRS are considered so unreliable that they are replaced entirely by imputed incomes derived from income tax records (Burkhauser *et al.*, 2017).

Secondly, even if we have the right sample, and even if the questions are answered accurately, the questions might be the wrong ones for the purposes of a microsimulation model. For example, in the FRS, the questions asked about wages and salaries are pretty close to those asked on a tax return or benefit application form, but the questions on self-employment incomes are far from what is needed for an accurate tax calculation.

3.10 Conclusion

This chapter has introduced the fundamental concepts and tools necessary for understanding tax-benefit microsimulation modelling and the distributional analysis of government policies. We began by recognising that policy changes inevitably create winners and losers across our diverse society, requiring systematic methods to understand their impacts on poverty, inequality and economic behaviour. The challenge lies in balancing redistributive objectives with maintaining appropriate economic incentives – redistributing income while preserving work incentives, or taxing harmful goods without disproportionately burdening vulnerable groups.

Central to this analysis are large-sample datasets, particularly the FRS, which provide detailed information about the incomes and circumstances of UK households. We have explored how these datasets are constructed through representative sampling, how grossing factors and differential weighting address response bias and how statistical methods like bootstrapping help quantify uncertainty in our estimates. The use of synthetic data, generated through AI techniques, offers promising solutions to privacy constraints while enabling wider access to analytical tools.

However, these powerful analytical methods come with important limitations. Survey data suffer from non-response bias; under-reporting of sensitive information like high incomes or expenditure on tobacco and alcohol; and questions that may not perfectly align with policy requirements. The technical, detached approach required for rigorous analysis can seem distasteful when dealing with deeply personal issues like poverty and fairness, yet this systematic framework proves essential for evidence-based policymaking.

As we progress to subsequent chapters, remember that microsimulation combines technical sophistication with real-world complexity. The measures and methods introduced here provide the foundation for understanding how policy changes ripple through our society, enabling informed decisions about the fiscal instruments that shape our collective future.

4

Understanding measures

Key foci

- Understanding equivalence scales and their role in measuring individual wellbeing within households.
- Comparing poverty measures: headcount, poverty gap and the Foster–Greer–Thorbecke index.
- Examining inequality through Lorenz curves, Gini coefficients and alternative measures.
- Balancing efficiency, fiscal neutrality and distributional objectives in tax-benefit design.

4.1 Individuals, families and households

Households Below Average Income (HBAI) describes the distribution of incomes of individual people, and almost all of what follows is about the welfare of individuals. But people are social beings. Most people live in households (those living alone can be thought of as one-person households). Others live in other arrangements: prisons, communes, barracks, care homes and the like, but, as we have seen, these are typically out of scope of our datasets.

The ONS defines a household as follows:

> A household comprises of 1 person living alone or a group of people (not necessarily related) living at the same address who: share cooking facilities and share a living room or sitting room or dining area. (Horsfield, 2016)

Note the need for shared facilities and shared rooms. The circumstances of the household as a whole affect the wellbeing of each individual member. There are two main issues here:

1. Larger households might be more efficient than small ones. A two-person household might not need twice the income of a one-person household to have the same standard of living. It is cheaper to buy food in bulk; a household might need only one fridge or cooker regardless of how large it is, and so on. Also, a member of a larger household might be able to specialise, for example, in paid or unpaid work.
2. Household members might not get an equal share of what is available.

We will consider these in turn.

4.2 Equivalence scales

A scale that reflects the different needs and capabilities of households of different sizes is known as an *equivalence scale*. If households did not become more efficient with size, and everyone had the same needs, then the equivalence scale would simply be 1 for a single-person household, 2 for a two-person household and so on. If there are economies of scale, the numbers might be 1 for a single, 1.5 for two-person, 1.8 for three. The scale might be lower for multi-person households with children, but higher for households with disabled or very elderly members.

You divide observed household income by the relevant scale to get *equivalised income* of the household, which is a measure of average wellbeing of the individual members. Recall that the Households Below Average Income figures we saw earlier use equivalised income (Department for Work and Pensions, 2024).

Where might we get such a scale? There is an equivalence scale implicit in some state benefits; for example, here are the scale rates for Universal Credit, a benefit paid to low-income families:

From this, you can see that if the scale for a single adult was 1.0, a two-adult household would be 1.57, and a two-adult, one-child household 2.42 (1.57 + 0.85). However, these benefit amounts must themselves have come from somewhere. Can we derive an equivalence scale from first principles?

One approach uses the regression techniques you learned in the previous week and the Living Costs and Food Survey we mentioned last time. The

Table 4.1 Scale rates for Universal Credit

Recipient	*£ per month*	*Proportion of single person*
Single person (age 25+)	400.14	1.0
Couple	628.10	1.57
Child	339.00	0.85

approach here dates back over 150 years, to the first ever systematic budget surveys, carried out in Germany by Ernst Engel. Engel was studying how shares of expenditure on different goods varied with income and with family size (Chai and Moneta, 2010). He made two observations:

1. Although on average rich families spent more on food than poor ones, rich families spent a smaller share of their income on food than poor families;
2. Larger families had a larger share of spending on food than smaller families with the same income.

Taken together, these give us a simple strategy to estimate equivalence scales: households of different sizes have the same wellbeing on average when their share of spending on food is the same.

Figure 4.1 illustrates one way of doing this, using the 2017/2018 edition of the Living Costs and Food Survey (LCFS) we discussed last time.

Total spending is plotted by each household on the x-axis against the share of food in total spending on the y-axis. Each dot represents spending by one household. The LCFS households are grouped into those with children (marked in orange) and those without children (in blue). The two solid lines show the average food consumption at each level of total consumption for our two classes of household – these are known as *Engel Curves* (Chai and Moneta, 2010). The curves are computed using the regression techniques you studied in the macroeconomics week.

Although there is a good deal of variation, the patterns Engel observed 150 years ago are there in this dataset.

Now we can calculate an empirical equivalence scale. Pick some share of food spending – a good one might be the median food share (11.6 per cent). That's the dashed horizontal line. Then we look up on the Engel Curves the level of total spending the two groups would on average need for this share. These are the points A and B on the diagram – for households with children, this is £747.90 (point B) and for those without, it is £525.38 (point A). The ratio between these is 1.423, which is our simple equivalence scale: our estimate is that families with children need 42 per cent more spending than families without children to enjoy the same standard of living.

A full analysis would do almost every aspect of this differently. You would want to allow for different household sizes and compositions, not just the presence or otherwise of children, and perhaps also other factors such as age, disability and the like. Nonetheless, we hope this shows you how a little bit of theory and a good dataset can be used to produce useful results in a straightforward manner. Much of the work of empirical economists, especially in the public sector, consists of doing simple exercises like this.

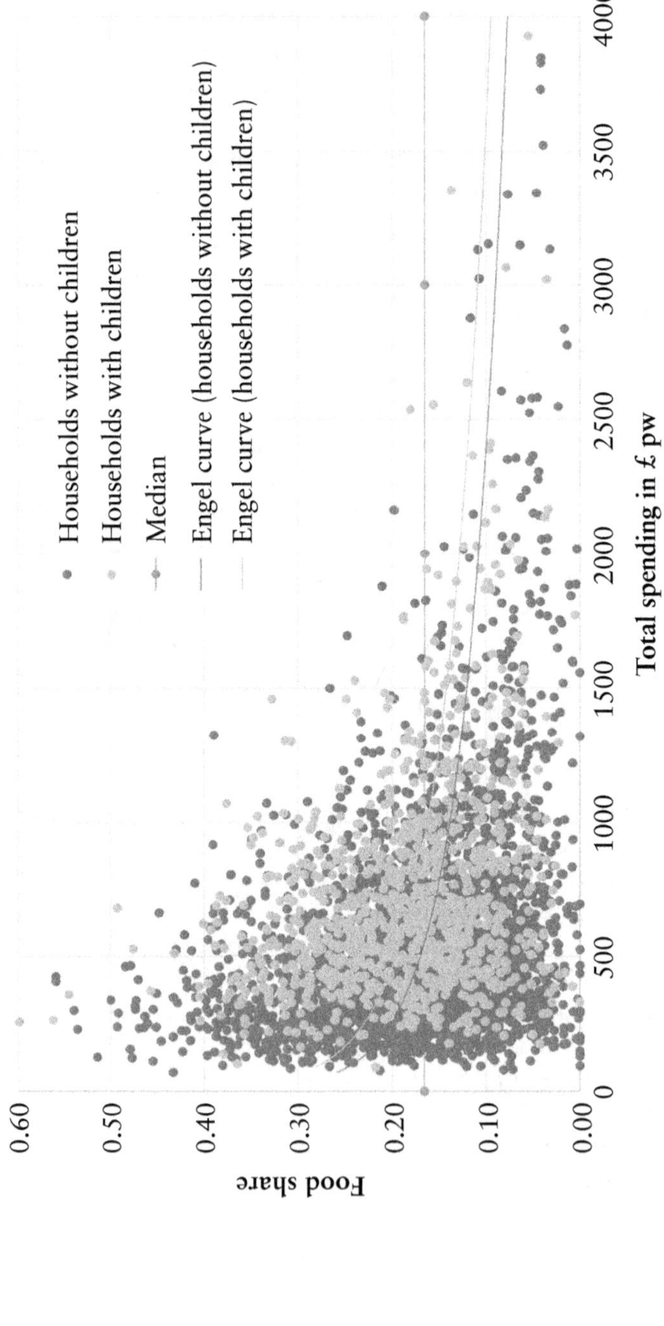

Figure 4.1 Food share mapped against total spend in £ per week. Calculations using 2017/2018 Living Costs and Food Survey.

Table 4.2 Modified OECD scale

Type	*Proportion of single person*
One adult	1.0
Two adults	1.5
Two adults, one child	1.8
Two adults, two children	2.1
Two adults, three children	2.4

The Households Below Average Income data we looked at earlier, which is equivalised using the *Modified OECD Scale* (Anyaegbu, 2010) is as follows:

Table 4.2 continues with an extra 0.5 for each extra adult, and an extra 0.3 for each extra child; the OECD defines a child as someone aged thirteen or under. The OECD scale is a standard scale used in many countries (Asghar Zaidi, Hagenaars and de Vos, 1994).

4.3 Unequal distribution within households

Once we have equivalised our household incomes, we need to assign it to household members. Typically, we just assign everyone the average household income. But this ignores the possibility of discrimination by gender, or other characteristics such as age or disability.

Making a different assumption requires somehow looking inside households to infer how sharing of goods and the allocation of tasks actually works in practice (Case and Deaton, 2003).

In principle, we can use budget surveys to examine this question, using variants of the approach above. If we can identify specifically male, female or children's goods in our survey (clothing might be an example), then we can measure how spending on these vary between, for example, households where women have significant income of their own (through work or perhaps benefit payments) and households where all the income accrues to men.

Alternatively, we could look at health or education outcomes – is shifting income between men and women associated with improvements in female health or school enrolment? There have been many studies, and the evidence seems mixed (Deaton, 2019). Consumption based studies tend to find no effect, while studies of health and education outcomes often show better outcomes in cases where incomes shifted from men to women.

4.4 Benefit units

There is a further subdivision of households we should briefly consider. Some state benefits such as Universal Credit or Job Seeker's Allowance are assessed over 'benefit units' – roughly speaking, adults living together as a couple and any children dependent on them. A household with a married couple and two children, and also an elderly parent, would be one household, but two benefit units, since the elderly parent would be assessed separately for means-tested benefits. In most modern analyses, benefit units are solely an indirect part of the modelling process, but in the past results were often presented at the benefit unit, rather than individual level. Interestingly, a recent re-examination of poverty statistics by the Social Metrics Commission (2024) uses benefit units – which it calls 'Sharing Units' – as its main unit of analysis.

4.5 Poverty

For our purposes, those in poverty are those whose command over resources falls below some minimum acceptable standard. To make this operational (something we can measure, and design programmes to alleviate), we need to establish what this minimum is – our poverty line. In reality, there is no single objective point above which people have an acceptable standard of life, and below which they do not; rather, there is a continuum. Stress levels, for example, worsen steadily the poorer people get, and then jump sharply as people approach and fall below a 'desperation threshold', which appears to coincide with the minimum income needed to satisfy basic needs (Nettle *et al.*, 2024). There are a variety of ways we could define such a standard; discussing these at length would take us off-topic, but an interesting recent approach is to use focus groups to gauge public opinion on what an acceptable minimum standard might be (Hirsch, 2019). And, as we have briefly noted, there are also multi-dimensional standards – recently the Social Metrics Commission has proposed one such for the UK (The Social Metrics Commission, 2024). But, for now, it is enough that an official poverty line exists – for the UK, since 1991, it has been defined as 60 per cent of median equivalised household income; looking back at Figure 3.1, this is the line marked '£390 pw' to the left of the chart; you can see straight away that, since the line falls towards the top of the second decile, about 18 per cent of the population is in poverty on that measure.

4.5.1 *Absolute and relative poverty*

Because the HBAI line is defined using the income of the year in question, it drifts up or down each year as median incomes rise and fall: it is a 'relative poverty line'. Indeed, poverty alleviation programmes will themselves change median incomes, and hence change the poverty line. For some purposes, therefore, we might also want to measure poverty against some unchanging standard: 'absolute poverty'. This can be done by picking an HBAI line for some reference year and, after adjusting it for price changes, applying it to subsequent years.

4.5.1.1 Aggregate measures of poverty

Once we have a poverty line, we can use our survey data to estimate the level of poverty in our society, and when we come to our microsimulation model in the next section, we can estimate how policy changes would change that level. The obvious way to do this is simply to count the number of people below the poverty line – a 'headcount' measure – and that is indeed what the official HBAI statistics do.

There is a problem with headcounts, however, especially when we come to designing anti-poverty programmes. Consider someone with income just below the poverty line – Alice, on (say) £349 pw – and someone far below the line: Bob on £203 pw. Cut Bob's benefits by £2 and use the money to pay for a £2 increase for Alice. Alice is now above the poverty line, so is removed from the poverty headcount. Bob is further below the poverty line but still counts for one on the headcount measure. We have reduced the poverty headcount by transferring money from a very poor person to a richer (though still quite poor) person. This is not just an academic point – some significant reforms to the benefit system have had exactly this effect (Dilnot and Stark, 1986), cutting support benefits for those on very low incomes and increasing support for the 'near-poor'. And targets for poverty reduction, such as those in the Scottish Government's Child Poverty Bill (Cabinet Secretary for Communities and Local Government, 2019) are always more easily attained by targeting the near-poor than the very poor.

It would therefore be good to have a poverty measure that never improves when we transfer money from a poorer person to a richer one – the idea that measures of poverty or inequality should never improve from an upward transfer is known as *Dalton's Principle* (Fishburn and Willig, 1984).

One obvious thing to do is to consider how far below the poverty line Alice and Bob are – Alice starts £1 below, and Bob £100. This leads to the poverty gap measure – summing up all the gaps for everyone gives the minimum amount that would have to be spent to eliminate poverty, *if* spending was perfectly targeted on the poor. (Poverty gaps are usually expressed as a fraction of the poverty line, so Alice's gap is 1/304 ≈ 0.003 and Bob's is 100/304 ≈ 0.328.) The poverty gap is useful, but still violates Dalton's Principle – to see this, suppose now Bob was in the same position as before, but Alice started £50 below the poverty line. The poverty gap is therefore £150 in total. Our transfer upwards of £2 from Bob to Alice makes no difference at all to this poverty gap – it is still £150, just distributed differently – £152 for Bob and £48 for Alice. Transfers upwards do not always worsen the poverty gap, again violating Dalton.

More sophisticated measures exist that do not violate Dalton's Principle. The most commonly used is the Foster–Greer–Thorndyke measure (Haughton and Khandker, 2009, pp. 9–34), sometimes known as the 'Poverty Severity Index'. This takes the proportional gaps, squares them, and then sums them – squaring the gaps means that the large gaps of very poor people like Bob become much more important in the final sum than small gaps of near-poor people like Alice. This means that our FTG measure for Alice and Bob would be 0.003^2 + 0.0328^2 ≈ 0.001. It can be shown mathematically that this measure can never be improved by an upwards transfer.

4.6 More sophisticated measures

Even more sophisticated measures of poverty exist; for example, a measure proposed by Amartya Sen (Hamilton, 2023) combines a measure of poverty with a measure of inequality amongst the poor (we come to inequality next).

The problem with ever more sophisticated measures is that they become progressively harder to explain to policymakers and the public more generally. And, of course, keeping civil society informed and on-side is a vital part of any successful anti-poverty strategy. Our microsimulation model can report all of these measures, and it can be a good exercise to consider which of them, if any, you'd want to report to different audiences.

4.7 Inequality

Inequality is a broader concept than poverty, defined across the whole population rather than just the poor. As with poverty, our job here is to take the intuitive notions we all have about whether some state is more or less equal than another and make them operational, so we can make reasonably precise statements about the inequality of society and how possible reforms might change it.

Table 4.3 Incomes of a small country

Person	*Income (£)*	*Cumulative population*	*Cumulative income (£)*	*Population share (%)*	*Income share (%)*
1	10.00	1	10.00	12.50%	6.90%
2	11.00	2	21.00	25.00%	14.48%
3	12.00	3	33.00	37.50%	22.76%
4	15.00	4	48.00	50.00%	33.10%
5	17.00	5	65.00	62.50%	44.83%
6	20.00	6	85.00	75.00%	58.62%
7	25.00	7	110.00	87.50%	75.86%
8	35.00	8	145.00	100.00%	100.00%
Total	**145.00**	8	**145.00**	**100.00%**	**100.00%**

We will start with a simple table and a diagram. In Table 4.3, column two, we show all the incomes of the people in a small economy. They have been sorted from the poorest at the top to the richest at the bottom. Next to that is the *cumulative population* – the sum of all the population up to that point. The first cell is 1, the next 2 (1 + 1) and so on. Then we have the sum of incomes up to that point (so the first is 10, the next 10 + 11 = 21 and so on). Finally, we have two columns which just re-express the cumulative populations and incomes as a share of the totals (the totals are recorded at the bottom); as with poverty, a lot of the work on inequality is done using proportions and shares rather than absolute levels. Since the total income is 145, and the poorest two people have 21, the share of the bottom two is 14.48 per cent (100*21/145), and so on.

With perfect inequality, the share of everyone but the top person is zero, the top person has 100 per cent. The graph in Figure 4.2 charts the cumulative population share on the x-axis against cumulative income share on the y-axis. This is the *Lorenz curve*, and, though simple, it is probably the best tool we have for thinking systematically about inequality.

The more equal a country is, the closer the Lorenz curve will be to the diagonal, and, conversely, the more unequal it is, the more the curve will be bowed away from the diagonal.

The *Gini coefficient* summarises this well, and it is the most widely quoted inequality measure. In Figure 4.2 we have shaded the area between the perfect equality diagonal and the actual Lorenz curve in yellow.

The bigger the yellow area the greater the inequality. The Gini coefficient just expresses this area as a percentage (sometimes as a proportion, so 0.2 instead of 20 per cent) of the triangle ABC in the diagram. Complete inequality gives a Gini of 1, and complete equality gives 0.

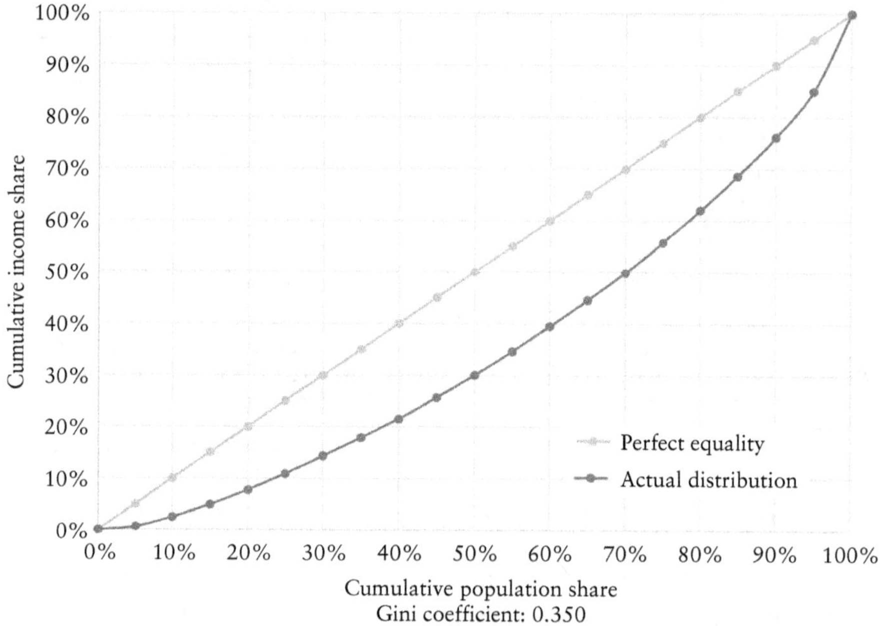

Figure 4.2 Income share mapped against population share

Table 4.4 Selected country Gini coefficients

Country	*Gini (%)*
Australia	35.8
Czech Republic	29.9
Denmark	28.2
UK	33.2
USA	41.5
South Africa	63.0

Table 4.4 from the World Bank shows some international comparisons of Gini coefficients (World Bank, 2025).

The UK has a high inequality by European standards, but a low one compared to the USA or South Africa. Figure 4.3 shows the UK Gini coefficient over time, using many years of our HBAI data we encountered earlier.

The 2008 recession actually *reduced* inequality on the Gini measure, mainly by wiping out some very high incomes in the financial sector.

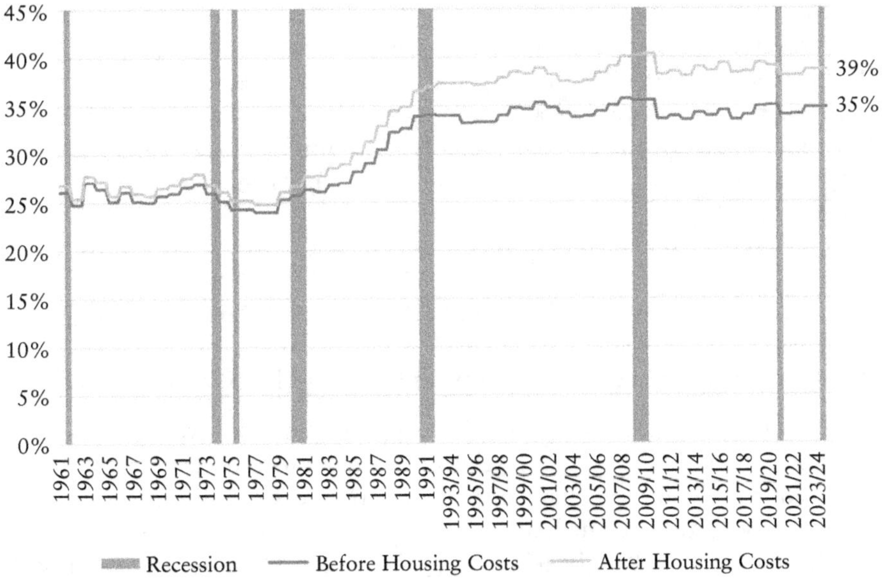

Figure 4.3 UK Gini coefficient between 1961 and 2024. Source: Department for Work and Pensions, 2024.

4.8 Advanced measures of inequality

There is a huge technical literature on inequality. Many other summary indices have been proposed, each with different desirable properties (Haughton and Khandker, 2009, pp. 101–119). For example:

- The *Theil index* has the feature that it can be neatly disaggregated to show the contribution of different groups to inequality; for example, the rise in UK inequality in the 1980s and early 1990s was accompanied by large changes in regional inequality. With the Theil index one can split changes in overall inequality into changes in inequality *between* regions (London v. the South East, for example) and changes *within* regions (greater inequality in London between financial workers and the rest);
- The *Atkinson index* allows inequality to depend not just on the distribution of income, but also on the analyst's (or society's) views on inequality ('Inequality Aversion');
- The *Palma index* (Cobham and Sumner, 2014) has recently become popular – it is simply the ratio between the share of the richest 10 per cent of the population and the poorest 40 per cent.

As with poverty measures, there is a tension between how sophisticated these measures are and how easy they are to explain to non-specialists. The Palma index, in particular, is very easy to explain, and so has become very popular, but it arguably lacks a strong basis – it clearly violates Dalton's Principle; for example, since upward redistributions within the bottom 40 per cent, the middle 50 per cent or the top 10 per cent, do not change the value of the Palma.

4.9 Illustrative distributional effects from different policies

What happens to poverty, inequality and mean and median incomes if:

1. Britain welcomes a group of Russian oligarchs? Answer: inequality ↑, poverty (both absolute and relative) ≈, mean income ↑, median ≈
2. Britain welcomes a group of penniless refugees? Answer: inequality ↑, poverty ↑, mean ↓, median ≈
3. All incomes in Britain increase by 5 per cent? Answer: inequality ≈, absolute poverty ↓, relative poverty ≈, inequality ≈, mean ↑, median ↑
4. All incomes increase by £10 pw? Answer: absolute poverty ↓, relative poverty ↓, inequality ↓, mean ↑, median ↑

4.10 Poverty and inequality of what? Income, consumption and beyond

Up to now we have used the term 'income', without worrying about what exactly we mean by it, or whether income is really the best thing to focus on. You may well have a reasonable idea of your family's income. But it is notoriously difficult to find a definition of income that fits every case, and one that can be made operational. The classic discussion of this in chapters 2 and 3 of the Meade Report (Meade, 1978). To see the problem, consider Alice and Bob. They have steady jobs on the same monthly salary, so on the face of it the same income, but Bob knows he will come into a large inheritance on retirement and Alice knows she will not. Clearly, Bob can enjoy a better lifestyle now than Alice, since Alice may have to divert much of her salary into pensions and savings. Likewise, compare Bob, on his steady income, with Cynthia, a TikTok sensation who has made a million pounds this year but who worries about being replaced by the next big thing in a matter of months. In the eyes of the Family Resources Survey (FRS), or indeed the tax authorities, Cynthia is by far the richer. But, if this is her one chance at success, can Cynthia really afford a lavish lifestyle?

This naturally leads to the thought that *consumption* would be a better thing to measure than income. The amount that Alice, Bob and Cynthia are consuming could be a good indicator of their view of their sustainable, or *permanent*, income. But in practice, consumption has problems of its own. Consider durable goods: in any given month, you either buy a fridge or you do not, and in either case, your spending on fridges is a poor indicator of your consumption of the service your fridge provides (Kay, Keen and Morris, 1984). So a comprehensive measure of consumption requires the imputation of some notional 'rental value' from all of a household's durable assets.

Housing is a particular problem in this regard, both for income and consumption measures. For those who own their houses, an 'imputed rent' would for many people be the largest element in their income, and, as can be seen from the frequent disputes over house valuations for local taxes, it can be very difficult to agree on what such a rental value should be. Many renters may have little or no choice about how much they pay. It is hard to tell whether rising rents reflect better quality housing, or simply a situation from which renters cannot escape. For these reasons, our official poverty and inequality measures are offered in before and after housing cost versions (Department for Work and Pensions, 2015).

Most studies of the poverty in the developing world measure consumption rather than income, for a related but distinct reason – small farmers, sharecroppers and peasants may well consume much of what they produce, only selling some, so any measure of cash income may well understate their wellbeing.

4.11 Incomes over time

The differing fates of Alice, Bob and Cynthia highlight the importance of considering the *intertemporal* nature of income and consumption. There are fewer steady jobs than there were in previous decades, but our surveys are mostly short-term; if they happened to pick Cynthia during her moment of fame she'll be recorded as very rich, and otherwise as very poor, whereas in reality if she's sensible she may have a modest but reasonable lifestyle for life. So our surveys may mistake *instability* in income for inequality (Blundell and Preston, 1998). With the rise of the 'gig economy', it is possible that much of recorded poverty represents people flitting in and out of jobs rather than permanent poverty. There is evidence that income volatility itself is harmful (Nettle *et al.*, 2024).

There is another important intertemporal aspect: people likely start out as a net recipient of benefits (such as Child Benefit) and public spending on education and health. As they age, there is a good chance they become a net contributor through taxation, perhaps with a period as a net recipient if they have a family of their own, before receiving State Pensions and perhaps social care towards the end of their life. So, you can view much of the tax-benefit system as adjusting a person's lifetime income rather than redistributing between groups. To capture this aspect, a long-run multi-year model is needed; that's not what we are presenting here, but we will briefly discuss such a model at the end of this week (Hills, 2004, pp. 184–206).

4.12 Broader indicators of wellbeing

Instead of single measures such as income or consumption, some advocate for multi-dimensional measures. These attempt to condense measures of income, education, health and personal freedom into a single index. Examples of these are the 'capabilities framework' of Amartya Sen (Sen, 1999), the United Nations Multidimensional Poverty Index (United Nations Development Programme, 2019) and, for the UK, the Social Metrics Commission Poverty Index (The Social Metrics Commission, 2024). These are appealing in some respects: reducing wellbeing to how much you earn, or how much you consume can seem distasteful, and, especially at the levels of countries or regions, it is certainly possible to have high incomes but poor outcomes for, say, health or education attainment. But there are problems with multidimensional indexes, too: if one aspect improves (health, say) but another worsens (education, perhaps), it is hard to say definitively that your index has gone up or down. And, although our main datasets have reasonably good data on many of the components of these indexes, in practice it can be very hard to operationalise these measures: as you will see, we can predict quite accurately the effects of fiscal changes on incomes or consumption, but predicting the effect on health or education attainment is much harder.

As well as these broad measures, there is sometimes concern about individual aspects; for example, fuel poverty (Department for Business, Energy and Industrial Strategy, 2019; Bradshaw and Keung, 2022), food poverty (Scottish Government, 2021) and recently period poverty (BBC News, 2019). As with the multidimensional measures, it may be difficult to operationalise these – you might need to augment the model we are about to look at with a *demand system* – a model which predicts how consumption of (e.g.) domestic fuel varies with income and prices (Deaton, 2019).

For all this, in what follows we will mostly be talking about changes in incomes, but you should keep these difficulties in mind. We cannot do everything, but that does not mean we should do nothing.

4.13 Incidence: who really pays taxes?

All the examples above and almost all of what follows are about things that directly affect people, by, for example, taking some of their income in tax, raising their wages or paying them benefits. But we can use microsimulation to study, for example, companies, farms or local authorities. This raises an important point: ultimately, the effects of a change to, say, the taxation of corporations or the funding of local councils falls on people, by changing, for example, dividends, local taxes or the quality of local parks, but the effect is at one remove from the policy. Resolving this indirection is known as finding the *effective incidence* of the change; the first-round effect is the *formal incidence*. For example, recent debates about the fairness of the United States tax code revolve around the question of whether corporation tax – which has been cut heavily in recent years – ultimately falls on wages or profits (Kay, 2005; Clausing, 2012; Saez and Zucman, 2019).

Considering the ultimate incidence of policy changes is important, but can be very difficult. Even the direct changes we are concentrating on here can have an incidence beyond those immediately affected – an income tax increase might cause higher prices in some industries, and so be 'passed on' to consumers who were not the direct targets of the tax. For the most part we will be considering first-round effects on the people directly affected by our policy changes – so, the formal incidence of the policy – but it is worth keeping in mind that the effective incidence may be different.

4.14 Incentives and fiscal neutrality

Mainstream economics starts from the premise that a properly functioning competitive market economy is the most efficient way of organising production and consumption for a modern society.

Economists think of an economy as a 'price system': where the market works well, prices reflect the relevant costs ('at the margin') of doing a thing, and people following these prices will be let 'as if by an invisible hand' to do the best thing (Smith, 1776). 'At the margin' is important here – it is the price of doing a little bit more of something that's the key thing – the price of the next litre of petrol you buy, or the wage for the next hour you work.

In designing a tax and benefit system, one common objective is therefore to distort market incentives as little as possible. There is a presumption in favour of low *marginal* tax rates on goods so the prices of things do not move away from their efficient level too much. In this context, we would consider labour to be a good that's bought and sold at a wage, so the presumption is for low marginal tax rates on earnings (We will discuss marginal versus average tax rates in more detail when we have the simulation model in front of us.) (Meade, 1978).

As well as low marginal rates, there is also a presumption in favour of broad-based taxation. Suppose a particular brand of baked beans was taxed, but all other brands were not. Since brands of beans are likely close substitutes, even if the tax rate was low, the taxed brand of beans would likely be wiped out – a pretty severe distortion. A tax on all beans would be less distortionary, a tax on all food better still, and a tax on everything best of all from this point of view. In the UK, most food, children's clothes and books are not subject to our 20 per cent Value Added Tax (VAT), while most other goods are. Economists at the Treasury have long had their eye on these exemptions, while politicians and their advisors have jealously guarded them, on both distributional and electoral grounds (both sides are right in their own way) (European Commission, 2011; Kay, 2012).

Sometimes subtleties in the tax code matter more than the headline tax rates. Consider corporation taxes – taxes on profits of companies. If a company is operating efficiently and making the most profit it can (maximising profits), then in principle it has no reason to change what it is doing if a proportion of those profits are taken away – its before-tax plan is still the best it can do. Neutrality in this case means careful attention to the detail of the tax code so the notion of profit for the tax corresponds to the notion of profit that the company seeks to maximise.

There are many important counterexamples. Collective action will always be required to supply 'public goods' (for example, defence) and to correct the distribution of income. Markets may fail altogether in some circumstances – where important information is unobtainable, for example (Stiglitz, 2016). Frequently the price that a free market would produce would not reflect the true marginal cost of things. Petrol pollutes, alcohol causes crime and illness, and so on – these are 'externalities' that are not priced in private transactions. In these cases, there is a good argument for having taxes that deliberately move the prices away from their free market level to reflect the full 'social' cost.

There is another sense in which we might want changes to the fiscal system to be fiscally neutral: we might want any change to have a net zero cost, so any tax cut is paid for by a spending reduction somewhere, and any benefit increase paid for by a tax rise. Proposals that fail to do this are often criticised in the media and parliament, but there might be good reasons to design a package of measures that is not zero-cost: for example if we want to boost demand in a time of recession, or if we believe our measures might improve the efficiency of the economy in the long run. In any event, it is always important to know what the projected net cost of proposals is, and to have a good story to hand if the cost is not zero.

4.15 Conclusion

This chapter has explored the fundamental concepts and measurement challenges central to understanding income distribution, poverty and inequality. We began by examining how individuals are organised into households and how equivalence scales help us account for economies of scale and differing needs within households of varying sizes and compositions. The Modified OECD scale provides a practical framework for converting household incomes into comparable measures of individual wellbeing, though questions about intra-household distribution remain complex.

We then investigated how poverty can be operationalised through poverty lines, distinguishing between absolute and relative measures. Beyond simple headcount measures, we explored more sophisticated approaches like the poverty gap and the Foster–Greer–Thorbecke index, which better satisfy Dalton's Principle by accounting for the depth and severity of poverty. Similarly, our examination of inequality introduced the Lorenz curve and Gini coefficient as standard tools, alongside alternative measures like the Theil, Atkinson and Palma indices, each offering different analytical advantages.

Throughout, we have emphasised the practical challenges facing policy analysts. The choice between income and consumption measures involves difficult trade-offs, particularly regarding housing costs and durable goods. Multi-dimensional wellbeing indices offer broader perspectives but sacrifice some analytical precision. The distinction between formal and effective incidence reminds us that policy impacts may differ from initial intentions.

Finally, we considered how efficiency concerns and market neutrality shape tax-benefit design, while acknowledging that deliberate departures from neutrality may be justified to address market failures or achieve distributional objectives. As we move forward to microsimulation modelling, these conceptual foundations will prove essential for designing and evaluating policy reforms that balance competing objectives of efficiency, equity and fiscal sustainability.

5

Building a tax-benefit model

Key foci

- Building functional tax-benefit models using Python and synthetic datasets.
- Understanding model validation through bottom-up and top-down approaches.
- Confronting limitations: non-take-up, static assumptions and formal versus effective incidence.
- Selecting appropriate analytical tools and accepting useful imperfection over unattainable perfection.

5.1 Building a tax-benefit model

We have covered a lot of ground quite fast: summary statistics, large sample datasets, data weighting, measuring poverty and inequality, measures of wellbeing, tax incidence and incentives. In this chapter, we discuss the practicalities of building a tax-benefit model. The accompanying workbooks, should you follow them, will walk you through building your own model of your own and using it to construct policy packages.

In essence a tax-benefit model is a simple thing. It is a computer program that calculates the effects of possible changes to the fiscal system on a sample of households. We take each of the households in our dataset, calculate how much tax the household members are liable for under some proposed tax and benefit regime, and how much benefits they are entitled to, and add up the results. If the sample is representative of the population, and the modelling sufficiently accurate, the model can then tell you, for example, the net costs of the proposals, the numbers who are made better or worse off, the effective tax rates faced by individuals, the numbers taken in and out of poverty by some change and much more.

5.2 Structure

The main issue we have not covered yet is how we actually do the tax and benefit calculations. The first issue to confront is that there are a lot of data to model: the standard guide to the UK tax system is Tolley's Guides (Redson, 2019).

The corresponding element for the Benefit System is the Child Poverty Action Group Welfare Benefits guide (CPAG, 2021), which is captured in Figure 5.1.

There is no royal road to creating the actual calculations; it is mostly a question of judgement – how much detail it is necessary to include, how best to use the available data and so on.

Figure 5.2 sets out a simple flowchart of the steps the model goes through.

Most of the steps here are hopefully familiar to you from earlier in the week; the one thing we have not discussed is *uprating*: our datasets are typically one to three years old by the time they are released, and wages,

Figure 5.1 Child Poverty Action Group's Welfare Benefits and Tax Credits Handbook 2019/2020

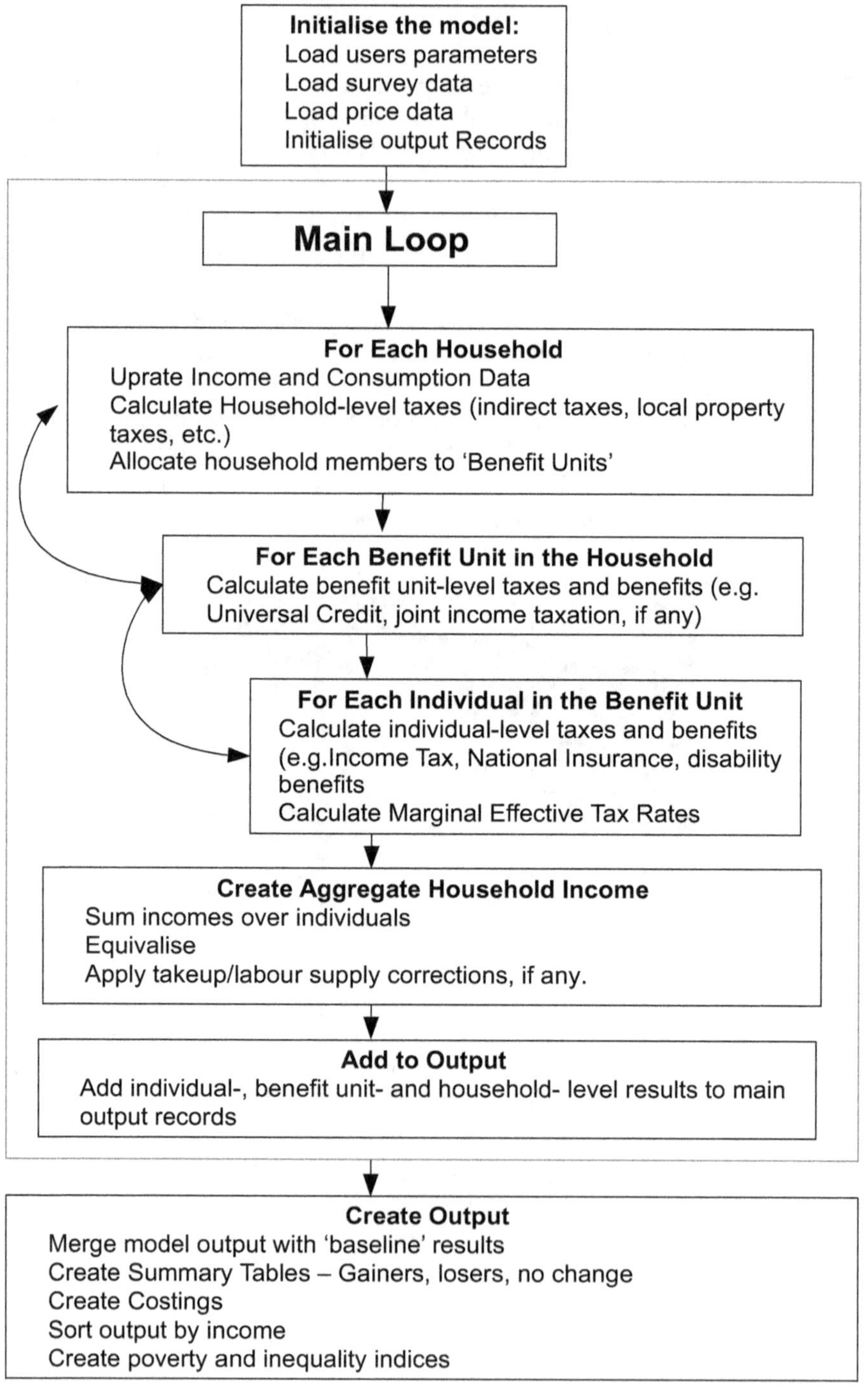

Figure 5.2 Model flowchart

prices and interest rates will have changed since the time of the interviews, so we multiply incomes, rents and consumption by amounts to reflect these changes.

5.3 How do we know the model is right?

A model of this sort inevitably gets quite big, and so there are lots of places it could go wrong. The model can be checked from the bottom up: are the individual calculations correct, is the survey data handled correctly, and so on. Or it can be tested top down: are the model's predictions for total amounts spent on benefits or raised in taxes close to what actually happens? In principle these two approaches are complimentary, but a model that is accurate at the individual level might actually be quite bad at predicting aggregates, and good performance at the aggregate level might hide significant errors in individual calculations.

5.4 Picking the right tool for the job

One of the key skills that is needed in applied economics is the ability to pick an appropriate tool for the job at hand, so it is worth us briefly exploring this change of tack.

Other tools that have been found useful in economics include the following:

- *Pencil and paper*: economics has a large inventory of simple but powerful graphics that can be applied to many situations – supply and demand diagrams, IS/LM, budget constraints and many others. The ability to sketch these is a key skill for an applied economist.
- *Spreadsheets*: these can be tremendously useful tools. But, like all tools, they are more appropriate for some tasks than others. Spreadsheets have been extensively studied (Panko, 1998; EuroSPRIG, 2019) and it is known that they are especially error-prone when dealing with complex logic or large amounts of data.
- *Statistical packages*: these are large computer programs that are optimised to produce, for example, the linear regressions you encountered earlier in this week, and in the macroeconomics week. Examples commonly used in economics include SAS (https://www.sas.com/en_gb/home.html), SPSS (https://www.ibm.com/analytics/spss-statistics-software) and Stata (https://www.stata.com/). Excellent free statistical packages are R (https://www.r-project.org/) and Gretl (http://gretl.sourceforge.net/).

- *Databases*: these are specialised programs that allow modelling, retrieval and updating of large amounts of complex data. Examples include Postgres and Oracle. Systems specialised in the fast processing of 'big data' are now appearing; an example is Apache Hadoop (http://hadoop.apache.org/).
- *High-level programming languages*: these are designed to express complex logic, such as the rules of the tax system, in a clear and efficient way. Examples that are widely used include Fortran (https://en.wikipedia.org/wiki/Fortran), Python (https://www.python.org/) and Julia (https://julialang.org/).

Sometimes large projects use many different tools, organised as *toolchains*; for example, a database to accumulate and retrieve data, a programming language to process it and a spreadsheet to display the results.

Although it is good to be aware of the options, it is impossible for a single person to master all of these things. But there may come a time in a large project where the best course is to employ a specialist, or to learn a new skill yourself – professional economists would normally be expected to know at least one statistical package, for instance.

On the other hand, sometimes the optimal tool is the one you are familiar with, rather than the technically perfect one. For example, the UK Treasury's tax-benefit model, IGOTM, is implemented in the SAS statistical system (Brice, 2015) rather than a conventional programming language: SAS is widely used in the UK Government, and that familiarity is judged to outweigh any awkwardness in applying SAS a little out of its natural domain.

5.5 Tax-benefit models: what could possibly go wrong?

Very simple modelling does not calculate what people and households will actually receive in benefits or pay in tax, but what *entitlements* to benefits and *liabilities* to tax are. This is modelling of *formal incidence*. People's entitlements and liabilities are important to know in themselves, but to go from liabilities and entitlements to what is actually received in tax and paid out in benefits requires a few extra steps that simple modelling does not take. For example, it is unable to account for behavioural changes in response to tax changes, for instance via adoption of new spending or work patterns or migration to different jurisdictions. This complexity is extremely important.

5.5.1 Unclaimed benefits

The Family Resources Survey (FRS) dataset records actual receipts of state benefits as part of its record of people's incomes. These recorded receipts are often different from the values a tax benefit-model predicts. In particular, there are often cases where a person is modelled to have an entitlement to some benefit but there is no recorded receipt. Typically, the modelled entitlement for these cases is relatively small. It is usual to interpret this as *non-take-up* – the modelled entitlements are correct but some people are choosing not to claim them, perhaps because of stigma or because the costs of claiming exceed the anticipated benefits. The fact that it is typically small amounts that seem to be unclaimed is consistent with this view (Fry and Stark, 1993), but it is also consistent with the view that we are making errors when we model entitlements and so the small entitlements that appear not to be taken up are actually just modelling mistakes (Duclos, 1995). Either way, the way to correct for apparent non-take-up is the same: we construct a statistical model a bit like the ones we have seen, except it predicts whether a modelled entitlement is taken up or not. Explanatory variables are the modelled entitlement and characteristics of the household, like age of the head of the household, presence of children and the like. Our little model does not have such a correction; since it is small entitlements that appear not to be claimed, we are not actually going to be all that far out when modelling total costs and the levels of household incomes, but we may be severely underestimating *caseloads* – the numbers of people receiving a benefit. Caseloads are very important for administrators, who need to know how many staff to hire and computers to buy, but arguably are less important for us than payments and incomes.

5.5.2 Errors with taxes

Similarly, it is often the case that the modelled amounts for direct tax liabilities (income tax and national insurance) are different from the tax payments recorded in the data. There could be lots of reasons for this, such as timing issues (recorded payments might be for liabilities from months or years ago) or data problems (especially for the self-employed). Unlike benefits, however, there is rarely any very clear pattern, with as many overestimates as underestimates, so that in aggregate tax-benefits usually predict total direct tax revenues quite well, at least once the high-income corrections discussed earlier have been applied.

This is not the case for indirect taxes, however. We discussed earlier how spending in household surveys on 'bads' such as alcohol and tobacco is much too low given what is known from customs data. It could be that people are usually honest with the survey interviewer about whether they drink, but then understate how much they drink, perhaps out of embarrassment (or drunkenness). If this is the case, then we can fix things simply by multiplying up the amounts people are recorded spending on alcohol – this is the standard correction used by most tax-benefit models. But suppose instead that the real reason for the understatement was that we were not interviewing enough drinkers. If that was the case, multiplying up the alcohol spending we do have would still give us the correct aggregate amounts, but would make our distributional analysis *worse* – it would look like an extra tax on alcohol would punish a few people really severely, whereas in fact the pain would be spread between more households.

This is an example in which improving the model's ability to forecast aggregates such as total tax revenues might *worsen* its accuracy at the level of individuals or households. The non-take-up problem discussed above is another example: since not everyone actually takes up benefits, a microsimulation model that mistakenly understates individual entitlements, and so gets all the micro-details wrong, might perform better in predicting aggregate costs than a model that gets entitlements right.

5.5.3 Changing behaviour

People may change their behaviour in response to changes to taxes and benefits, perhaps working more or less, or changing their spending on some good. Our model includes some of the key building blocks for an analysis of labour supply – it can calculate the *marginal effective tax rates (METRs)* for every person in the survey, and indeed complete *budget constraints*. We will discuss METRs and budget constraints next. The literature on the effects of taxes and benefits on the supply of labour is largely inconclusive (Blundell, 1992). Our understanding of the effect of taxes and price controls on demand for other goods is slightly firmer – for example, there's good evidence that minimum pricing for alcohol (Public Health Scotland, 2024) and the 'sugar tax' (Rogers *et al.*, 2024) have both had beneficial effects.

Models that do not allow for behavioural changes, as with take-up or labour supply here, are often referred to as *static* models, as opposed to *dynamic* models which do allow behavioural changes. It is important to note that dynamic models are not always preferable to static ones (Machlup, 1959).

5.5.4 Macroeconomic feedback

We have seen examples of how macroeconomic models try to capture important feedback in the economy. For example, a tax increase, all else equal, will reduce the amount households have to spend, and this decreases total demand in the economy, which in turn causes wages, profits and employment to be lower. Since incomes and spending are lower, the amount raised by the tax might be less than you'd predict from a static model such as ours (Wren-Lewis, 2016).

5.6 What is a good model?

The last few sections may have seemed like a long list of things we may not be measuring correctly or are ignoring, either to keep things manageable or because there is no known way of doing them correctly.

It is tempting to think that we should just wait for someone to build a model that fully allows for behavioural responses, calculates the true incidence of taxes, captures the true distribution within households, corrects for non-take-up and produces elaborate multi-dimensional measures of wellbeing. But no one will produce such a model any time soon, and even if they did, it would depend on so many strong assumptions that the output it produced would always be open to challenge, and the interactions in the model would likely be so complex that in practice you would get little insight into what was really going on.

It is always important for researchers to be honest about the limitations of their work (not least to themselves), but awareness of those limitations should not paralyse them. In practical tax-benefit modelling, the questions we are answering are not perfect – we have seen that at length. But they are important questions, ones which can be relatively easily explained, do not depend strongly on the analyst's prior beliefs, can be answered with a reasonable degree of precision and are genuinely useful in the design of policy. This is rare in economics, and should not be lightly given up.

5.7 Conclusion

We have studied most of the important concepts a professional in this field needs, got hands-on with a tax-benefit model and also carried out some ambitious policy design. This is a deliberately simplified model of a tax and benefit system. In reality, the UK or any other country's system has a bewildering array of taxes, tax bands, benefits and exemptions. But, at least in theory, these can be modelled using similar techniques as the ones described above. Then, we can make changes to the model and try to decide whether we think it is a 'fairer' or better way of taking money away from some people (taxes) and giving it to others (benefits).

Earlier, we expressed scepticism about whether a model that addressed all the limitations of this present one was feasible, and whether, if such an all-singing, all-dancing model was somehow built, it would actually be very useful. But interesting extensions in various directions have been made, and in this final section we will discuss a couple of them.

We have seen that poverty simulation is classic tax-benefit model territory. But how could we project forward over fifteen or more years? It turns out that we have already encountered the tricks that you need: reweighting and uprating. We saw above how, because of differential non-response, we needed to reweight our FRS dataset – i.e. give more emphasis to some households than others in the output – so that the final results matched known facts about the overall populations, such as the numbers of people of different ages and genders. We can extend this idea to produce weights so that our data match not current, but projected, levels. Likewise, for incomes, we can uprate the recorded levels in the data to match projections of three things from macroeconomic forecasters. Such projections exist: the ONS and Public Records Scotland produce long-run forecasts for populations and household composition and the Scottish Fiscal Commission produces income forecasts. Note that we are not forecasting populations and incomes *ourselves*; rather, we are making projections of poverty that are consistent with official forecasts.

6

Understanding advanced models

Key foci

- Tracing historical development from 1980s IGOTM/TAXBEN to contemporary Landman TTM applications.
- Demonstrating cumulative distributional analysis revealing £26 billion in regressive austerity cuts.
- Extending microsimulation to public services spending and forward-looking poverty projections.
- Balancing strengths (rigorous analysis, transparency) against weaknesses (static assumptions, sample limitations).

6.1 The historical context for tax and benefit microsimulation

The term 'microsimulation' in empirical economics refers to the method of simulating the impact of a policy or reform using an individual-level dataset combined with a computer program or application to perform the large number of calculations needed (Immervoll and O'Donoghue, 2008). In the context of tax and welfare policies, microsimulation normally involves the use of a tax-benefit model. A functional tax-benefit model requires the following elements to be in place:

1. One or more survey datasets with individuals (and the composition of those individuals into households) required to model the impact of tax and welfare policies;
2. Algorithms to calculate the impact of policies;
3. Some means of storing the parameters of the baseline (existing) tax and welfare system, plus modified versions of that system (for calculating the impact of reforms to the system);
4. Some means of calculating and displaying the results from the calculations.

Microsimulation modelling of tax and benefit policies in the UK first emerged in the 1980s – within the UK Government using IGOTM (the Inter-Governmental Tax-Benefit Microsimulation model), as in HM Treasury's analysis of distributional impacts of budgets on households (HM Treasury, 2024b), and outside government at the Institute for Fiscal Studies, which debuted its TAXBEN model in 1983 (Giles and McCrae, 1995). While survey datasets with sufficient sample sizes to conduct distributional analysis of tax and welfare policies had been collected in the UK from the early 1960s onwards (Goodman and Webb, 1994), it was not until the early 1980s that sufficient computational power existed in the computers of the day – first mainframe computers at universities or in government departments, and then desktop computers such as the IBM PC – to make microsimulation modelling of tax and welfare policies a tractable endeavour.

As well as the technical feasibility, the 1980s were a period of significant reforms to the tax and welfare systems in the UK. These included flattening and simplifying the income tax system, with the top rate of tax falling from 83 per cent in 1979 to 40 per cent in 1988; increases in indirect taxes, primarily the hike in the standard rate of VAT from 8 per cent to 15 per cent in 1979; and a range of benefit reforms, including the replacement of Supplementary Benefit with Income Support in 1988, most of which made claimants worse off. The 1980s were essentially a period of welfare austerity combined with cuts to direct taxes, which fuelled a need among researchers and commentators for distributional analysis of the impact of these reforms (Johnson and Stark, 1989).

6.2 The 2010s: modelling the impacts of austerity

The Landman Economics tax-transfer model (TTM) was launched in 2009, initially in response to a lack of tax-benefit modelling capacity within UK academic institutions, think-tanks and other research organisations. While the UK Government maintained IGOTM and the Department for Work and Pensions' Policy Simulation Model (PSM), and while there were two high-profile extra-governmental tax-benefit models in the late 2000s (the IFS's TAXBEN and EUROMOD at the University of Essex [Immervoll, O'Donoghue and Sutherland, 1999]), there was a lack of tax-benefit modelling expertise and capacity outside of these intellectual citadels. In particular, there was no obvious option for NGOs or other researchers who wanted to commission contract research and consultation on the distributional or cost effects of tax-benefit policies from a third-party provider. The IFS and EUROMOD rarely, if ever, accepted external research commissions, and the IGOTM and PSM models were for internal governmental use only.

In this environment, the establishment of the Landman Economics TTM was an important step forward: for the first time in the UK, a model was available for external researchers to commission research on the distributional and/or costing effects of tax and welfare policies.

In parallel with these developments on the research front, the political environment of the 2010s saw a renewed focus on the distributional effects of UK government policies as a result of the austerity measures implemented by the Conservative–Liberal Democrat coalition government of 2010–2015. This was followed by further austerity measures in the 2015–2017 and 2017–2019 Conservative governments, the former having a narrow parliamentary majority and the latter being a minority government with confidence and supply support from the Democratic Unionist Party of Northern Ireland.

In total, social security measures enacted during the fiscal events (Budgets and Spending Reviews or Autumn/Spring Statements) during the period between June 2010 and November 2019 resulted in a reduction of over £26 billion in social security spending by the fiscal year 2020/2021, relative to a situation in which benefits and Tax Credits had been maintained at their April 2010 levels and simply uprated by Retail Price Index inflation over the 2010s. This represented a cut in welfare expenditure of around 1.2 per cent of UK Gross Domestic Product based on the 2019/2020 nominal GDP figure (OBR *PSF Aggregates Databank* March 2024 [Office for Budget Responsibility, 2025]). In the face of reductions in spending of this magnitude, it is unsurprising that several organisations acted to commission research on the distributional effects of welfare cuts as well as accompanying changes to the tax system. Some of the major changes to the tax and welfare system over this period included:

- Real-terms increases in the value of the personal allowance for income tax (from £6,475 in the 2010/2011 tax year to £12,500 in 2019/2020, an increase of around 64 per cent compared to CPI inflation) (calculation comparing growth in the income tax personal allowance between the 2010/2011 and 2019/20 tax years with Consumer Price Index inflation over the period 2011 quarter 1 to 2020 quarter 1). CPI data are taken from ONS (Office for National Statistics, 2025a);
- An increase in the standard rate of VAT from 17.5 per cent to 20 per cent;
- Change from default uprating by the Retail Price Index or ROSSI Index to the Consumer Price Index for benefits, Tax Credits and tax thresholds;
- The introduction of Universal Credit, an integrated transfer payment for working-age people that replaced Working Tax Credit, Child Tax

Credit, Income Support, Housing Benefit and income-related Jobseeker's Allowance and Employment and Support Allowance (ESA). This has been rolled out gradually from 2013 onwards, with roll-out expected to be complete by the late 2020s (Mackley *et al.*, 2025);

- The benefit cap, which specifies maximum benefit levels for working-age families in receipt of Universal Credit or legacy out-of-work benefits;
- The two-child limit for claimants of Universal Credit, Child Tax Credit or Housing Benefit for claimants with two or more children born after April 2017.

6.3 Distributional analysis

An effective illustration of the peer-reviewed research produced by the Landman TTM is the analysis in Reed (2020). This includes most of the features of distributional analyses for which the TTM has been used since its inception in 2009. Three features of the analysis are particularly important.

First, the article takes a cumulative approach to analysing the impact of all tax and welfare reforms in the UK over a specific time period (from 2010 to 2017 in this case), rather than focusing on individual reforms in isolation. This is because the overall pattern of distributional impacts is the result of the interaction between a large number of specific reforms undertaken by the UK Government. For a comprehensive evaluation of the impacts of all policies taken together, a cumulative impact assessment is required.

Second, the article analyses distributional effects according to a number of different population composition variables. One crucial breakdown variable for assessing the distributional impacts of policies enacted since 2010 is by quantile of household income. Usually, decile is used as the quantile variable, dividing UK households into ten equally sized categories using grossing factors after ranking households from poorest to richest according to equivalised income either Before Housing Costs or After Housing Costs. Please see Francis-Devine (2025) for the definition of housing costs used in the Family Resources Survey (FRS) and the differences between Before Housing Costs and After Housing Costs income definitions (Francis-Devine, 2025). A decile breakdown is important for assessing the progressiveness or regressiveness of the set of modelled policies.

Figure 6.1 from Reed (2020) shows that the policy changes have a *regressive* impact across most of the household income distribution. That is, households lose more as a percentage of their net incomes in poorer deciles than richer households. The maximum average losses (around 10 per cent of net incomes) occur in decile 2. In contrast, deciles 8 and 9 actually gain from the reforms because reductions in average payments of income tax and

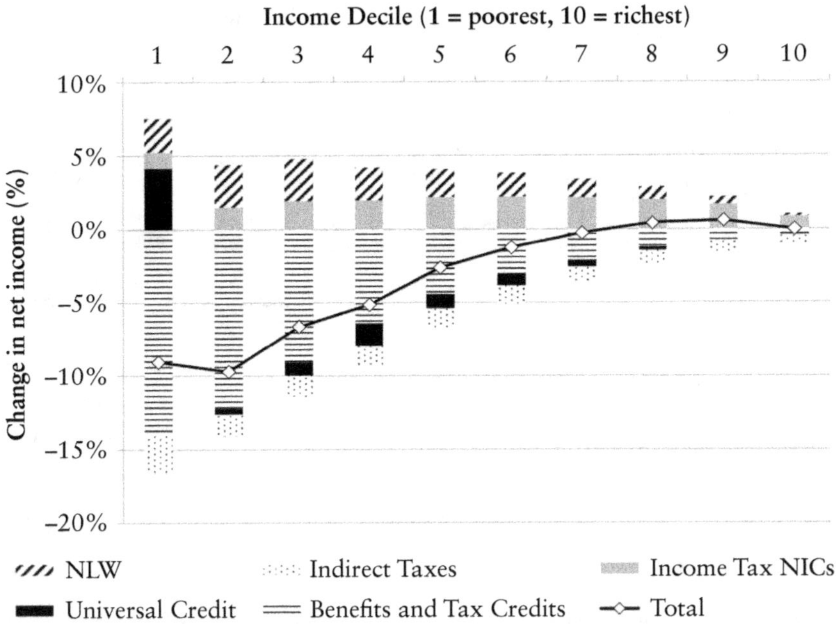

Figure 6.1 Landman Economics tax-transfer model analysis of percentage impact of reforms to taxes and transfer payments by household net income decile, 2021/2022 tax year in Great Britain

National Insurance Contributions more than compensate for the accompanying reductions in benefits and Tax Credits and increases in indirect taxes.

Other breakdown variables used in Reed (2020) and other distributional analyses using the TTM include many of the protected characteristics in the Equality Act, such as sex, ethnicity, disability and age. The ability to break the results down according to these variables made the TTM especially useful for analysis conducted for the Equality and Human Rights Commission in 2014 and 2018. This research assessed the extent to which welfare reforms since 2010 discriminated against disadvantaged and vulnerable groups in the UK (Reed and Portes, 2014; Portes and Reed, 2018b). Other breakdown variables relating to household or family (rather than individual) characteristics were also useful, including distributional breakdowns of policy impacts according to the number of children in the family. This is illustrated in Figure 6.2.

The model has also been used to analyse intersectional impacts of policies on groups facing multiple disadvantages, producing findings on the impact of gender and ethnicity (see Women's Budget Group *et al.*, [2017] for examples), subject to the sample size of the datasets used. The sample size limitation is discussed in more detail below.

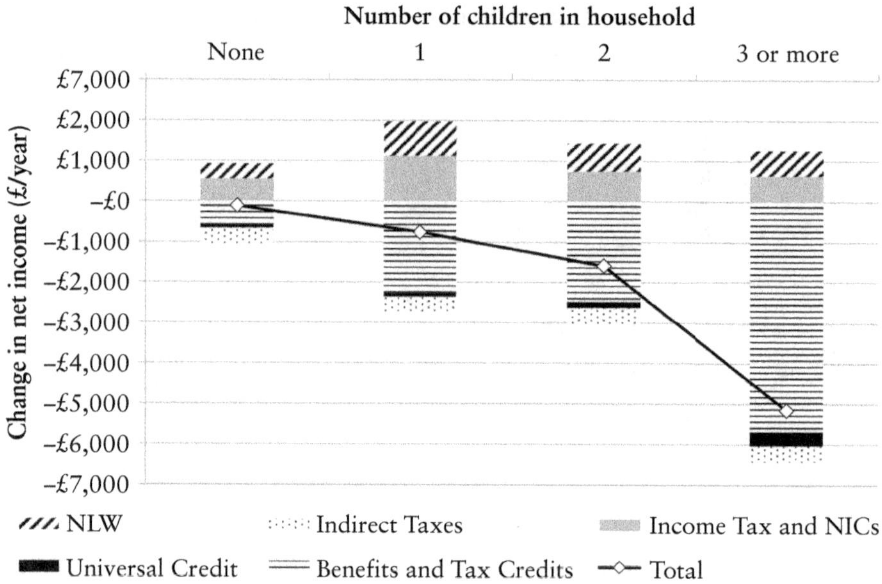

Figure 6.2 Landman Economics tax-transfer model analysis of cash impact of reforms to taxes and transfer payments by number of children in household, 2021/2022 tax year in Great Britain

Third, the distributional analyses distinguish between different types of policies. For example, Reed (2020) shows the effects of direct taxes (income tax and National Insurance Contributions), indirect taxes, benefits and Tax Credits and Universal Credit. This is important because different types of policy have very different distributional effects. Cuts to benefits and Tax Credits have a very regressive distributional impact, whereas the income tax and national institutuon contributions (NICs) changes follow an 'inverted U-shape' pattern, with households in the middle of the distribution gaining more in percentage terms than the poorest or richest households. The introduction of Universal Credit, compared to a situation where other changes to benefits and Tax Credits have been made, has a regressive impact across most of the distribution except for the lowest decile, where it results in an increase in average incomes. This is due to the assumptions made about take-up of UC compared to legacy benefits and Tax Credits, which are discussed in more detail elsewhere (Portes and Reed, 2018b).

Finally, the analysis in Reed (2020) also includes the impact of real-terms increases to the National Minimum Wage, which has been known as the National Living Wage since 2016. Even though this is not a tax or welfare policy in the traditional sense of the term, the UK Government claimed in the 2015–2016 period that the increase in minimum wage would largely cancel out the regressive impacts of cuts to benefits, Tax Credits and Universal Credit and that it was important to consider the minimum wage alongside the welfare cuts made in the summer 2015 Budget (Department for Business, Innovation and Skills, 2016). This is not the case: while the minimum wage increases offset a small proportion of the regressive impacts of welfare cuts, the overall picture (as shown by the 'total' line in Figure 6.1, which is a sum of all impacts) is still overwhelmingly regressive across most of the household income distribution.

6.4 Survey data considerations

The choice of survey dataset for a tax-welfare microsimulation model such as the Landman Economics TTM is crucial. The dataset needs to have detailed income information at the individual level (for modelling direct taxes and means-tested benefits, Tax Credits and Universal Credit) as well as information about benefit unit structure (for modelling eligibility for means-tested welfare payments). A benefit unit is a single adult or adult couple together with any dependent children. For modelling indirect taxes such as VAT and excise duties, the dataset also needs to have information on household expenditure patterns. The dataset also requires information on individual and household attributes, such as age and disability status at the individual level, number and age of children at the family level and housing tenure at the household level. These are important for modelling social security payments which are contingent on particular characteristics, such as the State Pension and Pension Credit for pensioners, and Housing Benefit for renters. Finally, the dataset should include information on a range of Equality Act protected characteristics, such as gender and ethnicity, to enable the analysis of distributional effects of policies according to these characteristics. This type of analysis is important to ensure that policies are not discriminatory as defined by the Equality Act 2010, and the Equalities and Human Rights Commission has commissioned analysis using the TTM to assess the distributional aspect of tax and welfare reforms by equality group at various points in the past decade (Reed and Portes, 2014; Portes and Reed, 2018a).

The default dataset for the TTM is the UK **Family Resources Survey** (around twenty-five thousand households per year; detailed information on income, benefit unit structure and individual and household attributes). The model can also run on:

- The **Living Costs and Food Survey** – smaller sample size (five thousand households per year), fairly detailed income information, **has expenditure information**.

- **Understanding Society – the UK Household Longitudinal Study (UKHLS)** – thirty thousand households per year, fairly detailed income information (not expenditure), **panel data** (reinterviews the same people year after year).

As a default, the TTM uses data from the UK FRS for analysis of direct taxes and welfare payments, and the Living Costs and Food Survey (LCFS) for analysis of indirect taxes. Both of these datasets have income information and data on a range of individual and household attributes, although the LCFS dataset does not contain detailed information on disability, which makes it difficult to analyse the impact of indirect taxes by disability status. This is one reason for the omission of indirect tax impacts from Figure 6.3, which looks at the impacts of tax and welfare policies according to the number of functional impairments across all adults in each household.

In recent years, the TTM has also been used to model distributional impacts using the UKHL) dataset, which has a panel dimension and so has some advantages in econometric terms over the FRS or LCFS, which are repeated cross-sectional samples. We discuss a specific example of the use of UKHLS data to extend the functionality of microsimulation modelling in

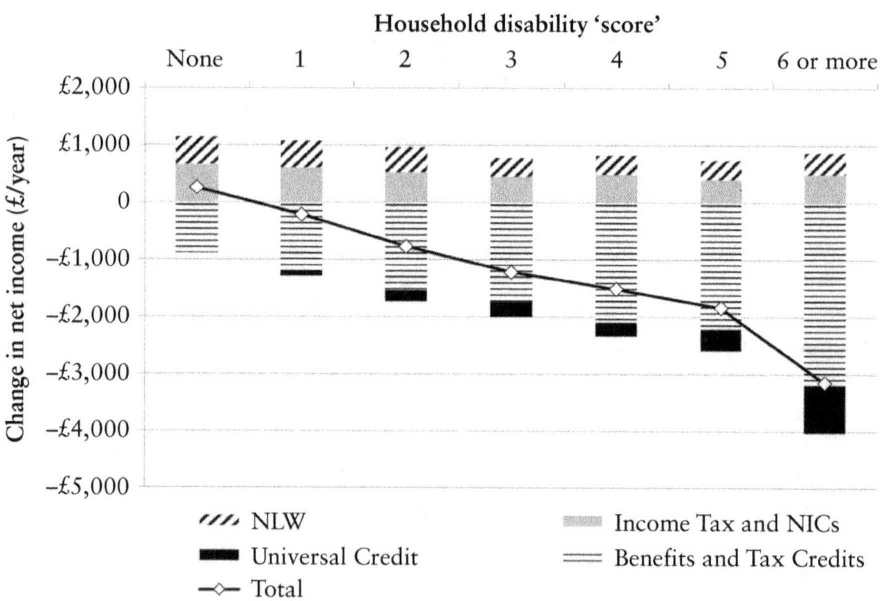

Figure 6.3 Landman Economics tax-transfer model analysis of cash impact of reforms to taxes and transfer payments by household disability score, 2021/2022 tax year in Great Britain

Chapter 5. Other datasets, such as the UK Wealth and Assets Survey (WAS), have also been used for modelling other aspects of the UK tax system in more detail. This includes analysis of the potential replacement of Council Tax by a 'proportional property tax', where the tax liability is a percentage of the valuation of each property, and the possible introduction of a wealth tax.

6.5 Strengths and weaknesses of the basic microsimulation approach

The microsimulation approach outlined in this chapter has a number of strengths and weaknesses as a tool for analysing the distributional effects of tax and welfare policies at the individual and household level. The main strengths of the approach are threefold.

First, the approach allows clearly defined quantitative analysis of the headline impacts of a set of policies, taken cumulatively. As set out above, the packages of tax and welfare reforms introduced by Conservative-led governments in the UK since 2010 had at least six major aspects to them and dozens of individual policy announcements. By using the TTM to analyse the cumulative impact of the policies, rather than separate analyses of each component or announcement, it was possible to make a holistic assessment of the impact of tax and welfare policies over the 2010s. This rigorous quantitative analysis enabled a conclusion that the impact of the reforms taken as a whole was overwhelmingly regressive across most of the income distribution. This message ran counter to the narrative being promoted by UK Government ministers at the time and provided a critical contribution to public debate on the regressive impacts of reforms.

Second, the approach facilitated use of information on Equality Act protected characteristics such as age, sex, disability and ethnicity in the survey datasets used for the model, as well as other household characteristics such as housing tenure and number of children. By doing so, it was possible to look at the impact of specific policies at a highly granular level, showing the impact on specific subgroups of the population who were particularly disadvantaged by austerity. Reed (2020) shows that households with three or more children lost more than £5,000 per year from tax and welfare reforms between 2010 and 2017, partly due to the two-child limit on premiums for housing benefits, Tax Credits and Universal Credit announced in the Summer 2015 Budget.

Third, the approach allows precise clarity about the modelling assumptions made when using the TTM to estimate distributional effects and other consequences of policy changes. The level of detail provided in the reports produced using the TTM – in particular Portes and Reed (2018a) – is designed to be sufficient to allow external researchers to replicate the results with their own models or open-source models such as UKMOD ('UKMOD', 2024). To facilitate this process in future, version 2 of the TTM will be a fully open-source model, available for third-party researchers to use on their own account, subject to survey dataset clearance from the UK Data Archive.

There are also several weaknesses of this static microsimulation approach. First, the approach is static and so does not consider the dynamic impacts of policies on outcomes such as labour supply (employment) or health. We discuss extensions to the TTM to handle dynamic aspects of microsimulation in Chapters 4 and 5.

Second, the limits of the sample size of the datasets used (around twenty thousand households per year for the FRS and around five thousand households per year for the LCFS) mean that not all distributional breakdowns are possible because the sample size of the population subgroups in the survey data becomes too small to support reliable statistical analysis. This limitation has been partially overcome by using multi-year pooled datasets, with Reed (2020) using a four-year pooled sample of FRS and a six-year pooled sample of LCFS.

Third, some Equality Act protected characteristics are omitted from the End User Licence (EUL) version of the survey datasets available from the UK Data Archive (University of Essex, 2024) for confidentiality reasons. This means that the EUL versions of the FRS and LCFS do not contain information on sexual orientation or gender reassignment of survey members.

Fourth, sample size also makes it hard to examine effects by country or by region in England. A cross-country analysis is particularly important after 2015 given the additional powers granted to Scotland to vary income tax rates and introduce changes to the disability and carer benefits regimes, and the subsequent divergence between Scotland and England.

Finally, there are some limitations in the tax and welfare policies that can be modelled using this technique due to the nature of the survey datasets. For example, the standard EUL datasets do not have local authority identifiers, which means that distributional changes due to restrictions to Local Housing Allowance in the private sector, and localisation of Council Tax Support, can only be modelled approximately. The impact of increased use of sanctions in the welfare system from the early 2010s onwards is also difficult to model using the FRS, as the dataset does not contain any variables for whether benefit or Universal Credit claimants are subject to a sanction at the time of interview. It is, however, possible to assess the impact of welfare sanctions using different techniques based on administrative data. See Reed (2014) for an example of this.

6.6 Britain's fiscal moving parts

The full parameter set for a basic tax-transfer model contains around two hundred parameters. The most essential ones for direct taxes and benefits are as follows:

Direct taxes.

Income tax system in England, Wales and Northern Ireland (parameters in annual terms):

- **Personal allowance** – the amount someone can receive per year before paying income tax at the basic rate (currently £12,570).
- **Basic rate** – the percentage income tax rate between the personal allowance and the higher rate threshold of £50,270 – currently 20 per cent.
- **Higher rate** – the percentage income tax rate above the higher rate threshold up to the additional rate threshold of £125,140 – currently 40 per cent.
- **Additional rate** – the percentage income tax rate above the additional rate threshold – currently 45 per cent.

National Insurance system for employees and self-employed people:

- **Main employee rate** – between Primary Threshold of £242 per week and Upper Earnings Limit of £967 per week (currently 8 per cent).
- **Main self-employed rate** – between Lower Profits Limit of £12,570 per year and Upper Profits Limit of £50,270 per year (currently 6 per cent).

Welfare benefits:

Universal Credit is the main means-tested benefit for adults below State Pension age of sixty-six, and their children (parameters in monthly terms):

- **Standard single rate** – monthly payment for single person aged twenty-five or over (currently £393.45).
- **Standard couple rate** – monthly payment for a couple, both aged twenty-five or over (currently £617.60).
- **Rate for first child** – monthly payment for first child (currently £333.33).
- **Rate for second child** – monthly payment for second child (currently £287.92).
- **Taper rate on earned incomes** – the rate at which UC is withdrawn for every £1 of earned income over the work allowance (currently 55 per cent).
- **Maximum number of children for support** – sets a limit on the number of children for whom UC child payments are made (currently in force; max number: 2).

Child Benefit is a per-Child Benefit for children that is means-tested for very high earners (parameters in weekly terms):

- **Rate for first child** – weekly payment for first child (currently £24.00).
- **Rate for second and subsequent children** – weekly payment for other children (currently £15.90).

State pension is the main non-means-tested benefit for pensioners (over the State Pension age of sixty-six), based on previous contributions (parameters in weekly terms):

- **New State Pension (for pensioners who retired from 2016 onwards)** – weekly payment based on full contributions record: currently £221.20.
- **Old State Pension (for pensioners who retired before 2016)** – weekly payment based on full contributions record: currently £169.50.

Pension Credit is the main means-tested benefit for pensioners (over the State Pension age of sixty-six) (parameters in weekly terms):

- **Single Pensioner Guarantee Credit** – currently £227.10.
- **Couple Pensioner Guarantee Credit** – currently £346.10.

By changing the different values for the tax and benefit parameters in the fields, we can answer the following illustrative questions:

- How much do increases to tax or NICs raise (or vice-versa for tax cuts)?
- How much do increases in welfare benefits for working-age adults, children or pensioners cost?
- What are the impacts of various changes to the tax/benefit system on poverty and inequality?
- What are the impacts of various changes to the tax/benefit system on the distribution of household incomes?

6.7 Extending the usefulness and functionality of tax and welfare microsimulation

As well as being used to assess the distributional impacts of actual tax and welfare reforms over a given period (e.g. from 2010 to 2017 in Reed, 2020), the Landman TTM can be used to simulate the current and future impact of hypothetical policies. It can also be used to simulate the impact of changes in employment or household demographics on overall distributional measures such as the level of poverty or inequality in the UK population. In the last decade, the TTM has been used for three forecasting exercises of this type (listed in chronological order):

1. Forecasting the increase in working-age employment necessary to meet the (then current) targets for child poverty in 2020 following the Coalition Government's cuts to welfare expenditure (Reed and Portes, 2014).
2. Forecasting changes to poverty (including child poverty, but also working-age and pensioner poverty) over the period 2015 to 2030 (Harrop and Reed, 2015).
3. Forecasting child poverty in Scotland up to the fiscal year 2030/2031 as required by the Child Poverty (Scotland) Act (Scottish Parliament 2017), which included a set of child poverty targets to be achieved by 2030 (Harrop and Reed, 2015).

Harrop and Reed (2015) use base data from the then-most-recent FRS (2011/2012) and make adjustments to the data to simulate the impacts of changes to employment rates and earnings inequality ('predistribution' characteristics of the labour market) compared to the impacts of potential changes to tax and welfare policies ('redistribution') over the 2015–2030 time period. Central forecast projections for employment and earnings are taken from the Office for Budget Responsibility (OBR). The model also takes account of changes to the age structure of the economy as forecast by the Office for National Statistics (ONS) in its population projections, reweighting the FRS using a technique developed by Creedy using New Zealand data (Creedy, 2003).

The research shows the interplay between 'predistributive' policies, including promoting higher employment and higher earnings through policies such as legislating for all public sector jobs to pay a real living wage, and 'redistributive' policies through the tax and welfare system, such as 'triple lock' uprating of benefits and Tax Credits and significant real-terms increases to Child Benefit. It is important to note that the real Living Wage, as calculated each year by the Living Wage Foundation, is higher than the National Living Wage, which is a statutory minimum wage set by the UK Government. The Living Wage Foundation provides an explanation of the differences between the two measures (Living Wage Foundation, 2025).

Returning to this report almost a decade later, many of its central projections for the evolution of poverty and inequality in Britain over the 2020s seem depressingly accurate. For example:

> The implications of fifteen years of flat incomes for low-income families are hard to contemplate. Stagnant incomes would mean there would be no chance of reducing the number of families who are really struggling to make ends meet. Emergency food banks would move from being a temporary phenomenon of the economic crisis to an entrenched feature of British life. And people in rented accommodation would see their living standards fall the most, as

> an ever higher slice of their incomes would have to go towards housing costs before any other bills were paid. (Harrop and Reed, 2015, p. 4)

This analysis with Andy Harrop is an excellent example of the capacity of the TTM to facilitate and inform debate about future tax and welfare policies, developing a forward-facing narrative rather than just analysing the impact of policies introduced in the recent past – important as that analysis is.

6.8 Analysing the distributional impact of spending on other public services

Real-terms cuts to transfer payments received by individuals and households (benefits, Tax Credits and Universal Credit) over the period since 2010 are only one dimension of austerity, albeit an important and fiscally significant one. Changes to 'in-kind' public spending, such as health, social care, Sure Start and other early years programmes; schools, higher education, public transport, social housing and the police; are also an important aspect of austerity since 2010. For example, the June 2010 Budget from the incoming Coalition Government announced cuts of almost £20 billion per year to departmental spending by 2014–2015 *excluding* social security (Office for Budget Responsibility, 2025). While the mix of cuts was subsequently adjusted in the 2010 Autumn Statement and subsequent fiscal events so that cuts fell more heavily on welfare and less heavily on in-kind public spending, there were still around £17 billion of real-terms cuts to in-kind spending by 2015–2016 as a result of announcements at fiscal events between the June 2010 Budget and the 2014 Autumn Statement (Office for Budget Responsibility, 2025). This means that it is crucial to analyse spending on public services more generally alongside traditional tax-welfare microsimulation analysis.

Analysis of public services spending outside of cash transfer payments has not traditionally been a feature of microsimulation tax-benefit modelling. There are some exceptions, such as the Office for National Statistics' annual publication, *The Effects of Tax and Benefits on Household Income* (Office for National Statistics, 2023), which is based on Living Costs and Food Survey data and includes some in-kind services, while Sefton estimates the distributional effect of public services spending as part of the social wage (Sefton, 2002). The Landman Economics Public Spending Model (PSM), which was originally developed in 2009–2010 and used for the first time to analyse the impact of the projected departmental cuts in HM Treasury's Autumn 2010 spending review (Horton and Reed, 2010), expands the functionality of the TTM to include the distributional impact of cuts to public services spending.

Modelling the distributional impact of spending cuts requires two indispensable types of data at a minimum. One is a source of data on aggregate spending broken down by spending category. The Landman Economics Public Spending Model uses data from HM Treasury's *Public Expenditure Statistical Analyses* (PESA) publication (HM Treasury, 2024a), which provides breakdowns of spending on different areas of public services broken down using the United Nations' Classification of Functions of Government (COFOG) system (United Nations, 2000). PESA provides a breakdown of spending totals and spending per head of the population for each country in the UK as well as for the nine regions of England.

The second source of data required is on usage of services. The model allocates spending cuts as falling on people who use public services. The distributional analysis of the impact of spending cuts outlined in Reed (2017) used version 1 of the Landman Economics PSM, which is based on data from five different UK survey datasets: the FRS (schools, higher education and social housing and social care for the elderly and disabled); General Lifestyle Survey (healthcare and museum and gallery attendance); Living Costs and Food Survey (public transport); British Crime Survey (police services); and the British Household Panel Survey (family social care services) (Reed, 2017).

The estimation of public service usage according to different individual and household characteristics, such as net income decile, family demographics, age, ethnicity, disability, etc., was a complex process in version 1 of the PSM. This involved using the FRS as the master dataset and matching in probabilities of usage of different categories of public service via regressions on each of the four other datasets used in the model, with explanatory variables common to the FRS and each of the other datasets. Reed (2017) provides an overview of the econometric procedures involved for mapping spending categories on to the FRS (Reed, 2017, pp. 122–123). The report for the Equality and Human Rights Commission by Reed and Portes provides a more detailed description of the methodology (Portes and Reed, 2018a). Overall, the model assigns just under three-quarters of public spending in the constituent countries of the UK to individuals using the service use variables across the five micro-datasets. The remaining quarter is mainly categories of spending such as defence, environmental protection, foreign aid and debt interest, which cannot be assigned to specific individuals in the UK.

The results for the impact of public spending between 2010 and 2015 show that spending cuts to in-kind services have a regressive impact as a proportion of 'final income', which is defined as net income *plus* the value of in-kind services received in 2015. The cuts are largest for the lowest decile of net incomes, at almost 8 per cent of final income, and smallest for the top decile, at around 1.5 per cent (Reed, 2017).

Overall, the Landman Economics Public Spending Model has played an important role in the 2010s and early 2020s by providing means of gauging the size and distributional effect of public spending cuts across the four countries of the UK. Since Reed (2017), development of the model has continued. Reed and Portes provide a detailed assessment of the impact of spending cuts across England, Scotland and Wales in a report for the Equality and Human Rights Commission (Portes and Reed, 2018a), while Reed and Portes do the same for Northern Ireland (Reed and Portes, 2021). The latter report, for the Northern Ireland Human Rights Commission, also uses version 2 of the Landman Economics Public Spending Model. This model uses a single survey dataset (the UKHLS) to model all the service use variables. This simplifies the econometrics of modelling service use considerably, while also opening up the possibility of a holistic analysis of (direct) tax, welfare and other spending changes over the period from 2010 to 2026 using a single dataset, which would produce an almost fully integrated TTM and PSM (with only indirect taxes not included in the UKHLS model).

6.9 Understanding the likely impacts of fiscal changes

Imagine a hypothetical Britain in which the Chancellor of the Exchequer has been told by the Office for Budget Responsibility that UK economic performance has increased, so that £20 billion extra per year is available to spend on cutting taxes, increasing welfare benefits or a combination of the two. Imagine, further, that the Chancellor has a firm commitment to reducing poverty. It is important to assess first which reforms deliver the biggest 'bang for the buck' in terms of reducing poverty (using the headline measure in the model outputs, which is the proportion of households below 60 per cent median income after housing costs) and, then, which reforms are best at reducing *deep* poverty.

To assist the Chancellor, there are some illustrative statistics below on the cost (or the gain) to the Government from various reforms (to the nearest billion pounds in most cases):

Income tax:

- Reducing (*increasing*) the Personal allowance by £1,000 per year raises (*costs*) £7 **billion.**
- Increasing (*reducing*) basic rate by 1 per cent raises (*costs*) **£6 billion.**
- Increasing (*reducing*) higher rate by 1per cent raises (*costs*) **£2 billion.**
- Increasing (*reducing*) additional rate by 1 per cent raises (*costs*) **£0.9 billion.**

National Insurance Contributions:

- Increasing (*reducing*) employee NICs by 1 per cent raises (*costs*) **£5 billion.**
- Increasing (*reducing*) self-employed NICs by 1 per cent raises (*costs*) **£0.3 billion.**

Universal Credit:

- Increasing (*reducing*) single and couple monthly adult payments by £100 per month costs (*raises*) **£8 billion.**
- Increasing (*reducing*) per child payments by £100 per month costs (*raises*) **£6 billion.**
- Reducing (*increasing*) the rate at which UC is withdrawn when earnings increase (the 'taper rate') by 10 per cent costs (*raises*) **£8 billion.**
- Removing the two-child limit on UC costs **£2 billion.**

Child Benefit:

- Increasing Child Benefit by £10 per week costs **£6 billion.**

Pension Credit:

- Increasing single and couple Pension Credit payments by £10 per week costs **£15 billion.**

State pension:

- Increasing the State Pension by **£10** per week costs **£5 billion.**

It is clear that these are often expensive payments.

6.10 Conclusion

This chapter has traced the development and application of tax-benefit microsimulation modelling in the UK, demonstrating how computational advances have transformed our capacity to analyse distributional impacts of fiscal policy. Beginning with the emergence of models like IGOTM and TAXBEN in the 1980s, we have seen how microsimulation has evolved from a specialised technical exercise into an essential tool for policy analysis and public debate.

The Landman Economics TTM exemplifies the modern capabilities of microsimulation, combining detailed survey data with sophisticated algorithms to produce comprehensive distributional analysis. The model's application to analysing austerity measures during the 2010s revealed how cumulative policy changes – totalling over £26 billion in social security cuts by 2020/2021 – had overwhelmingly regressive effects across the income distribution. This analysis provided crucial empirical evidence that challenged official government narratives and informed public understanding of policy impacts on vulnerable groups.

We have explored how microsimulation extends beyond traditional tax-benefit analysis to encompass public services spending and forward-looking poverty projections. The integration of protected characteristics analysis enables assessment of potential discrimination, while forecasting capabilities allow policymakers to evaluate alternative policy pathways. However, important limitations remain: static models cannot capture behavioural responses, sample sizes constrain analysis of small subgroups, and some policy impacts – particularly sanctions and localised effects – prove difficult to model accurately.

As microsimulation tools become more accessible through open-source development, their potential for informing evidence-based policy design grows substantially. The interactive exercises demonstrate how even simplified models can illuminate trade-offs between poverty reduction, inequality, and fiscal sustainability, equipping the next generation of analysts with practical skills for rigorous distributional analysis.

7

Exploring tax-benefit systems

Key foci

- Modelling three Basic Income schemes showing dramatic poverty reductions and progressive distributional effects.
- Using within-between models to establish causal relationships between income and health outcomes.
- Estimating health impacts: 124,000–1,005,000 depression cases prevented annually across schemes.
- Calculating economic returns: £3.87–£19.65 billion in QALYs and substantial NHS cost savings.

7.1 Simulating the impact of welfare reforms and accompanying tax changes: the example of Basic Income

In addition to being used to model the impact of tax and spending reforms and forecast the impact of future reforms (as shown in Chapters 3, 4 and 5), the tax-transfer model (TTM) can also be used to model the potential impact of policies which have never been introduced at a large scale in the UK. One such policy is Basic Income – a non-means-tested, non-taxable payment to every individual citizen in the UK. Standing provides an excellent introduction to the economic and ethical case for Basic Income as a policy that would help address the interlocking current crises – what he calls the 'eight giants' – blocking the path to a Good Society: inequality and the associated rise of rentier capitalism (Standing, 2021), insecurity, household and corporate debt, stress, precarity (Standing, 2011), automation and Artificial Intelligence, extinction (through ecological crisis) and the rise of right-wing populism in politics (Standing, 2020). Standing argues that 'a Basic Income and an income distribution system in which it is an anchor would help to weaken the threat posed by all eight of the modern giants blocking our route to a Good Society' (Standing, 2020, p. 40).

The most recent applications of the TTM have been in modelling the distributional effects and costings of various Basic Income packages as well as the effects of Basic Income on health. Most of the earliest microsimulation modelling of Basic Income schemes used data from North America, where many of the earliest pilot schemes of Basic Income were initiated.

Forget uses administrative health data to analyse the impact of MINCOME, a Basic Income programme that ran in the town of Dauphin in the province of Manitoba in Canada between 1974 and 1979 (Forget, 2013). The research uses propensity score matching (based on age, sex, family size, urban or rural residency setting and family type) to control for differences between the treatment and control group. Forget finds that there was an 8.5 per cent reduction in the hospitalisation rate for MINCOME participants relative to the control group from other areas of Manitoba who did not receive the Basic Income, particularly for accidents and injuries and mental health. Widerquist gives a roundup of the results from other North American Basic Income pilot studies in the 1970s (Widerquist, 2017). In the UK context, Torry (2019) presents the results of a number of microsimulations of the distributional impacts and costs of Basic Income using the EUROMOD tax-benefit model, while Martinelli presents costings and distributional results using the Institute for Public Policy Research tax-benefit model (Martinelli, 2020).

Standing (2020) recommends that a future UK government conduct a series of pilot studies to determine if a Basic Income would have the anticipated beneficial effects, or any negative effects, and what the costings of a full roll-out might be. The Welsh Government launched a Basic Income pilot for care leavers in 2022 (Welsh Government, 2022; Holland *et al.*, 2024; Mathur *et al.*, 2025). In the Canadian context, Forget and Frankel examine the evidence from the Income Support programmes introduced in Canada during the COVID-19 pandemic, which were neither universal nor unconditional, but the public discussion around these schemes highlighted some of the challenges faced by advocates of Basic Income looking to make the case for the introduction of Basic Income; namely, fears that the upfront costs of a Basic Income scheme are 'unaffordable' and would require government borrowing that would fuel inflation (Forget and Frankel, 2024). We address these fears specifically in my research covered in this chapter. There are also worries – in Canada as in the UK – that a Basic Income will discourage work. We do not directly address the labour supply implications of Basic Income but we would note that as Forget and Frankel point out, and as is confirmed in the reviews of evidence on the labour supply effects of existing pilot studies by Miller (2017) and Widerquist (2017), the estimated negative labour supply effects based on pilot studies of Basic Income are small, if they exist at all. In fact, some studies show *positive* labour supply impacts arising from the introduction of Basic Income.

7.2 Static distributional modelling of Basic Income schemes and accompanying tax packages

Howard Reed's report for the Compass thinktank with Stewart Lansley (Reed and Lansley, 2019) uses the TTM to model two variants of Basic Income schemes:

- Scheme 1: a 'fast-track' scheme, which would pay £60 per week to adults aged eighteen to sixty-four, £40 per week for each child aged under eighteen and £175 per week for pensioners aged sixty-five or over. This would be introduced over the course of a single parliament.
- Scheme 2: A 'slow-track' scheme, which would pay £80 to working-age adults, £50 per week for children and £180 per week for pensioners. This would be phased in more gradually over a period of ten years or longer.

It is essential to consider the funding mechanism for a Basic Income alongside the introduction of Basic Income payments. While it is not necessarily the case that a scheme needs to be fiscally neutral (increased expenditure on the Basic Income being matched by increased tax receipts and reduced spending on existing benefits), in the first round, large-scale money creation to fund a Basic Income without any fiscal backing from increased taxation is likely to be inflationary. Lansley and Reed (2019) suggest funding Basic Income Scheme 1 via a combination of a) savings from abolishing existing benefits, including Child Benefit and the state Retirement Pension which are superseded by the Basic Income payment; and b) direct tax increases, including abolishing the income tax personal allowance, increasing the basic, higher and additional rates of income tax by three pence in the pound and a 12 per cent rate over the whole range of employee and self-employed National Insurance Contributions (Lansley and Reed, 2019). For Scheme 2, we recommend the establishment of a sovereign wealth fund, the returns from which would grow over time to enable the scheme to be fiscally neutral over a period of fifteen or more years.

The distributional impacts of Scheme 1, as modelled using the TTM, are dramatic: child poverty, measured as the proportion of children in households whose median net equivalised household income falls below 60 per cent of median net household income, falls from around 29 per cent to only 18 per cent, while the Gini coefficient on inequality of household disposable income falls by 4 percentage points.

The schemes featured in Lansley and Reed (2019) are essentially 'starter' Basic Income policies, with the level for working-age adults set not far above the Jobseeker's Allowance/single adult Universal Credit payment, which is currently £90.50 per week or £393.45 per month. The British benefits system is one of the least generous in the OECD for an unemployed single adult of working age, ignoring housing support and just focusing on Jobseeker's Allowance or the UC equivalent (Whiteford, 2022). Our proposed Basic Income rates for children are substantially higher than the current rates of Child Benefit in the UK, but this mainly reflects the fact that Child Benefit is a particularly low and formerly universal payment to children, which needs to be supplemented by Child Tax Credit or Universal Credit for low-income families. The rate for pensioners is also much higher than the working-age payment, but this reflects the fact that pensioners retiring after April 2016 in the UK with a full National Insurance Contributions record receive a basic State Pension which is considerably higher in real terms than the pre-2016 system, and the pension rises according to the 'triple lock' rule – the highest of CPI inflation, average earnings growth or 2.5 per cent – each year. Thus, even a starter Basic Income scheme needs to be sufficiently high for pensioners to ensure that there is not a large number of losers from the scheme, which involved a rate of at least £175 in 2019 when the analysis was published.

The more recent analysis by Reed *et al.* (2023) aims to address a criticism levelled by Martinelli (2020) among other authors, that any Basic Income scheme beyond a starter scheme would be too costly to be a viable replacement for the current, largely means-tested, welfare system. We model three different schemes at widely differing levels of generosity, ranging from Scheme 1, an updated version of the Lansley/Reed starter scheme, to Scheme 3, which pays Basic Income at the level of the MIS as defined by researchers at the University of Loughborough for the Joseph Rowntree Foundation (Centre for Research in Social Policy, 2025).

The MIS payment levels in Scheme 3 are much higher than for Scheme 1. Table 7.1 sets out the details of tax-benefit configuration. For example, the adult payment in Scheme 3 is £230 per week compared to £63 per week in Scheme 1. Gross expenditure on the Basic Income schemes rises as generosity increases, with Scheme 1 involving gross expenditure of around £274 billion. Scheme 2, a halfway-house between the starter scheme and full MIS payments, costs £464 billion while Scheme 3 costs £678 billion (to the nearest billion pounds in each case).

Income tax rates are adjusted upwards across the three schemes to achieve fiscal neutrality, combined with reductions in expenditure on means-tested benefits, Tax Credits and Universal Credit and the elimination of Child Benefit and the current State Pension. For Scheme 1, the magnitude of tax increases required is similar to Lansley and Reed (2019). For Scheme 3, we abolish employer and self-employed National Insurance Contributions and replace them with income tax rates of 65 per cent (basic rate), 85 per cent (higher rate) and 95 per cent (additional rate). These direct tax rates

Table 7.1 Basic Income payments by household types

Period	*Scheme 1*		*Scheme 2*		*Scheme 2a*		*Scheme 3*		*Scheme 3a*	
	Week	*Year*	*Week*	*Year*	*Week*	*Year*	*Week*	*Year*	*Week*	*Year*
Under 18	£41	£2,132	£63	£3,276	£41	£2,132	£95	£4,940	£41	£2,132
Single adult under 65	£63	£3,276	£145	£7,540	£145	£7,540	£230	£11,960	£230	£11,960
Single adult aged 65+	£190	£9,880	£190	£9,880	£190	£9,880	£230	£11,960	£230	£11,960
Couple under 65	£126	£6,552	£290	£15,080	£290	£15,080	£460	£23,920	£460	£23,920
Couple + one child	£167	£8,684	£353	£18,356	£331	£17,212	£555	£28,860	£501	£26,052
Couple + two children	£208	£10,816	£416	£21,632	£372	£19,344	£650	£33,800	£542	£28,184
Basic income tax rate1	23%		40%		48.20%		40%		65%	
Higher income tax rate	43%		60%		68.20%		60%		85%	
Additional income tax rate	48%		70%		78.20%		70%		95%	

are certainly high, raise real prospects of public opposition and would require significant investment in anti-avoidance measures at HM Revenue and Customs to be effective if introduced in one go. However, the point of including them in the chapter is to show that it is possible to fully meet the cost of a Basic Income using increases in personal tax alone.

Because income tax and national insurance contributions (NICs) payments are modellable in the TTM, their inclusion in the reform packages modelled by Lansley and Reed (2019) and Reed *et al.* (2023) makes it possible to assess the distributional effects of a revenue-neutral Basic Income package in a holistic and comprehensive manner. In reality, it is likely that Basic Income would be funded by a range of different tax measures, including taxes on wealth, corporations and polluters, as well as income. Much broader tax measures are outlined elsewhere (Common Sense Policy Group, 2024a).

As Table 7.2 illustrates, the distributional effects of all three Basic Income schemes are extremely progressive. Scheme 1 results in an increase of almost 140 per cent in average incomes in the lowest decile of households, while Scheme 3 results in an increase of 534 per cent in the lowest decile (i.e. average income rises by more than six times!) and a 50 per cent increase in the second decile, with net income in the top decile falling by just over 30 per cent. AHC child poverty falls from 27.3 per cent in the current tax and welfare system to 12.5 per cent – which would be the lowest level of child poverty recorded since 1977 – in Scheme 1, and 3.8 per cent in Scheme 3. Table 7 of Reed *et al.* (2023) shows a wider range of outcomes for the impact of each scheme on poverty and inequality.

Part of the reason why the distributional effects of the Basic Income schemes are so large for the poorest households in the income distribution is that take-up of Universal Credit and legacy means-tested benefits and Tax Credits is considerably less than 100 per cent, which leads to some

Table 7.2 Distributional effects of Basic Income

		2022 baseline	*Basic Income*
Poverty (after housing costs)	**Children**	29.2%	13.5%
	Pensioners	10.1%	16.6%
	Working-age adults	15.0%	11.2%
Poverty (before housing costs)	**Children**	20.1%	6.6%
	Pensioners	21.7%	14.2%
	Working-age adults	20.2%	15.5%
Inequality	**Before housing costs**	0.353	0.3
(Gini, household incomes)	**After housing costs**	0.394	0.331

households in the lowest decile having very low incomes. Because Basic Income is universal by design, it addresses the problem of non-take-up directly and acts as a powerful tool for reducing inequalities at the low end of the income distribution.

7.3 Dynamic modelling: health impacts of Basic Income

Observational and experimental associations between income disparities and health have been established in studies and reviews examining, for example: self-rated health (Kondo *et al.*, 2009; Davillas, Jones and Benzeval, 2019; McCartney *et al.*, 2019; Reche, König and Hajek, 2019); mortality (Kondo *et al.*, 2009; McCartney *et al.*, 2019); biomarkers (Davillas, Jones and Benzeval, 2019); child health and wellbeing outcomes (Cooper and Stewart, 2021); mental health among children and young people (Pickett and Wilkinson, 2015; Parra-Mujica *et al.*, 2023; Villadsen *et al.*, 2024); and adult mental health (Tibber *et al.*, 2021; Akanni, Lenhart and Morton, 2022; Thomson *et al.*, 2022). Supporting Pickett and Wilkinson's causal review (2015), Adeline and Delattre's (2017) analysis endorsed both the Absolute Income Hypothesis (a positive and concave effect of income on health) and the Income Inequality Hypothesis (that income inequalities affect the health and wellbeing of nearly all members of a society). A recent review (Shimonovich *et al.*, 2024) has questioned the Income Inequality Hypothesis, but in controlling for individual level income in a multilevel framework to examine the causal effect of income inequality, it may over-control for factors on the causal pathway. The balance of evidence supports the notion of an increase in the quantity, security and predictability of income being the 'ultimate "multipurpose" policy instrument' (Mayer, 1997).

Alongside this building evidence, though not necessarily because of it, recent UK governments have committed to a 'prevention agenda' (Department of Health and Social Care, 2018) in improving population health, with more specific goals incorporated into the 2019 NHS England Long Term Plan (NHS England, 2019). There is longstanding evidence on the need for economic interventions to address population health (Working Group on Inequalities in Health, 1980; Marmot *et al.*, 2010, 2020) and existing approaches are proving inadequate means of reducing the burden on reactive services, with rates of mental health problems (McManus *et al.*, 2016) and physical impairments (Department for Work and Pensions, 2024b) continuing to rise.

Basic Income is a largely unconditional, secure, regular payment to all permanent residents to support basic needs regardless of employment status or income. It has been proposed as an upstream intervention to improve population health by increasing income size and security (M. T. Johnson *et al.*, 2022a). We anticipate that Basic Income would work through the following pathways shown in Figure 7.1.

For our purposes here, we need to combine analysis based on a 'within-between' model – which is intended to support causal inference from

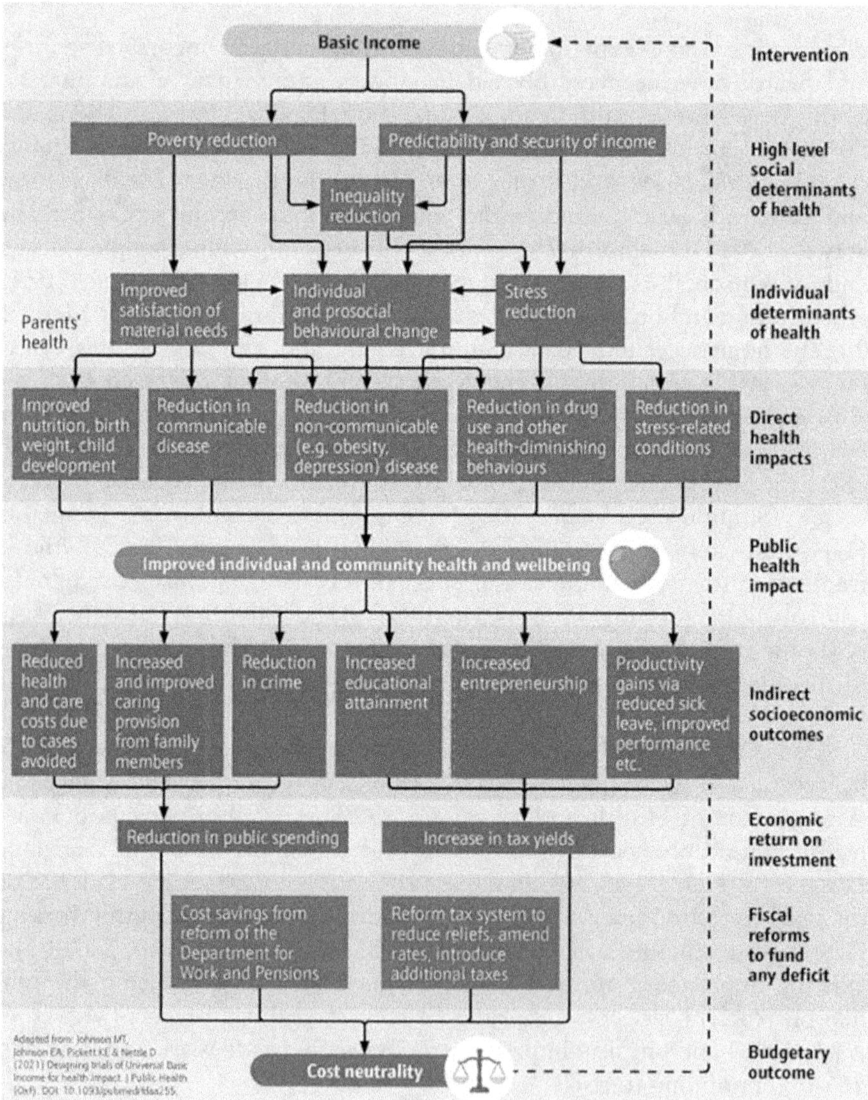

Figure 7.1 Logic model for health impacts of Basic Income

observational data – using data from both Understanding Society: The UK Household Longitudinal Study (UKHLS) and the Family Resources Survey (FRS) to microsimulate the effects of three proposed Basic Income schemes on mental and physical health among UK adults over the age of eighteen (Reed, Johnson, *et al.*, 2024).

We seek to answer the following questions:

1. To what extent would cases of mental and physical health problems be affected by Basic Income schemes?
2. What is the likely social return on investment resulting from the health effects of Basic Income schemes in terms of quality-adjusted life years (QALYs) and their UK-relevant willingness to pay value?
3. What are the likely cost savings for the NHS and personal social services as well as patients?

In answering these questions, we build on previous work both within our team and that of others. Our own previous work (Chen *et al.*, 2023; Parra-Mujica *et al.*, 2023; Villadsen *et al.*, 2024) has focused on mental health among adolescents and young adults, while that of others has generally excluded physical health (Thomson *et al.*, 2024). This study therefore fills several important gaps in the literature.

7.4 Finding the right panel data

The modelling of the relationship between health variables (explained in detail below) and net equivalised household income (with other individual and household characteristics used as control variables) is carried out using Waves 1–12 of the UKHLS, with data collected between 2009 and 2022 (Institute for Social and Economic Research, 2023). The UKHLS draws on interview data from approximately forty thousand households per wave to present socioeconomic, demographic and health data of individuals living in private households in the UK. The UKHLS modelling uses a balanced panel of individuals with data for all twelve waves of the UKHLS, which is a much smaller, but still highly reliable, sample at just under seven thousand individuals per wave (Reed, Johnson, *et al.*, 2024).

The Landman Economics TTM, running on data from the 2021–2022 FRS dataset, is used to microsimulate net equivalised household incomes under three different Basic Income schemes, described below. The regression coefficients from our analysis of the relationship between health variables and income, controlling for other household and individual characteristics, are used to predict the improvements in population health arising from each Basic Income scheme.

We used this as the basis for our microsimulation's synthetic population, weighted for additional characteristics found in the 2021–2022 FRS dataset.

7.5 Calibrating the tax-transfer model

We used the TTM to microsimulate the distributional household income effects of three Basic Income schemes and, with a new module, the health effects resulting from that redistribution. The schemes were broadly designed to provide pathways towards attaining the MIS. MIS is the income needed by different types of households to reach a socially acceptable living standard, as determined by members of the public with support from experts (Davis *et al.*, 2022). The three Basic Income schemes modelled were the following, based on those in Reed *et al.* (2023) and uprated according to the latest MIS:

Scheme 1 – Starter (per week): £50 per child; £75 per adult over eighteen and under sixty-five; £205 per adult aged over sixty-five

Scheme 1 is fiscally neutral in static terms and does not include savings and returns from investment elsewhere as a result of its introduction. It is affordable within the current fiscal context in the UK. No additional funding from the Exchequer and no net increase in taxation is required.

Scheme 2 – Intermediate (per week): £75 per child; £185 per adult under sixty-five; £205 per adult aged over sixty-five

Scheme 2 is a midpoint between the lower and higher levels. It is not fiscally neutral but can be funded by a range of means.

Scheme 3 – MIS level (per week): £100 per child; £295 per adult under sixty-five; £295 per adult aged over sixty-five

Scheme 3 ensures that all families reach the MIS level. It has a significant up-front cost but can be funded by a range of means.

These schemes would minimise losses for low-income households and the amount of disruption involved in moving to a new Income Support system, while enjoying broad public support. For instance, these schemes have been found to have support among critical 'Red Wall' voters in Wales and the Midlands and the North of England (M. T. Johnson *et al.*, 2022b).

The level of payments in each of the schemes is based on existing analysis by Reed *et al.*, uprated according to the UK Consumer Prices Index (CPI). Some of the components of MIS, such as food and energy, have experienced inflation rates much higher than the overall CPI average of around 10 per cent (Reed *et al.*, 2023). This means that the MIS scheme, for example, has risen by more than 28 per cent compared with our 2022 report (Reed *et al.*, 2023).

In the schemes, the main non-means-tested benefits in the UK benefits system (Child Benefit and the State Pension) are replaced by Basic Income. Basic Income payments are counted as unearned income to calculate Universal Credit – the main UK means-tested benefit for people on low incomes – which results in a one-for-one replacement. However, a small disregard is applied for Schemes 1 and 2 so that low-income individuals and families are better off under Basic Income than the baseline system. In Scheme 3, payments are sufficiently high that no disregard is necessary. Schemes 2 and 3 are not fiscally balanced (i.e. increases in tax revenue do not match the cost of Basic Income expenditure, net of any reductions in other benefits), but the costs are static and do not take account of any behavioural changes or savings that may be made in other areas as a result of improved productivity, reduced crime etc.

Following this economic microsimulation, we estimated effects on cases of depressive disorders and physical health problems (as measured by self-reported SF-12 Mental Components Summary [MCS-12] and Physical Component Summary [PCS-12] scores), quality-adjusted life years (QALYs) (calculated from SF-12 to SF-6D score) and willingness to pay value gained, as well as direct NHS, personal social services and patients' associated cost savings with regard to depressive disorders only.

Figure 7.2 shows a graphical representation of the modelling process.

7.6 Statistical analysis and outcomes

We used a within-between model (estimated using the UKHLS balanced panel shown in Table 7.1) to examine associations based on both increases or decreases in individuals' income compared with their average over time (the within component) and individuals' average income compared with the average of the population (the between component) on the one hand and health on the other. Net equivalised household income is the sum of net monthly incomes from all household members, adjusted by the OECD-modified equivalence scale (Office for National Statistics, 2015) to account for households of different sizes and compositions. In all results, we mean household income, even when we refer to an individual's income. Following

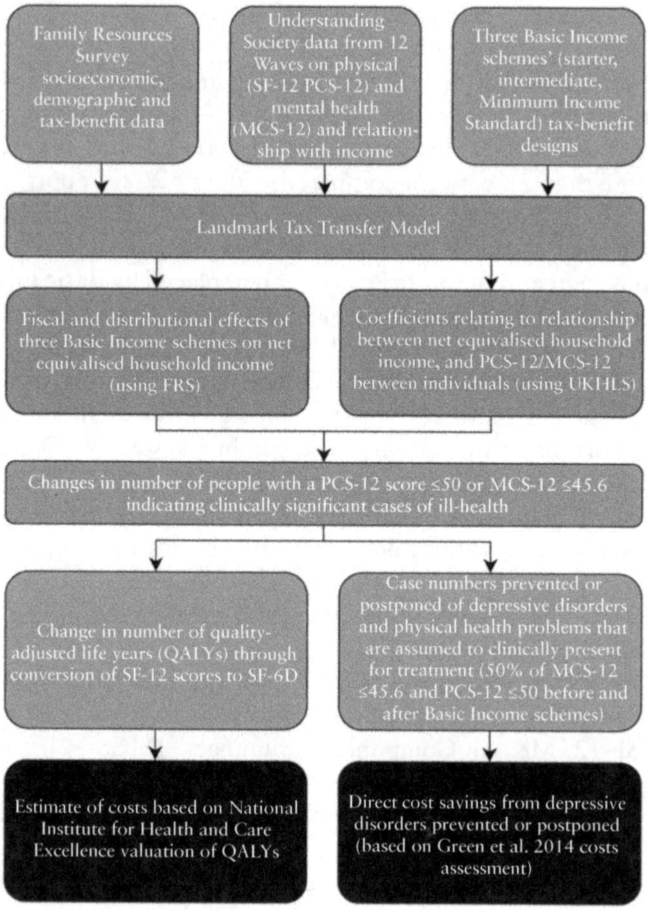

Figure 7.2 Modelling process diagram

the definition in national statistics, a household is defined as one person living alone, or a group of people (not necessarily related) living at the same address who share cooking facilities and share a living room, sitting room or dining area. A household can consist of a single family, more than one family or no families in the case of a group of unrelated people.

We believe that this model incorporates a number of key income-based drivers of health, including temporary and permanent income shocks, objective inequality and subjective social status inequality, to greater or lesser extents. The significance of income variations on anxiety and depression has been indicated by recent natural experiments, which have shown that the reduction in available resources has immediate and significant mental health impacts (Nettle, Chevallier, *et al.*, 2023). It does not, however, capture what we anticipate through our model of impact to be very substantial benefits from Basic Income of increased security of income and protection from destitution for a very large proportion of the population in even relatively highly paid jobs.

Using Stata 15 (StataCorp, 2017) to run this model, as in our previous studies (Chen *et al.*, 2023), we found that increases in income and higher average income are associated with better mental and physical health.

These findings fed through to our microsimulation modelling. Contrasting with our previous project, which used two separate microsimulations (economic and then health) in a hybrid serial arrangement, here we used the coefficients from the 'between' components of the UKHLS income model to forecast changes in population health in the FRS, based on the changes in net income arising from the counterfactual net equivalised household income distributions as microsimulated using the Landman Economics TTM.

In this study, we used the between-individual components because Basic Income would be a permanent rather than transitory change in income levels. The within coefficients mainly capture transitory variations in income. There is also an essential aspect of between-individual income which has subjective and prospective impacts on individuals. There is substantial and increasing evidence (see, for example, Wilkinson and Pickett's *Spirit Level* (Wilkinson and Pickett, 2010) for a summary) that inequality is causally related to outcomes, not just objective income levels. The between measure captures this (at least to some extent).

The TTM runs on Python 2.7. Detailed methodology for the TTM is available in Portes and Reed (2018b), and Women's Budget Group, Runnymede Trust, RECLAIM and Coventry Women's Voices (Women's Budget Group *et al.*, 2017). For uses of the TTM for microsimulation and varying assumptions, examples and details can be found in Reed and Portes (2014) and Harrop and Reed (2015).

7.7 Health economic measures

We examined the effects on case numbers of depressive disorder and physical health problems prevented or postponed; QALYs and associated UK-relevant willingness to pay, social value gained; years of life gained; as well as direct NHS, personal social services and patients' associated cost savings based on depressive disorders alone. Because this study is concerned with the public health impact of Basic Income, we have used NICE valuation of a QALY (£30,000) (NICE, 2022), rather than the current Treasury Green Book valuation, which is £70,000 in 2020/2021 prices (Government Finance Function and HM Treasury, 2022).

The estimated reductions in healthcare costs and increases in QALYs are calculated using the FRS data based on the coefficients from the UKHLS health-income model. To estimate the confidence intervals in the UKHLS model, we used a bootstrapping procedure on the 12-wave UKHLS balanced panel sample, randomly drawing (with replacement) from the sample of individuals with a full twelve waves of observations in the data. The bootstrapping procedure used a thousand repetitions to estimate the upper and lower 95 per cent confidence intervals for the income variables in the MCS-12 and PCS-12 regressions. The estimated changes in PCS-12 and MCS-12 scores arising from modelled changes in income, resulting from the introduction of each Basic Income scheme, were then converted into estimated changes in SF-6D score using the proprietary conversion algorithm from QualityMetric (2022) and the University of Sheffield (2024b).

Costs for anxiety and depression treatment were informed by the usual care arm of the CADET randomised control trial (Green *et al.*, 2014). We estimated and report two different cost perspectives: a) the UK NHS and Personal Social Services (Third Party Payer) perspective; and b) a broader perspective that included resource use from primary/community care (e.g. GP, mental health worker, social worker), secondary care (e.g. hospital admissions, psychiatric rehab ward, outpatient appointment), social care (e.g. daycare centre, drop-in club), informal care from friends/relatives (e.g. hours per week help from friends/relatives) and other patient costs (e.g. OTC medications, travel costs) to estimate the total cost of anxiety and depression. We uprated all costs to 2023 British pounds using the CPI. We further assumed that only half of the modelled individuals that reported symptoms of anxiety or depression would seek treatment and thus incur healthcare costs. This assumption was roughly informed by the Adult Psychiatric Morbidity Survey (McManus *et al.*, 2016). We extended this assumption to cases of physical health problems on the basis that producing conservative estimates is likely to have fewer real-world negative effects when assessing the cost-benefit of a policy like Basic Income than the alternative.

7.8 Health measures

We controlled for whether individuals were depressed or had symptoms indicating a physical health problem in the previous period, as well as sex, age and ethnicity; whether the individual was born in the UK and in which region or rurality; their highest qualification, marital status, employment status and attrition (people dropping out of the survey in specific waves).

Health variables of interest are presented as follows:

7.8.1 SF-12

The SF-12 (v2) survey (Ware, 2002) is a widely used tool to assess an individual's health-related quality of life, generating two summary scores: the Physical Component Summary (PCS-12) and the Mental Component Summary (MCS-12). We use an overall SF-12 score as well as MCS and PCS scores as outcome variables using our within-between model. Additionally, we create a dichotomous variable for cases of depressive disorder which takes the value of 1 if the individual's score is ≤ 45.6 and 0 if it is ≥ 45.7 (Vilagut *et al.*, 2013). In the case of the PCS-12, we use a threshold for clinically significant symptoms of a physical health problem of ≤ 50 (Soh *et al.*, 2021). The items comprising SF-12 can be found in the UKHLS Wave 12 questionnaire (Institute for Social and Economic Research, 2022). The scoring system used can be found in Ware *et al.* (2002).

7.8.2 SF-6D (SF-12)

SF-6D (Brazier, Roberts and Deverill, 2002) is a preference-based measure of health which enables the calculation of QALYs and therefore economic evaluation and cost-effectiveness of interventions. Originally developed to derive utility values from items in the SF-36 measure of health, an index based on seven items in six dimensions from SF-12 was created in 2004 (Brazier and Roberts, 2004), denoted by SF-6D (SF-12). The dimensions cover, with UKHLS variables in parentheses, physical functioning (scsf2a), role limitations (scsf3a and scsf3b), social functioning (scsf7), pain (scsf2a), mental health (scsf6c) and vitality (scsf6b). Each dimension has between three and five levels with 7,500 possible health states based on one selection in each dimension (Brazier and Roberts, 2004). The valuation study was undertaken in the UK.

We used software from QualityMetric (QualityMetric, 2022) to convert SF-12 scores into SF-6D scores, which were then used to calculate the change in QALYs for the UK population arising from the redistribution of income through the Basic Income schemes with their accompanying funding mechanisms.

7.8.3 Quality-adjusted life years (QALYs)

QALYs are a widely recognised standardised measure of health outcomes, including those that are not directly comparable, commonly used in health economics and health technology assessment (Drummond *et al.*, 2015; Kaplan and Hays, 2022). QALYs capture not only the increased life expectancy resulting from an intervention but also the improvements in health-related quality of life, with a year in perfect health assigned a QALY value of 1, while a year of less-than-perfect health receives a value less than 1. Patient wellbeing is assessed in the physical, social and psychological domains, and QALY weights are empirically assigned to each dimension. In the context of this study, QALYs enable policymakers and stakeholders to compare the cost-effectiveness of Basic Income with other health interventions and make informed decisions about resource allocation to maximise health gains. Additionally, QALYs incorporate a time dimension, useful to consider the duration of health improvements resulting from long-term policies.

Each QALY has been assigned a value of £30,000 based on NICE guidance which suggests that between £20,000 and £30,000 per QALY gained as a result of an intervention may be deemed cost effective (NICE, 2012). The Treasury's Green Book proposes a much higher value of £70,000 but this generally relates to other non-health expenditure interventions such as those related to transport (Government Finance Function and HM Treasury, 2022). In order to consider the broader impact of the intervention for assessment of Basic Income as a welfare policy intervention, the results we produce can be multiplied by 2.33.

7.8.4 Years of life gained

In order to calculate differences in life expectancy, we use multipliers (conditional on gender and age) for men and women of each year-of-age group in the FRS data. The multipliers are derived from McNamara *et al.* (2023). The gender- and age-specific multipliers are used to produce an estimate for years of life expectancy gained, conditional on QALYs gained, for men and women in each age group. These are then summed across the whole (grossed-up) FRS population to produce estimates for total years of life gained for each Basic Income scenario.

7.9 Initial findings

Table 7.3 shows the number of cases of anxiety and depression and of clinically significant physical health symptoms prevented or postponed under each scheme. Between 124,000 (95% confidence interval [CI]: 86,000 to 150,000) and 1.005 million (95% CI: 845,000 to 1.402 million) cases of depressive disorders and 118,000 (95% CI: 70,000 to 156,000) to 1.042 million (95% CI: 881,000 to 1.612 million) cases of physical health problems

Table 7.3 Modelling results indicating per year depressive disorders cost savings with confidence intervals in parentheses from different perspectives

Basic Income Scheme	*Mental health (anxiety and depression) cases avoided or prevented*	*Physical health cases avoided or prevented*	*QALYs*	*Value of QALYs*	*Number of years of life gained*	*NHS and personal social services cost savings, assuming 50% of cases diagnosed and treated*	*Total (including patients' related) cost savings, assuming 50% of cases diagnosed and treated*
1: £50 per child; £75 per adult over 18 and under 65; £205 per adult aged 65+	124,000 (86,000 – 150,000)	118,000 (70,000 – 156,000)	129,000 (86,000 – 172,000)	£3.87 billion (£2.58 billion –£5.16 billion)	169,000 (113,000 – 226,000)	£126 million (£88 million – £154 million)	£563 million (£392 million – £686 million)
2: £75 per child; £185 per adult under 65; £205 per adult aged 65+	537,000 (446,000 – 747,000)	548,000 (457,000 – 833,000)	375,000 (252,000 – 499,000)	£11.28 billion (£7.57 billion – £14.98 billion)	494,000 (331,000 – 656,000)	£549 million (£455 million – £763 million)	£2.449 billion (£2.032 billion – £3.404 billion)
3: £100 per child; £295 per adult under 65; £295 per adult aged 65+	1,005,000 (854,000 – 1,402,000)	1,042,000 (881,000 – 1,612,000)	655,000 (440,000 – 870,000)	£19.65 billion (£13.21 billion – £26.10 billion)	860,000 (578,000 – 1,143,000)	£1.026 billion (£872 million – £1.432 billion)	£4.579 billion (£3.893 billion – £6.391 billion)

could be prevented or postponed each year depending on the scheme. The table presents modelling results indicating cases of depressive disorders and physical health problems, with confidence intervals in parentheses, among adults over the age of eighteen prevented or postponed in 2023.

Table 7.3 shows that between 129,000 (95% CI: 86,000 to 172,000) and 655,000 (95% CI: 440,000 to 870,000) QALYs could be gained, valued at £3.87 billion (95% CI: £2.58 billion to £5.16 billion) to £19.65 billion (95% CI: £13.21 billion to £26.10 billion). The savings are independent of the cost of the investment, the framework for which has been outlined previously (Reed *et al.*, 2023).

7.10 Understanding the findings produced

These microsimulation findings indicate that Basic Income schemes could provide a significant benefit to the mental and physical health of adults, a large social return on investment and substantial savings for the health and social care system as well as in costs incurred by patients. The three Basic Income schemes reduce income inequality and increase the average incomes of the lowest quintile (poorest 20 per cent) of household net equivalised incomes in particular. It is this boost to income for low-income households that drives the projected increases in population health arising from the introduction of Basic Income.

Previous studies in a UK context have estimated impacts focusing on mental health alone and/or particular age groups. Compared with Parra-Mujica *et al.* (2023) and Chen *et al.* (2023), which also use UKHLS data to examine the relationship between income and mental health and microsimulate impacts based on Basic Income schemes respectively, this article expands analysis to all adults, rather than focusing on sixteen- or eighteen-year-olds to eighteen- to twenty-four-year-olds, and covers both mental and physical health. Physical health, in particular, has not been assessed or modelled comprehensively in previous studies. Similarly, Thomson *et al.* (2024), which was published after our findings had been produced and drafted, focuses exclusively on mental health and adults aged twenty-five to sixty-four. Thomson *et al.*'s analysis also uses an alternative measure of mental health, GHQ-12, whereas SF-12 has an established and rigorous process of translation to QALYs using NICE guidelines. Green Book value can be produced by using a 2.33 multiplier.

This study uses validated measures from a large-scale, long-running and nationally significant household Longitudinal Study. It also builds on an economic microsimulation model that has previously been subject to peer review. For the first time, it has provided an estimate of potential health impacts of Basic Income schemes across the adult population. It is, however, based on observational data and assumes that low income is causally related to depressive disorders and physical health problems and that increasing income can fully reverse the risk. The association between income and mental health has been shown in experimental and observational studies. Recent evidence from the cost-of-living crisis supports the assumption that reduction in non-committed money has a causal effect on mental health (Nettle, Chevallier, *et al.*, 2023). However, the heterogeneity of cash transfer schemes and other policies intended to redistribute income and the heterogeneity of reported mental health outcomes make evidence synthesis difficult. Large, representative trials of Basic Income that capture comprehensive and comparable data in the real world are crucial (E. A. Johnson *et al.*, 2023b). There remains an opportunity to model the health impacts of changes through all pathways identified in Figure 7.1 on all major disease types. This would enable much greater specificity in the types of health problems addressed and associated savings, including when extrapolating from trials.

As discussed above, we believe that the 'between' coefficient from our analysis most closely resembles the impact of a permanent change in income from a Basic Income, also reflecting the cumulative and subjective impacts of inequality. There remains, however, a challenge with regard to income quintiles being the average across the country, as differences in living costs might have a significant impact on people's day-to-day experience and material conditions. We are currently examining a measure that would more accurately reflect the effect of people's uncommitted income while also being usable within microsimulation.

It is important to note that the cost-of-living crisis, and the high inflation period in the UK and much of the wider world in 2023, has compressed and is likely to further compress household incomes, accelerating the situation in public health further by negatively affecting the pathways set out in Figure 7.1. This suggests that our modelled estimates are conservative and that research on Basic Income policies is continuing to build both in relevance and in political and public health salience. There is evidence to suggest that the redistributive impacts of Basic Income schemes will benefit women more than men, who have lower incomes on average, and lower-income groups more than higher-income groups (Reed *et al.*, 2023). It is also assumed that additional needs relating to disability will be provided by supplementary conditional payments (Johnson, Reed and Johnson, 2023). There is no evidence that Basic Income produces negative labour market participation outcomes. Indeed, Basic Income reduces the participation tax rates associated with negative income tax schemes – that is, the loss of benefits as income from work increases – tax rates which are identified by Martinelli as particularly affecting lower-income households (Martinelli, 2017).

The findings have relevance to policymakers in indicating that upstream economic interventions have the potential to improve population health; reduce the burden on downstream, reactive health services; and address the long-term increase in both the prevalence of long-term health conditions and impairments and the associated health and social care costs. Clinicians are increasingly faced with patients presenting with problems that are fundamentally socioeconomic in nature, or the result of socioeconomic factors. Given that they are asked by the government to take part in welfare claim and other social processes, there is a need for clinicians to make their voices heard in relation to policy development to ensure that they can continue to do their jobs effectively and support better health and wellbeing for their patients.

Again, with caveats regarding the likely underestimate of impact, the savings from the NHS and from patient-related costs could cover the full economic cost (including salaries and all other associated costs and overheads per year) for between 7,481 (under Scheme 1) and 61,184 (under Scheme 3) additional hospital-based band-5 nurses per annum (Jones and Burns, 2021). Physical health NHS and personal social services savings are more difficult to calculate. However, it is reasonable to anticipate that they may be even higher, given that the 2022/2023 clinical commissioning groups (CCG) budget for mental health, learning disability and dementia services in England is just £13.3 billion, or 13.8 per cent of the total (Baker and Kirk-Wade, 2023).

The methods we have employed take into account any prospective negative impacts from an increase or decrease in income at different points in the income distribution. It is important to note that there is some evidence that increases in income at the top end of the distribution have increasingly diminishing returns, such that there may actually be a decrease in health at the absolute top end. There is evidence of increased mortality and accidental deaths in US studies of infrequent cash transfers, for example following the annual Alaska Permanent Fund distribution or the biannual Eastern Cherokee payment, perhaps due to increased, stored-up activity (M. T. Johnson *et al.*, 2022a). This speaks to the importance of other pathways within our model of impact, beyond objective income increases, particularly regularity and security of income. There is no reason to believe that such issues would arise in a Basic Income system with distributions occurring weekly or monthly.

We believe that this study represents a first step in establishing much broader health impacts of prospective Basic Income schemes. However, further work is required to understand the impact of such schemes through all of the pathways identified in our model of impact. Experimental studies, while difficult due to the need to replicate Basic Income at a large scale in order to imitate a full policy effectively, would provide greater certainty with regard to health impacts and policymaker confidence. However, our study indicates that the health savings and returns on investment could be substantial.

7.11 Conclusion

There is now widespread consensus that reforms over the last fifteen years have made Britain more unequal and have had a particularly adverse impact on some of the most vulnerable children and adults in the country – those in low-income households, people of colour, disabled people and children in large families in particular. Statistics from analysis using the Landman Economics TTM are regularly cited in Hansard (Abrahams, 2016; Matheson, 2018) and in the national media (Portes, 2018; Andrews, 2023). It is essential to emphasise that enhanced microsimulation necessarily improves the quality of debate around tax and welfare policies in the UK and its constituent countries.

The use of the TTM to forecast a range of future economic outcomes – such as poverty and inequality – and the potential impacts of changes to tax and welfare policy on these outcomes helps provide important insights that can inform longer-term debate. This is critically important in a field that tends to be dominated by thinking on a time horizon that is no longer than the five-year limit of the next parliamentary term. Meanwhile, introducing modelling of the impact of cuts to spending on public services into distributional analysis using the Landman Economics Public Spending Model significantly enhanced the quality of debate over the impacts of austerity in the 2010s and beyond.

Modelling Basic Income schemes in recent years has helped Basic Income move from a somewhat esoteric policy option to a more central position in public debates over the future of welfare. While neither of the two major parties in the UK made any commitment to Basic Income for the 2024 General Election, the Green Party has both committed to introducing a Basic Income and increased their share of the vote and their parliamentary representation in elections between 2019 and 2026.

More recent developments on the modelling of the potential positive health impacts of introducing a Basic Income are important in policy terms. The projections suggest both increased population health and reduced health inequalities, which are generally regarded as intrinsic goods, and also positive productivity impacts and reduced pressures on public spending on health, social care and criminal justice. The potential of these outcomes to increase tax yields and reduce budgetary pressures then provide potential fiscally neutral packages of tax-benefit reforms, partially obviating the need for large-scale tax rises. A more sophisticated and broader treatment of these downstream impacts of Basic Income is an urgent requirement for future research. The research outlined in this book has contributed to enabling that work to take place and to inform more ambitious forms of social policy.

Strengths:

1. Allows rigorous quantitative analysis of the impact of policies.
2. Results can be broken down by a range of characteristics (household income, but also individual attributes e.g. age, gender, ethnicity, disability).
3. Making the model open source allows other researchers to replicate the results (the new version of TTM is being open-sourced on GitHub).

Weaknesses:

1. Static modelling (this does not consider behavioural effects, e.g. changes in work effort; or longer-term effects, e.g. health impacts). *These can be added in, however.*
2. The sample size of the datasets limits the scope for two-way (or three-way) breakdowns, and also makes geographical breakdowns below regional level difficult.
3. Data available from the UK Data Archive (https://www.data-archive.ac.uk/) omit some important variables for confidentiality reasons (e.g. gender reassignment, religion).
4. Some policies cannot be analysed due to limitations in the survey data (e.g. Universal Credit sanctions).

8

Quantitative evidence on impacts and social feasibility of reforms

Key foci

- Introducing TriplePC's integration of economic microsimulation, health impacts and public preferences.
- Using conjoint analysis to reveal trade-offs: high tax acceptance when poverty dramatically decreases.
- Demonstrating public preferences for wealth/carbon taxes over borrowing to fund progressive policies.
- Challenging assumptions about the Overton Window with evidence of strong redistributive support.

8.1 The challenge of social feasibility

For the past five decades, industrialised countries have been broadly committed to trickle-down economic policies that have radically increased inequality (Piketty and Saez, 2014). This shift has been advanced through the justification of absolute societal gains. The UK Conservative Party, in particular, has argued that reducing the tax burden on the wealthy stimulates economic activity that would incrementally improve the welfare of those in all subsequent strata of society (Thatcher, 1975). Any increase in inequality has been justified through reference to any absolute material gain among the worst off on the grounds that such impacts improve the interests and wellbeing of all members of society. There is evidence that the opposite may be true.

Wilkinson and Pickett (2010) provide a substantive overview of the impacts on inequality on society: as inequality rises, crime and social disorder increase, and health, among other social goods, decreases. Not only does the distribution of risk increase among particular groups, but morbidity (diseases and health conditions) and mortality (deaths) increase overall (Marmot *et al.*, 2020). Marginal absolute gains among the worst off do not mitigate impacts. Indeed, Bartram's analysis of 1981–2020 World Values Survey and European Values Study data shows that, in spite of economic growth over the last forty years, 'in wealthy countries increased inequality has a substantial negative impact on life satisfaction, while in poorer countries any effect (positive or negative) is small' (Bartram, 2022, p. 2). He notes that UK life satisfaction in 2018 was similar to that during recession-hit 1981, when inequality was much lower (British Sociological Association, 2022).

In the UK, there is evidence both of higher rates of anxiety and depression among lower-SES groups, and bi-directional causality. Not only are conditions affected by SES: they also affect income (Wilson and Finch, 2021), compounding inequality. We have argued that data from longitudinal studies and some controlled trials of income interventions indicate that the primary driver is income to health (Nettle *et al.*, 2024). This is likely the case for a large number of other health conditions, but depression is critical given that it has long been suggested as the most costly disease to society (Lecrubier, 2001) and the leading cause of disability worldwide (Bernardi and Johns, 2021). If governments are serious in their 'prevention' strategies, there is a genuine need for upstream socioeconomic interventions that address the source of morbidity and broader social pathologies: material inequality.

Evidence on voting participation suggests a political challenge. Those from lower-SES groups (Hill and Leighley, 1992) and those with mental health conditions, in particular, are less likely to vote than average (Sund *et al.*, 2017). Ojeda and Pacheco found that 'self-rated health is associated with a lower probability of voting in one's first election' and 'depression is related to a decline in turnout over time' (Ojeda and Pacheco, 2019). Ojeda argues that this is because depression reduces motivation by instilling a sense of hopelessness and imposes somatic burdens that reduce capacity for participation. He argues that this creates a political cycle of depression:

> 1) individuals with depression are unlikely to participate in the political process, 2) the lack of participation leads to underrepresentation and a lack of policies that benefit those with depression, and 3) the lack of beneficial policy outcomes perpetuates the experience of depression. And so it repeats. (Ojeda, 2015, p. 1240)

There is evidence that the clustering of anxiety and depression among lower-SES groups has played a significant role in recent electoral outcomes. For example, there is evidence both of association between income and increased support for 'leave' in the UK's 2016 Referendum on EU Membership (Stark, 2017) and that psychological traits like anxiety and depression positively predicted support for 'leave' and Trump in 2016 (Obschonka *et al.*, 2018). There are two contrasting explanations for this trend. First, the campaigns focused on increasing control, including by claiming to support particular constituents against competitors for material resources (The Atlantic, 2016). This provides means of mitigating a source of anxiety and depression. Second, Bernardi and Johns argue that those with depression or depressive traits support the politics of the least upheaval. With regard to Brexit, they argue that there was a shift from pre-referendum support for 'remain' to post-referendum 'leave' in order to 'make the issue go away' (Bernardi and Johns, 2021). These two explanations highlight a tension in preferences among lower-SES voters, who are disproportionately affected by anxiety and depression, between increasing control and mitigating unpredictability, since the means of delivering the former require a degree of reform beyond the *status quo*. The very voters who stand to benefit most from change may have a psychological disposition against the uncertainty bound up with that change.

A second challenge to redistribution is that those from higher-SES groups, who are more likely to vote, are less likely to benefit from redistribution and may, in fact, lose out through increased taxation to fund redistribution. Indeed, policymakers, who are much more likely to be well off, fall into this category (Dickins, 2023; E. Johnson, Thew, *et al.*, 2025). That is to say, the very people responsible for addressing inequality have a personal interest in not pursuing policies to address it. Evidence on concern for relative gains suggests that this is a crucial consideration: voters are less likely to support policies that impose a personal net loss to achieve a net gain for others. Moreover, people's perception of their socioeconomic status and their potential exposure to tax increases means that they may believe that they are at risk of losing out, even when they stand to benefit significantly.

Thirdly, battleground constituencies also have older populations. Older voters are more likely to be more secure materially, both by acquiring wealth throughout their working lives, owning homes outright and having access to guaranteed Basic Income-style payments through their pensions. We have shown elsewhere that age and wealth predict evaluation of Basic Income (Johnson, Johnson and Nettle, 2022).

These challenges mean that politicians often conclude that redistribution is a vote loser. In the UK, the consequence has been that the present Labour leadership has eschewed radical redistributive policies and focused on New Labour-style technocracy combined with English identity politics. This may assuage concerns about the previous leadership's ambivalence towards English national identity, but leaves open the possibility of much longer-term electoral problems. The trend of PASOKification – the loss of support for progressive parties the more they favour the *status quo* – suggests that the more unequal a society becomes, the less likely it is to be able both to function and to support centre-ground parties. This creates a hypothetical downward cycle, in which the worst off expand in number, lose faith in government and support right-wing parties. As a consequence, public health diminishes, social disorder increases and the means by which to address the overall trend are reduced by lack of electoral success among progressive parties.

Elsewhere, we have argued that increased awareness of exposure to the risk of destitution among the population has increased support for equality-promoting measures that enhance security (Nettle *et al.*, 2021). Our findings suggest that Basic Income, as a radical redistributive measure, has high (~75 per cent) levels of approval both in the UK and US and within 'Red Wall' constituencies (Johnson, Johnson and Nettle, 2022). Figure 8.1 indicates raw levels of support for the policy in Red Wall constituencies and nationally.

At a time of permacrisis, the need for transformative evidence-based policymaking is urgent and great. Often, policymakers regard the transformative policies capable of addressing these crises as beyond the 'Overton Window', which is used to describe actions consistent with public acceptability (Mackinac Center, 2025).

In this chapter, we work through a series of examples of evidence produced regarding economic, health and electoral outcomes to frame the evidence produced in your own microsimulation to persuade relevant stakeholders. We explore ways of presenting evidence for different stakeholders, such as civil servants, third sector bodies and academics. We focus on the following questions:

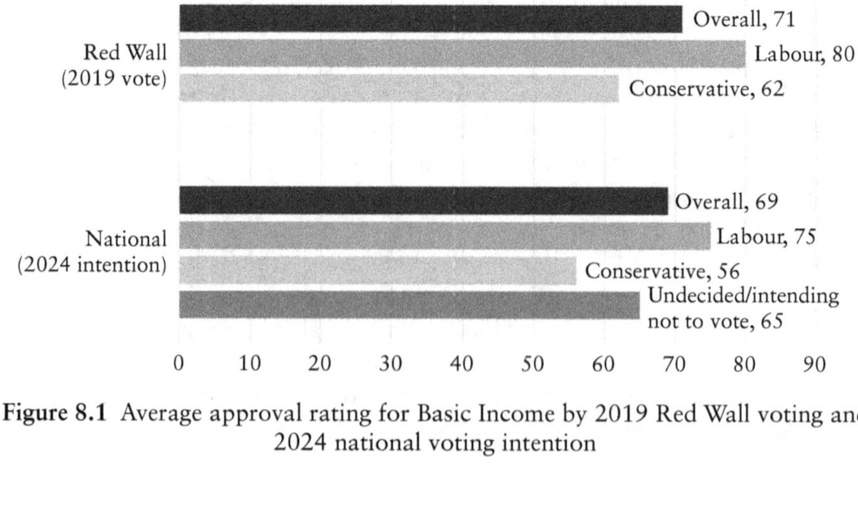

Figure 8.1 Average approval rating for Basic Income by 2019 Red Wall voting and 2024 national voting intention

- What evidence matters?
- How can the Overton Window be shifted?
- How should we engage with different stakeholders?

In this chapter, we outline two means of examining and shifting an Overton Window-based roadblock.

First, we set out conjoint analysis, which elicits preferences on trade-offs between features and outcomes of policy, and means of combining that with data on microsimulation evidence on impacts of health, health economics and economic impacts. This enables coherent analysis of existing preferences.

Second, we set out adversarial co-production of narratives to shift public opinion. This approach involves working with opponents of evidence-based policy to develop means of persuading potential beneficiaries to support introduction. This emerging approach has been deployed in examination of public preferences with regard to welfare reform, but can be applied to a wide range of policy areas. We outline the history of co-production before setting out the process by which adversarial co-production was developed. We then describe the impact of adversarial co-production on public preferences on Basic Income. This enables us to set out challenges and opportunities for those with an interest in addressing our crises, serving to stimulate genuine debate on longstanding assumptions about the limits of evidence-based policy and public opinion.

We begin by setting out means of combining quantitative, conjoint evidence with public opinion data via the Public Policy Preference Calculator: TriplePC.

8.2 Combining microsimulation and public opinion data

There are many measures that might actually be popular with the public, but measures that policymakers have been unwilling to consider because of uncertainty about their electoral consequences.

Perhaps the best example in the UK is the Social Democratic Party–Liberal Party Alliance's 'Dead Parrot' merger manifesto of January 1988 (Crewe and King, 1995b). This proposed the abolition of Child Benefit and the imposition of a uniform rate of VAT to raise money for an anti-poverty programme. Although this had been modelled in detail, fear of the electoral consequences among members of parliament meant the manifesto was abandoned within a day. The resulting confusion and indecision arguably caused long-lasting damage to centrist politics in the UK (Crewe and King, 1995a). The UK's zero-rating for food and children's clothing remains politically untouchable to this day despite the orthodox economic arguments in favour of a uniform rate (Crawford, Keen and Smith, 2010). The problem is that evidence on the electoral feasibility of a VAT extension is unclear, especially if it was part of a package that used the money raised for poverty reduction or other appealing policies. As such, we need an approach that allows us to examine preferences under actual circumstances in which trade-offs are required.

One of the key actual outcomes of policy in this area relates to health. There is strong evidence that welfare policies can have a substantial effect on population health (Johnson *et al.*, 2022). A stark reminder of the real impact of worsening population health can be seen in the proportion of the UK population with a long-standing illness, disability or impairment which causes substantial difficulty with day-to-day activities. This is estimated to have risen from 19 per cent in 2011/2012 to 24 per cent in 2021/2022, an increase of 3.9 million people (Department for Work and Pensions, 2024b). Interestingly, the proportion among State Pension age adults has remained the same between 2011/2012 and 2021/2022, at 45 per cent, whereas for working-age adults it has increased from 16 per cent to 23 per cent and for children the figures are 6 per cent to 11 per cent. This suggests that increases in prevalence are not simply the effect of an ageing population (Department for Work and Pensions, 2024b).

In that context, it is essential that policymakers invest real thought in realising the Government's prevention agenda (Department of Health and Social Care, 2018), which was incorporated into the 2019 NHS England Long Term Plan (NHS England, 2019). Four and a half decades on from the Black Report, which highlighted the role of material circumstances on health inequalities (Working Group on Inequalities in Health, 1980), a decade and a half on from the Marmot Review (Marmot *et al.*, 2010) and half a decade since its 'ten-years-on' update (Marmot *et al.*, 2020), which highlighted worsening trends in inequalities, there is good reason to examine and tackle social determinants of health (Johnson *et al.*, 2022).

There is ample evidence that financial insecurity causes ill health, including evidence from recent natural experiments during the cost-of-living crisis (Nettle *et al.*, 2024; Nettle, Chevallier, *et al.*, 2025). Conditional, means- and needs-based welfare systems in high-income countries are associated with below-average health outcomes (Shahidi *et al.*, 2019; E. Johnson, Thew, *et al.*, 2025) and increased psychological distress prevalence (Wickham *et al.*, 2020). We have suggested several explanations (Johnson *et al.*, 2022): schemes are 'insufficient to offset the negative health consequences of severe socioeconomic disadvantage' (Shahidi *et al.*, 2019); conditionality and assessment inflict stress (Dwyer *et al.*, 2020) and create perverse incentives for health-diminishing behaviour (Johnson *et al.*, 2022); and focusing on the poorest fails to mitigate broader determinants that affect society as a whole (Marmot *et al.*, 2010). As such, there are good reasons to build on findings of systematic reviews of cash transfer schemes that resemble Basic Income, such as Gibson *et al.* (2020), which indicate positive impacts on mental and physical health, hospital attendance and health-related behaviour, such as alcohol and drug use (Gibson, Hearty and Craig, 2020). In the absence of UK randomised controlled trials (RCTs), there is a need to explore prospective impacts via microsimulation.

There are existing health simulations for the UK. Public Health Scotland's Informing Interventions to Reduce Health Inequalities (Triple I) tools focus on comparing the effects and costs of a range of tax-benefit changes (including a Basic Income) as well as non-economic programmes, such as a lifestyle weight management service, speed limits of twenty miles per hour or Alcohol Brief Interventions. Effects and costs modelled are based on premature deaths, years of life lost and hospital stays, with changes in population health and inequalities as the key measures. It does not model either the economic impacts on household types or public preferences. Indeed, most other health microsimulations tend to model the economic effects of health, rather than the other way round, meaning that assumptions of causality are problematic (Schofield *et al.*, 2017).

There is then a need for microsimulation with a public-facing user interface that enables automated assessment of economic and health impacts as well as public preferences between different welfare and tax policies. The Public Policy Preference Calculator (TriplePC) does this. The model has three strands:

1. Estimating the likely electoral popularity of possible policies.
2. Deriving relationships between income and health, in a form suitable for use in a microsimulation.
3. Integration of strands 1 and 2 into a microsimulation tax-benefit model.

Understanding the underpinning relationships between these strands enables the development of evidence capable of informing policymakers more cohesively than unintegrated data.

8.3 Public preferences: conjoint analysis

Since the late twentieth century, welfare states have faced a number of challenges related to demographic and economic trends, such as deindustrialisation; ageing populations; immigration; and rising precarious employment. These challenges have driven varied processes of retrenchment, expansion and recalibration in welfare systems (Armingeon and Bonoli, 2006;

Taylor-Gooby *et al.*, 2017). In the past few decades, most OECD countries have tightened eligibility conditions for receipt of benefits, particularly in relation to job search requirements and conditions about citizenship or residence, ostensibly to deal with concerns about moral hazard (Knotz, 2018). In the UK, the level of support provided to working-age adults relative to average wages has fallen over time, particularly for single people.

Recently, there has been a surge of academic and policy interest in novel welfare models such as Basic Income (Wispelaere and Morales, 2016), minimum income guarantee (Statham, Parkes and Gunson, 2021) and participation income (Atkinson, 2015; McGann and Murphy, 2023). These proposals are often pitched as a response to a series of crises, from the Global Financial Crisis of 2007–2008 to the COVID-19 pandemic and its aftermath, as well as means for addressing persistently high poverty and inequality rates that existing systems have failed to mitigate (Chen *et al.*, 2023; Parra-Mujica *et al.*, 2023). However, as we have seen in Chapter 5, these interventions require the reversal of long-term trends in policy, and, in some cases, considerable fiscal reform.

Public support for welfare systems is generally high, especially for encompassing policies such as pensions (Svallfors, 2010). However, expressions of support for single policies can be misleading. Both public support for higher government spending and public support for lower taxation can be found in the same populations when each of these is presented in isolation (Bremer and Bürgisser, 2022a). Similar observations apply to institutional design features: descriptions of Basic Income schemes often elicit strong approval, but so do descriptions of welfare schemes based on very different principles, such as those involving high levels of conditionality (Roosma and van Oorschot, 2019; Nettle *et al.*, 2021; Laenan, 2023). Thus, the pertinent question is not whether people support a policy in some absolute sense. Every policy is a bundle of features, some of which will be perceived as positive and some of which as negative. The critical questions are as follows: which features increase net support?; which decrease it and by how much?; and how do people trade off the various features against one another?

Early models assumed that preferences for welfare transfers were driven by fairly narrow self-interest: voters who could expect to gain directly in income would favour the expansion of the welfare system, whereas those who might be net contributors would favour its contraction (Meltzer and Richard, 1981). In fact, the predictive power of personal expectations of gain or loss, though real, is not as clear as first thought.

In addition to personal gain, voters also appear to be concerned about outcomes for the population at large, and particularly the effect on poverty (Bechtel and Liesch, 2020). These broader concerns are not limited to those who identify as left-wing. Indeed, the impact of left–right political orientation, though measurable, is not as strong as might be expected (Johnson, Johnson and Nettle, 2022). The widespread concern about poverty is consistent with a tradition of research in behavioural economics showing that, in distributional questions, people tend to have preferences for a distribution that includes consideration of the effect on the welfare of the worst off (Charness and Rabin, 2002; Kameda *et al.*, 2016). This hints at preferences consistent with what John Rawls described as 'maximin': maximise the minimum to ensure that the worst off are as well off as possible (Rawls, 1971). The preference for positive population-level consequences may not be limited to the wellbeing of the worst off. People may also want a welfare system to reduce inequality, reduce stress or improve physical health (Johnson *et al.*, 2020; Nettle *et al.*, 2021, p. 20; Johnson, Johnson and Webber, 2022), though the strength of these preferences relative to those for other features has not yet been tested.

One difficulty with eliciting preferences on features of welfare systems is that, all else being equal, the public tend to prefer public spending on most social goods. There are majorities of the public in most countries in favour of public expenditure on key areas of the welfare state (Jensen and Petersen, 2017). However, that support is reduced when people are presented with trade-offs between higher spending and higher income tax burdens. It is this trading-off that enables translation of general positions on distribution into specific preferences on policies. Using a conjoint experiment, Häusermann *et al.* find that in Switzerland, opposition to restrictive pension reform can be overcome if salient compensation is provided to certain groups (Häusermann, Kurer and Traber, 2019). Barnes *et al.* use a multivariate choice experiment in the UK to find that, in general, people favour higher taxes to fund key policy areas, but that younger respondents are less likely to support tax increases (Barnes, Blumenau and Lauderdale, 2022). Bremer and Bürgisser also use a conjoint experiment, in Germany, Italy and the UK, and identify a hierarchy of social policy priorities, with pensions and education at the top, family policies in the middle, and labour market policies lower down (Bremer and Bürgisser, 2022a). The relative importance of each policy area is heightened by material interests: pensioners see pensions as particularly salient, and adults with children prioritise family policies.

Along with the cost and the population consequences, people may be concerned with institutional design features, including the nature and consequences of entitlement. An influential idea in this area is that people rely on a 'deservingness heuristic': they want to see resources restricted to deserving recipients (Jensen and Petersen, 2017; Roosma and van Oorschot, 2019). Deservingness and its interpretation have influenced conjoint work on the acceptability of Basic Income proposals. Rincon in Spain (2023), and Rincón, Vlandas, and Hiilamo in Finland (2022), used conjoint designs to explore the relative preference for Basic Income versus conditional or non-universal alternatives. In the Spanish sample, they found that the universality of Basic Income had a negative effect on popularity: preference could be increased by restricting entitlement to citizens of the country. In Finland, by contrast, it was the unconditionality that was negatively valued: preference could be increased by including a requirement to demonstrate need. In both studies, taxing capital or the highest incomes to fund the policy – making the rich pay – increased preference. Stadelmann-Steffen and Dermont, in a comparative study in Spain and Finland, restricted the universe of policies under consideration to different forms of Basic Income (2020). In both countries, they found that more restrictions on the eligible population (making recent immigrants ineligible) increased the preference for the policy, and a very low level of payment was dispreferred to a more generous one. Since the study only considered Basic Income schemes, which are by definition unconditional, the effect of unconditionality on preference was not evaluated.

Overall, then, there is evidence that deservingness concerns can be influential. However, we do not know how strong these concerns might be as drivers of preference relative to costs in terms of taxation, or preferences for poverty reduction and other positive population consequences, since these different dimensions are rarely put together in the same survey. Moreover, we do not know what deservingness means to populations, given that criteria of deservingness presumably differ according to time and place.

In recent years, conjoint analysis has become increasingly popular as a method for eliciting the public's relative valuations of competing policy goods (Hainmueller, Hopkins and Yamamoto, 2014; Bansak *et al.*, 2023). This is a survey-based technique originally developed as a market research tool, to examine how consumers value characteristics (sweetness, colour, alcohol content, etc.) of goods. Recently, the technique has become popular as a method for discovering the public's relative valuations of competing economic or social policies (Bremer and Bürgisser, 2023). Respondents are repeatedly invited to choose their preferred policy design from a pair of policy configurations. The configurations vary in terms of a series of attributes (payment size, conditionality, etc.) whose levels are randomly permuted. This allows researchers to estimate the average impact of any particular feature attribute-value on preference for the policy. Critically, the strength of preference or dispreference for several different policy attributes can be simultaneously estimated and measured on comparable scales. Research comparing conjoint survey experiments to actual votes has shown that the conjoint results are good predictors of voting outcomes (Bansak *et al.*, 2023).

We used a conjoint experiment to assess the nature and strength of public support for different features of potential welfare schemes using a conjoint survey experiment with eight hundred British residents (Nettle *et al.*, 2025a; Johnson *et al.*, 2023). The attributes that we varied cover the schemes' generosity (e.g. size of payment), conditionality (e.g. residency, work), funding mechanism (e.g. tax, borrowing) and outcomes (e.g. effects on poverty, health). We examined the relationship between design preference and demographic characteristics such as sex, age, self-reported financial position and political orientation.

Participants were asked repeatedly to choose their preferred welfare policy from sets of two. Each time, the two policies contained the same input (design) and outcome (health and distributional) attributes but with randomised levels in each (e.g. payment sizes of £63 per child, £145 per adult and £190 per pensioner; poverty decreased by 25 per cent etc.). Each participant completed fifteen choice tasks. Each option within each task was defined by ten attributes. Each attribute had three to nine possible levels. Table 8.1 shows the full list of ten attributes with between three and nine levels each. Attributes were chosen on the basis of previous research conducted by the programme team examining aspects of welfare policy of relevance to public opinion as well as critical aspects of policy design (Johnson, Johnson and Nettle, 2022; M. T. Johnson *et al.*, 2023).

All options were fully randomly generated from the possible combinations. Instructions in the survey explained that participants might prefer some features in one policy and some in the other, but they needed to consider which policy they preferred overall. The attributes on which the policies varied were explained in greater depth prior to the first choice task, and then described just with brief phrases during the choice tasks themselves. Note that many of these randomly generated pairs are totally implausible. This is integral to how a fully randomised conjoint analysis works: by generating all the possible combinations, things that are actually correlated in real life (e.g. tax rates and poverty rates) are rendered orthogonal to one another. It is this that allows identification of their independent marginal effects.

Relative to the UK population, the sample contained an over-representation of people who voted for the left to centre-left Labour Party at the 2019 general election (44.3 per cent of those in our sample who voted versus 32.1 per cent election result); and an under-representation of those who voted for the right to centre-right Conservative Party (31.8 per cent versus 43.6 per cent election result).

We simultaneously estimated the average impact of preference or dispreference for particular feature attribute-value on preference for policies overall using comparable scales through computation of Average Marginal Component Effects (AMCEs) (Hainmueller, Hopkins and Yamamoto, 2014) from linear probability models. The AMCE for a given level of an attribute can be interpreted as the marginal effect on the probability of choice of the

Table 8.1 Conjoint experiment attributes and levels

Attribute	*Levels*
Payment size	• Child – £0; Adult – £63; Pensioner – £190 • Child – £41; Adult – £63; Pensioner – £190 • Child – £0; Adult – £145; Pensioner – £190 • Child – £41; Adult – £145; Pensioner – £190 • Child – £63; Adult – £145; Pensioner – £190 • Child – £63; Adult – £190; Pensioner – £190 • Child – £95; Adult – £190; Pensioner – £230 • Child – £41; Adult – £230; Pensioner – £230 • Child – £95; Adult – £230; Pensioner – £230
Income tax	• Basic rate – 20%; Higher rate – 40%; Additional rate – 45% • Basic rate – 30%; Higher rate – 50%; Additional rate – 60% • Basic rate – 40%; Higher rate – 60%; Additional rate – 70% • Basic rate – 48%; Higher rate – 68%; Additional rate – 78% • Basic rate – 50%; Higher rate – 70%; Additional rate – 80% • Basic rate – 65%; Higher rate – 85%; Additional rate – 95%
Other funding	• Increased government borrowing • Removal of income tax-free personal allowance • Corporation tax increase • Tax for businesses based on carbon emissions • Tax for individuals based on carbon emissions • Tax on wealth • VAT increase
Poverty	• Decreased by 100% • Decreased by 75% • Decreased by 50% • Decreased by 25% • Decreased by 10% • Decreased by 5% • Increased by 5% • Increased by 10% • Increased by 25% • Increased by 50%
Inequality	• Decreased by 50% • Decreased by 25% • Decreased by 10% • Decreased by 5% • Increased by 5% • Increased by 10% • Increased by 25% • Increased by 50%

(*Continued*)

Table 8.1 (Continued)

Attribute	*Levels*
Life expectancy	• 0 more or less years on average • 5 fewer years on average • 3 fewer years on average • 1 less year on average • 1 more year on average • 3 more years on average • 5 more years on average
Anxiety and depression	• Same number of cases • 50% fewer cases • 25% fewer cases • 10% fewer cases • 5% fewer cases • 5% more cases • 10% more cases • 25% more cases • 50% more cases
Conditionality	• People in and out of work are entitled • People who are not disabled are required to look for work • Only people in work are entitled • Only people out of work are entitled
Means-testing	• People with any or no amount of income are entitled to the full benefit • Only those with incomes less than £20k are entitled to the full benefit • Only those with incomes less than £50k are entitled to the full benefit • Only those with incomes less than £125k are entitled to the full benefit
Universality	• Anyone residing in the UK for more than six months are entitled • Only citizens and permanent residents are entitled • Only citizens are entitled

attribute being at that level compared to the reference level, averaging across the possible levels of all other attributes. Through randomisation and a high number of pairwise comparisons, this allows us to quantify the causal effect of including specific levels of individual reform elements on the support for the entire reform package, compared with the support for a reform package that contains the baseline level (status quo) of this particular reform element (Nettle, Chrisp, *et al.*, 2023; Nettle *et al.*, 2025a).

For sub-group analysis, we used ANOVA to test formally whether including interactions between the subgroup identity and the attribute improved model fit. We then compared the marginal mean probabilities of choice for each attribute level between subgroups and used z-tests to establish where the significant differences resided. All analyses were carried out using the cregg R package (Leeper, 2020). Data and code for the underpinning analysis can be found at https://doi.org/10.17605/OSF.IO/HTSQC.

We found

- A preference for more generous payments than less generous ones.
- A strong preference for decreases in poverty (compared to the status quo).
- Preferences on tax rates depended on the broad effects of the policy package. Increasing personal income tax rates were popular if the package they were part of also decreased poverty, and unpopular otherwise.
- A preference for a wealth tax, carbon taxes and increased corporation tax, as opposed to increased government borrowing.
- A significant positive effect of a large reduction in inequality, and a significant negative effect of a large increase in inequality. However, the effects for inequality were weaker than for poverty.
- Other health and wellbeing consequences also had some significant marginal effects above and beyond those of poverty and inequality. An increase in life expectancy of five years was significantly preferred to the status quo, and a decrease in life expectancy of five years significantly dispreferred.
- A dispreference for increased rates of anxiety and depression relative to the status quo, and there was a slight preference for policies that decreased them sharply.
- No strong preference for or against means-testing or other restrictions on eligibility.
- Mild differences between left- and right-supporting participants, in the expected directions.
- No significant variation by gender or between rich and poor.
- Older people were significantly less keen on high income tax schemes and, curiously, less concerned with health consequences (Nettle *et al.*, 2025a).

Higher personal income tax rates were dispreferred if they left the current poverty rate unchanged, or increased it. However, income tax increases were favoured if they also decreased poverty. Even for very high marginal rates (50 per cent basic rate, 70 per cent higher rate, 80 per cent additional rate), the net preference shift was positive if the accompanying reduction in poverty was sufficiently dramatic. Note that this figure is a conservative estimate of the support for policies that increase tax rates but have positive societal outcomes, since respondents also placed some value on reductions in inequality and improvements in health, in addition to their valuation of reductions in poverty. Given that poverty reduction would be likely to affect inequality and health, the total valuation of policies that reduce poverty might thus be slightly higher than the figure suggests.

The fundamental trade-off between personal income tax rates and the rate of poverty was present for both Conservative and Labour voters alike. However, the set of acceptable resolutions of the trade-off was somewhat different. Labour voters would not accept poverty increases even to keep personal income tax low, and would accept the highest income tax rates in order to achieve a large reduction in poverty. Conservative voters would accept modest increases in poverty to keep income tax rates low, and would not accept the highest rates even if poverty could be completely eliminated. Nonetheless, even Conservative voters would accept income tax rates considerably higher than the status quo (40 per cent/60 per cent/70 per cent) as long as these were accompanied by large reductions in poverty.

Our findings suggested that significant reform to the current welfare system would be popular. This is due to the high value placed, population-wide, on poverty reduction and its positive sequelae. This was sufficiently high to more than offset aversion to tax increases. The findings suggest that the public are much more favourable to redistributive government action than might otherwise be assumed.

Income tax rates and poverty rates were not the only determinants of choice. Sources of funding such as wealth taxes and carbon taxes on corporations or individuals were positively valued compared to increasing government borrowing. This may well be because they were perceived as allowing the social goods of a generous system without individuals having to reduce their disposable earned incomes. This is understandable in the context both of an escalating cost of living that has left even those in well-paid work in fuel poverty (Bradshaw and Keung, 2022; Keung and Bradshaw, 2023) and the trend in recent decades for relative increases in wealth and decreases in wages (Bourquin, Brewer and Wernham, 2024). As with the net acceptability of higher income taxes, there seems to be a disconnect between what public acceptability research shows and current opinion in policy circles. For example, other recent UK research shows high levels of public support for a wealth tax (Rowlingson, Sood and Tu, 2021), but the Labour Government recently ruled out proposing one on the ostensible grounds of political unfeasibility (Crerar, 2023) despite increasing calls by senior Labour figures to do so (Walker, 2025).

There was some evidence that, above and beyond the effect of the scheme on poverty, a positive value was attached to the following: decreases in inequality (especially for young people and Labour voters); improvements in life expectancy (especially for older people); and avoidance of increases in anxiety and depression (especially for younger people). These effects were substantially weaker than the preference effects of the poverty rate. In one sense, our findings accord with behavioural economic evidence that people tend to be 'intuitive Rawlsians' (Charness and Rabin, 2002; Kameda *et al.*, 2016): when considering our schemes, the population consequence that most influenced our respondents was indeed the rate of poverty, which roughly equates to the wellbeing of the worst off. However, our findings show that people are not *strictly* intuitive Rawlsians. Above and beyond the absolute gains for the worst off, respondents cared about effects on inequality, as well as health and wellbeing. This was particularly true when the impacts on inequality and health – in either direction – were large.

Conjoint analysis permits, therefore, much more nuanced and precise analyses of public preferences than traditional polling. It enables policymakers to understand the real-world implications of trade-offs between policy design and outcome in order to project electoral feasibility. This is critical in a representative democratic society.

8.4 Modelling health outcomes

Given the importance of health to people's assessment of welfare policies, we modelled two health measures: mental health and life expectancy. We built a model relating SF-12 scores (Ware, 2002) to income and demographic characteristics. SF-12 is a widely used measure of an individual's health-related quality of life, with two summary scores: the Physical Component Summary (PCS-12) and the Mental Component Summary (MCS-12). The model is estimated over twelve waves (2009/2011–2020/2022) of Understanding Society: The UK Household Longitudinal Study (UKHLS) (Institute for Social and Economic Research, 2023) and the panel data belonging to it (Reed, Nettle, *et al.*, 2024).

Our health model is estimated using the 'between' individual coefficient from a fixed effects 'within-between' model, which combines the effect on physical and mental health of both an individual's income in one wave v.

their average across waves, and their average across waves compared with the sample average.

The model is a reformulation of the standard Mundlak model and has a significant advantage in being able to retain the flexibility of random effects models while reducing concerns about bias that fixed effects models address (Bell and Jones, 2015; Bell, Fairbrother and Jones, 2019). The within-between model conceptually captures several key income-based drivers of health, including:

- Temporary income shocks (within component), which see individuals' income increase or decrease in one wave compared to their average.
- Permanent income shocks (between component), which see an individual's average income either be closer to or further away from the population average.
- Objective inequality (between component), which sees differences between individuals' average income, which is calculated over a longer, enduring period.
- Subjective social status inequality (between components), which is the psychological phenomenon driven, in part, by income inequality.

It does not, however, capture what we anticipate through our model of impact (Johnson *et al.*, 2022) to be very substantial benefits from systems such as Basic Income of increased security of income and protection from destitution for a very large proportion of the population in even relatively highly paid jobs. We use the between-individual coefficient in our modelling because changes to the welfare system are more likely to reflect permanent income shocks.

The SF-12 regressions (Reed, Johnson, *et al.*, 2024) are broadly in line with a previous study in relation to young people's mental health undertaken by the author team using UKHLS data (Chen *et al.*, 2023; Parra-Mujica *et al.*, 2023). There is a full literature review in Reed *et al.* (Reed, Nettle, *et al.*, 2024) which highlights the breadth of evidence indicating a causal relationship between increased income (throughout the distribution but especially at the lower end) and health. The review also highlights studies with apparently confounding results or differences in interpretation, which can be explained by researchers attributing greater causal value to paid employment than income from welfare. This is partially reflected in Katikireddi and colleagues' (Thomson *et al.*, 2021) logic model. There is good reason to believe that the attributions needed to create a functioning integrated model of public opinion and health are well-evidenced, including via Nettle *et al.*'s cost-of-living study, which provides considerable evidence of the immediate impact of financial distress (i.e. a reduction in non-committed money) (Nettle *et al.*, 2024).

8.4.1 Mental health

We create a binary variable for cases of depressive disorder which takes the value of 1 if the individual's imputed MCS-12 score is ≤ 45.6 and 0 otherwise (Vilagut *et al.*, 2013).

8.4.2 Life expectancy

We impute life expectancy from SF-12 in three steps:

1. Convert SF-12 scores to SF-6D (Brazier, Roberts and Deverill, 2002), using software from QualityMetric (QualityMetric, 2022). SF-6D is a preference-based measure of health.
2. Use the SF-6D score to calculate quality-adjusted life years (QALYs). QALYs are a widely recognised standardised measure of health outcomes commonly used in health economics (Drummond *et al.*, 2015; Kaplan and Hays, 2022).
3. Calculate life expectancy from QALYs using multipliers conditional on gender and age. The multipliers are derived from McNamara *et al.* (2023).

When estimating how an increase in net incomes translates into a gain in QALYs for a given person in the UKHLS sample, we assume that the implementation of a tax-benefit change gives rise to a permanent change in incomes and hence a permanent change in SF-6D score for each sample member. We calculate the change in SF-6D for each individual based on their predicted change in SF-12 scores in the income to SF-12 regressions. In other words, we assume that a tax-benefit scheme policy is introduced permanently. The change in SF-6D for each sample member is then translated into a change in QALYs using the mapping between the SF-6D metric and QALYs as defined by SF-6D's creators (University of Sheffield, 2024a). This change in QALYs is summed across the UKHLS sample, grossed up to population level and treated as an annual impact of the policy. These annual impacts can be summed over the number of years that the policy is in operation. It should be noted that we use SF-6D rather than SF-6Dv2 which was not available at the time of undertaking the study.

8.4.3 Responsiveness to income changes

These estimates are then integrated directly into the microsimulation model. As modelled, mental health appears rather unresponsive to changes in income. For example, choosing the most generous benefit increases from the options from the Conjoint Analysis – a package costing £430 billion – would reduce the number of adults with critically low SF-12 scores (below 45.6) by about 3 per cent.

8.5 Microsimulation: the TriplePC model

As discussed in Section 8.3, respondents have preferences over inputs (income tax rates, payment sizes, etc.) and outcomes (poverty and inequality levels, numbers of mental health cases, etc.). We use microsimulation to bridge between them.

The analysis uses a heavily adapted version of Scotben (Stark, 2024), an open-source microsimulation model of Scotland written in the Julia programming language, but is being converted to Landman. Scotben is a conventionally structured static tax-benefit model, in the family of models branching out from the Institute for Fiscal Studies' TAXBEN (Johnson *et al.*, 1990). For this project, we extended the scope of the model to Great Britain using a single 2021/2022 wave of Family Resources Survey (FRS) data (Department for Work and Pensions, 2014). The model covers the whole of the UK personal tax and benefit system, including local taxes, with some minor exceptions such as Scottish Best Start grants. As a base, we use the tax and benefit system as of Q3 2023, and all incomes, wealth and consumption are also uprated to 2023 Q3. We use the 2021/2022 FRS sample weights as is. The entire model (minus, because of licence restrictions, the main dataset) is available as a GitHub repository (Stark, 2024). As discussed below, the model has a web interface – this has its own GitHub repository (Stark, 2014): keeping the model's interfaces separate allows the model itself to be uncluttered with otherwise unneeded web handling code and libraries.

We used the AMCEs from the conjoint experiment for each component of any welfare policy the user wishes to specify through the interface from the data of Nettle *et al.* (2025a). In the conjoint methodology, these are assumed to have an additive effect on popularity. That is, for example, the popularity of a policy combining high income taxes, carbon tax and a decrease in poverty, which will be the sum of the negative marginal effect on popularity of the high-income tax, the positive marginal effect on popularity of the carbon tax, the positive marginal effect of the poverty reduction, and so on. This summation is the popularity outcome returned by the model.

The outcome questions are phrased as changes (e.g. '50 per cent fewer cases of anxiety and depression', 'poverty increased by 50 per cent'). A particularly tricky question arising from this is how to establish a baseline for comparison. The conjoint experiment survey had no 'keep things as they are' option for the tax and benefit inputs, so there were two options for the TriplePC:

1. Using a tax-benefit system some way from the current one as a baseline and assuming that the outcome changes represent changes in poverty, health, etc. from that point, rather than changes from the actual current situation.
2. Using the current system as the baseline, but then the default output will have significant deviations for the outcome variables.

Neither of these choices is good, but on balance we decided 1) was the least bad. It makes the conjoint popularity output much easier to understand; with option 2) we would be applying large changes in poverty and inequality to the base conjoint results, which would make those results very unintuitive. The chosen baseline therefore comprised the first (default) option from each set in Table 8.1 above:

- Benefits: £0 pw per child, £63 per week per adult and £190 per week per pensioner, with these replacing Child Benefit and the State Pension;
- Taxes: current non-Scottish income tax rates, bands and allowances, applied across the whole UK including Scotland;
- Net cost of the scheme met by additional borrowing.

We discuss how we interpret and model these changes in more detail in the next section, but the upshot is that our modelling starts some distance from the actual existing system. The relatively large payments to each adult (offset somewhat by the abolition of Child Benefit) mean that the scheme costs a net £108 billion per annum. The adult payments reduce headcount poverty by 3 per cent but child poverty rises by 0.7 per cent, since the Child Benefit abolition more than offsets the gains to parents from the adult payments. There are small decreases (less than 1 per cent) in adults with depression. All the results from the model are relative to this new baseline. This is not ideal and is certainly a lesson for future work.

8.6 Income tax rates

The conjoint experimental survey had six income tax rate options with a basic, higher and additional rate in each (see Table 8.1). The first of these options is the current non-Scottish UK income tax rates, which we take as the base. Scotland has its own five-rate system. Because of the need to impose a uniform base case, we impose the 'Rest of UK' three-rate system as the baseline in Scotland too, so we start from a position where Scottish low earners pay slightly more than in reality, and high earners less.

All other options represent rate increases. We assume the corresponding thresholds are as present. Since we have to remain consistent with the conjoint analysis, only the six rate groups in Table 8.1 are presented to the user, though the model can handle any combination of rates and thresholds. We assume no behavioural responses to changing tax rates and make no corrections for under-reporting of incomes beyond that embodied in the FRS sample weights.

8.7 Benefits

The payment size question in the conjoint survey was about a hypothetical system of payments that most closely reflects the simplicity of Basic Income (Reed *et al.*, 2023). There were also questions about eligibility, means-testing and citizenship (see Table 8.1, above). It is not clear how this proposed system of cash transfers should interact with the existing tax and benefit system, especially bearing in mind that the question is not how an expert believes they should interact, but what was most likely in the mind of the conjoint respondents. It is reasonable to assume:

1. Means-tested benefits are retained. A wrinkle here is that the UK has two means-tested benefit systems operating: the 'legacy' Tax Credit-based system and the new Universal Credit (UC) that is gradually supplanting it (House of Commons Library, 2020). For simplicity, in our modelling we assume all households have been transitioned to UC.
2. Most other benefits, including the State Pension and Child Benefit, are abolished and replaced by the cash transfers.
3. Needs-based benefits such as those based on sickness or disability, like Personal Independence Payment (PIP), are retained.

The least generous set of options (child – £0; adult – £63; pensioner – £190) is taken as the base value. Compared to the actual system, this means that we are starting from a social security system that's considerably more expensive (because of the adult payments), but where pensioners are usually slightly worse off (£190 v. £203.85 for the new State Pension) and families with large numbers of children not on means-tested benefits are worse off, since the cash transfer to children is zero in the default case and the payments to adults are not always enough to compensate. We do not adjust taxes to meet these extra base costs. For eligibility, means-testing and citizenship options, it seemed plausible that at least some of the respondents might be aware of the means and eligibility tests from existing benefits. Consequently, we model the eligibility rules that apply to the 'legacy' UK benefits: Working Tax Credit and Income Support/Employment Support that are in the process of being phased out, and the means-tests are taken from the new Universal Credit (Child Poverty Action Group, 2022).

8.8 Modelling other funding options

Table 8.1 includes a number of 'other funding' options that are worth discussing briefly. There is ambiguity in some of these options. A wealth tax or carbon levy could be implemented in many ways, for instance; we make what we hope are reasonable assumptions for these cases, but for the microsimulation to be fully consistent with the conjoint survey we would have to know what was in the minds of the respondents. This section discusses how we tackled modelling three of these options.

8.8.1 'Increase in VAT'

Our FRS dataset has no expenditure data. The main UK source of household expenditure data is the Living Costs and Food Survey (LCFS) (Office for National Statistics, 2019a). To model the complex set of VAT exemptions and zero-rated goods (HM Revenue and Customs (HMRC), 2022), we have three choices:

1. Switching the primary dataset to be the LCFS. The LCFS, then known as the Family Expenditure Survey (FES), was the primary dataset of all UK tax-benefit models until it was supplanted by the FRS. The LCFS remains the source used in the Treasury's IGOTM model (Brice, 2015). But, to model other options such as wealth taxes, we would still need other datasets. Switching between multiple different datasets, and hence slightly different base outcomes, and depending on which options were being modelled, could be confusing.
2. Imputing expenditure data onto the FRS via a demand system. This seems appealing as the model would be consistent with economic theory; expenditure could vary with tax rates, and, in principle, we could use the demand system to calculate changes in economic welfare rather than just estimate cash changes. But it is infeasible to build a demand system with fine enough detail to adequately model the complex set of exemptions and zero-rated goods.
3. Assigning LCFS records to our primary FRS dataset using data matching, which is the option we chose.

Matching is not a precise science (Leulescu and Agafitei, 2013). Matching variables were chosen to roughly mimic those known to be statistically important in consumption modelling. We used the following variables (all at household rather than individual level):

- Tenure (owner occupation, private renting, etc.);
- Region of the UK;
- Number of rooms in the dwelling;
- The age of the household representative person (HRP) – the HRP is defined as the person with the highest income in the household, or the eldest if there is no non-benefit income;
- Broad household composition (families with children, single-person households, etc.);
- Any wages in the household;
- Any pension income received;
- Any self-employment income received;
- HRP is unemployed;
- HRP is non-white;
- Any female adult in the household;
- Any disabled person in the household;
- Number of children in the household;
- Total number of people in the household;
- Gross household income.

The Julia source file 'src/MatchingLibs.jl' in the GitHub repository contains the full calculations used (Stark, 2023b); throughout the development process we have tried to write code that is intelligible to non-specialists, though the manipulations needed to get the two data sources consistent can be fiddly.

The broad strategy is to give a score of 1 if each attribute matches exactly between the two datasets (exactly the same region, for example) and a score of 0.5 if a coarser match is possible (e.g. both households are in any region in the North of England). The highest total score is then the match (Stark, 2023a).

In aggregate, our current VAT modelling under-predicts revenues by about 50 per cent: we model £102 billion for VAT revenues as against actual revenues for 2022/2023 of £160 billion (HM Revenue and Customs (HMRC), 2022). There are well-known problems with under-reporting LCFS expenditure data, such as alcohol and tobacco spending (Stark *et al.*, 2025), which will account for much of this. For this exercise, we provide a crude fix by grossing up all the expenditure records by 1.5. Undoubtedly, this is an area we can improve on.

8.8.2 'Tax on wealth'

Modelling wealth is tricky for three reasons:

1. Our primary FRS dataset has limited information on wealth, mainly intended to help model benefit eligibility tests.
2. The form this wealth tax should take is not specified.
3. Wealth taxes are held to be particularly easy to evade or avoid (Scheuer and Slemrod, 2021).

To solve the first reason, we impute data from the Wealth and Assets Survey (WAS) (Office for National Statistics, 2019b) onto the FRS households. We chose to do this using a simple linear regression of three categories of wealth (pensions, housing and financial/other assets) against household characteristics that are common to FRS and WAS. In retrospect, regression-based imputation was likely a mistake and matching will be used in future versions.

For the form of the tax, we were guided by the Wealth Tax Commission (Advani, Chamberlain and Summers, 2020). We followed their recommendations of excluding pension wealth, having an allowance of £500,000 and having the tax payable over five years, though we deviated from the Commission in applying the tax to aggregate household wealth rather than individual wealth (Chamberlain, 2020).

Even when payable over five years, as recommended by the Wealth Tax Commission, the payments from wealth taxes needed to fund some of the more generous benefit schemes can exceed net income for many families, especially elderly families who have high housing wealth. Most likely the scheme would need to be augmented by an income-related rebate scheme, or some scheme to defer until death.

8.8.3 'Corporation tax increases'

Building a plausible micro-data based model of corporation tax is difficult and not something that could be contemplated for this project. In any case, for a household-based microsimulation model, what matters is the incidence of the tax on the households. This could be on profits, or passed on in price increases or real wage reductions (Atkinson and Stiglitz, 2015). If we make a simple 'small country' assumption – that the rate of return on capital and the price of tradable goods are set exogenously on world markets – then corporation tax is ultimately incident on (private sector) wages and self-employment income. Therefore, we calculate the tax increase needed to meet the costs of the benefit increase and reduce the wage bill by that amount. Note that as the wage bill falls, direct tax revenues also fall, but in a non-linear way because of the tax allowance and progressive tax rate structures, so finding the correct corporation tax increase requires the use of our root-finder. In practice the rates needed for the more generous benefit increases can be implausibly large, exceeding in some cases total UK Corporation's Gross Profits.

8.9 Model flow

Putting all this together, a model run has five main stages:

1. The user selects from the payment size, income tax, other funding, conditionality, means-testing or universality options from Table 8.1.
2. The model then calculates net incomes for each person in the FRS households given these choices.
3. These net incomes are in turn plugged into the equations discussed in Section 8.2 to give us estimates of changes to the prevalence of depressive disorders and mortality.
4. The model next calculates gainers and losers, revenues and costs and also changes in poverty and inequality.
5. Finally, the model calculates conjoint public preferences based on points 1 to 4 above and displays the results.

The model has a simple single page web interface, publicly available at https://triplepc.northumbria.ac.uk/. Figure 8.2 shows this in action. The user has selected a relatively generous benefit increase (top left panel), partially paid for by income tax increases (top centre). The bottom half of the screen shows the results, relative to the base discussed in Section 8.3 above. Health results are in the bottom row, showing small mental health improvements. The net cost of this scheme is £118 billion (right middle panel). Poverty and inequality are both reduced (centre left panel). The Conjoint analysis is in the centre: the scheme is more popular by 4.7 points than the baseline due to the popularity of the poverty and inequality reductions and the benefit increases, though this is partly offset by unpopular tax increases.

8.10 Lessons learned

One important lesson for similar future work is the need for good coordination between conjoint analysis and microsimulation modelling at the outset of the project. In our case, the conjoint analysis was conducted ahead of microsimulation modelling work. Consequently, microsimulation requirements were largely fixed by the questions in the conjoint survey. This has several consequences:

- The model could present only a very limited set of options for taxes and benefits compared to the model's underlying capabilities. The system used for the survey – Qualtrics – had a hard limit on the number of attributes that could be included, which meant that it was not possible to ask about basic and higher tax rates individually. It might also

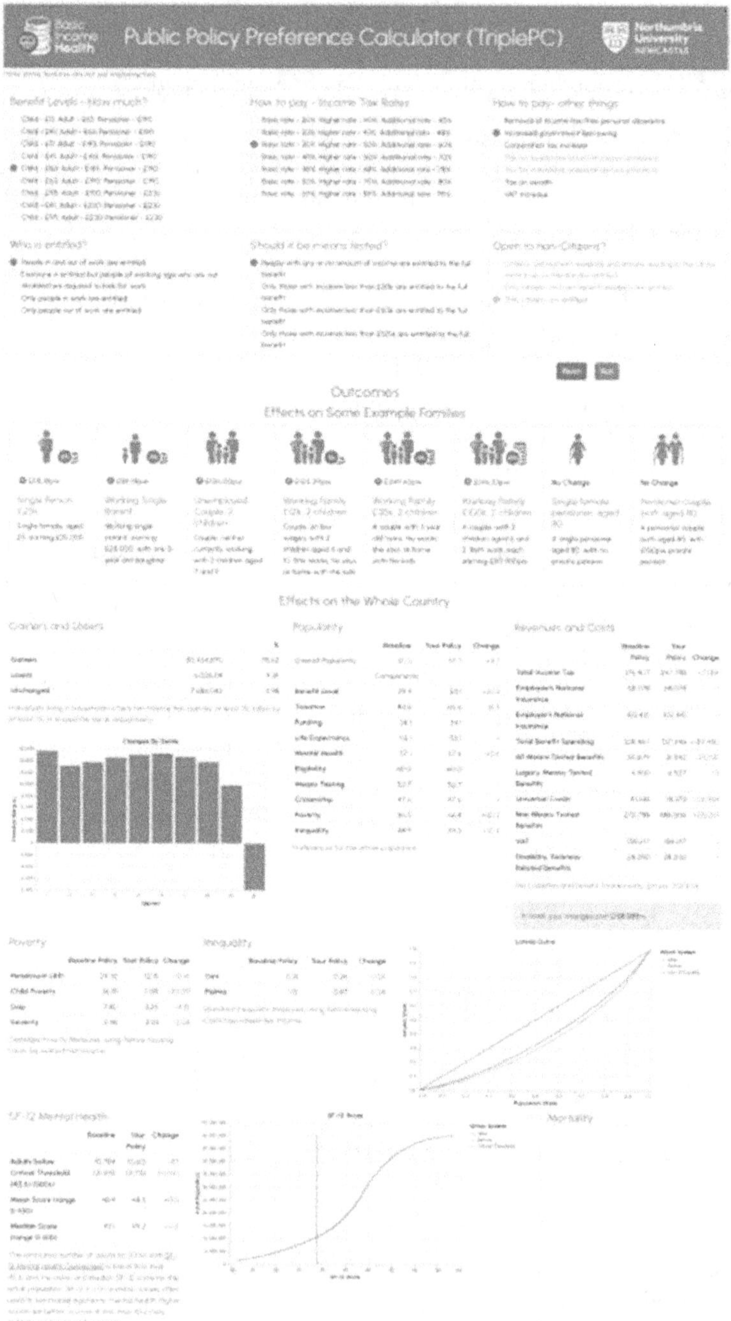

Figure 8.2 TriplePC interface example scenario

have increased respondent load to an unacceptable level and therefore reduced the quality of the preference data.

- The meaning of options such as 'tax on wealth' should, where possible, be made clearer in order to provide a clear direction for modelling.
- Co-development of a conjoint survey and microsimulation might have enabled respondents to see accurate consequences of their preferred policies for incomes and health.
- Some of the options in the survey, such as VAT increases, were quite burdensome to model in the time available.
- Careful thought must be given to the definition of the base case the model is comparing against.

There are also interesting questions about how to best present results of a model with such diverse outputs. For instance, since one is a stock and the other a flow, can we count payments by a household from a wealth tax in the same way as payments for income tax? And should we be imputing a monetary value to any health improvements?

Finally, there is the question of uncertainty. Although it is technically straightforward to quantify uncertainty by running the model multiple times and reporting ranked outcomes, we are reluctant to do so, because we feel that it gives a false sense of certainty by implying that the principal uncertainties around microsimulation models can be captured with a few extra loops. Some sources of error can be quantified by bootstrapping, such as sampling errors in the data, the regression error terms and, to some extent, uncertainty around matching. However, the critical sources of error in microsimulation models – specification and implementation errors in programming and inappropriate data – cannot be quantified in this way. And in any event, a bootstrapping model would be too slow to be useful interactively, unless run on more processors than it is feasible to fund for this project. The best defences are instead a good test suite, clearly written code and openness and we are happy to have made all data freely available.

TriplePC illustrates the importance and practicality of using conjoint data to provide instant analysis of the political implications of welfare packages, but also learned some important lessons on how best to conduct integrated microsimulation and conjoint analysis.

8.11 Conclusion

Friedrich Hayek, who has inspired the nation's economic policies since 1979, saw the post-war recovery as being the start of a slippery slope toward communism. Even though every single outcome of importance to people improved consistently between 1945 and the 1970s without threatening democracy in the slightest, Hayek believed that the involvement of the state in the economy and its role in taxing wealth to secure citizens was a source of grave injustice (Hayek, 1944).

The consequence of rolling back the state from 1979 onwards has been hugely damaging to the UK, particularly in regions outside the South East of England: we produce very little; low- to middle-income countries put our infrastructure to shame; and workers' exposure to financial insecurity is unprecedented in generations.

Labour's commitments to do little of substance in government reveal thinking from a bygone era in which tax, rather than low and insecure pay and crippling costs of privately supplied essentials, was foremost in people's minds. Since the election, the folly of those commitments has become clear. This is now an unpopular government that has tied itself in knots committing not to do the very things that the public want it to do (YouGov, 2025a, 2025b). All of the available evidence suggests high levels of support for tax and spend for good reason – the public recognise that there is no alternative within the private sector (Common Sense Policy Group, 2024b).

The point of this chapter is that the basic elements of economic and health evidence produced via microsimulation clearly need to be connected to public opinion evidence. In the next chapter, we will examine means of narrating that evidence effectively.

9

Persuading the politicians: how to deploy evidence to influence policy

Key foci

- Adapting adversarial collaboration to develop persuasive policy narratives with firm opponents.
- Demonstrating a three-stage process: screening opponents, co-producing narratives, testing persuasive effects.
- Showing statistically significant support increases among initial policy opponents.
- Addressing political challenges: rebuilding faith while resisting chaos narratives from opponents.

9.1 Changing people's perspectives: adversarial co-production of narratives

Establishing real existing policy preferences must always be seen as the first of two policymaking stages. It tells us only that people have preferences on account of the information available at any given time. It is simply wrong to assume that those preferences are fixed, even though they may hint at enduring principles with regard to concern regarding equality, deservingness and other issues. One of the most significant differences between centrist and right-wing politics in recent years is that the latter have engaged in long-term campaigns of persuasion via the media and other actors. Increased support for Brexit, for Reform and for a number of economically regressive policies at electorally critical periods indicates the success of these approaches and the failure of centrists to understand both the need for change and the means of persuading the populace of the value of those changes.

This is important to recognise insofar as centrists have often promoted co-production as an important feature of policymaking. Often described as a social science 'buzzword' (Adelle *et al.*, 2020, p. 1), co-production has emerged as one of the key concepts in understanding knowledge–policy interactions (Bandola-Gill, Grek and Tichenor, 2023, p. 276) and is associated with the involvement, for example, of users of public services in their design and delivery (Bovaird, 2007). It acknowledges the need for improved policymaking, but, as we will see, in a way that often seems at odds with the seriousness of the period of permacrisis with which policymakers are faced. With high levels of disengagement from politics (Uberoi and Johnston, 2022) and high levels of disregard for politicians, the UK's future depends on the capacity of policymakers to persuade an alienated electorate to support measures that will mitigate poverty, inequality and the climate emergency. This is particularly important in highly distressed 'left-behind' communities targeted for Levelling Up by the Conservative Government of 2019–24, which constituted an attempt to improve the infrastructural, economic, social and health outcomes of less affluent parts of the UK (Department for Levelling Up, Housing and Communities, 2022).

There is good reason to understand the role that forms of co-production might play in this and how it can address two issues that represent an equipoise in public policy. On the one hand, Bandala-Gill suggests that preference for technocratic legitimacy leads to the presentation of quantitative evidence disconnected from the political legitimacy associated with people's values (Hornikx, 2018; Bandola-Gill, Grek and Tichenor, 2023). The rejection of apparent economic expertise by supporters of Brexit has been presented as evidence of this deficit. On the other hand, we have argued that the opposite has become true, with policymakers, in the wake of Brexit, believing that citizens of left-behind communities in particular hold fixed value-based positions that preclude the presentation and implementation of evidence-based transformative policy (Johnson, Johnson and Nettle, 2022). As a consequence, politicians have elected to support conservative social and economic positions in order to appear sensitive to existing value sets, rejecting the capacity for persuasion (M. T. Johnson *et al.*, 2023). In this regard, policymakers take people's positions, as represented in focus groups, as fixed and they alter their public positions accordingly. Thus, the evidence base they end up incorporating into policy is that of voters' expressed positions in bizarrely circumscribed and circular forums, rather than actual evidence of impact. While this suggests elements of co-production, it is actually deleterious to citizens themselves, since it necessarily leads to evidence-based policies (EBPs) being rejected.

Social science is subject to a similar or greater degree of methodological contention. In particular, colleagues find themselves in disagreement over the feasibility of policy, especially where there is a critical need for intervention and a strong evidential basis for implementation. Those in public policy and politics often hold that there is an 'Overton Window' of policies acceptable to the public that provides parameters for action. There is a belief that the public, including those who are likely to benefit most from implementation, will reject policies for value-based or cognitive reasons that evolve slowly over time and not in response to the presentation of the policy itself. There is widespread belief that transformative policy, of the sort needed to address chronic health and economic inequalities or the climate emergency, sits outside the window, shifting policymakers' appraisal of 'sensible' policies towards approaches that are inadequate or actually exacerbate harm.

This is apparent in the case of 'nudging', which formed a central pillar of public health mitigation and messaging during the pandemic. Nudging revolutionised debate on the implementation of social policy, with Thaler and Sunstein presenting policymakers with means of avoiding 'big state' intervention, non-coercively influencing behaviour toward evidence-based ends (Thaler and Sunstein, 2008). Shove's 'ABC model' holds that policymakers change attitudes by informing individuals of the costs of behaviour and providing incentives for change (Shove, 2010). Their approach holds two critical deficits. First, as Dowding notes, this privatises responsibility for action and suggests that active state intervention is unjust or counterproductive, abrogating policymakers of responsibility for outcomes (Dowding, 2020). Second, and more critically, there is an emerging body of evidence to suggest that nudging does not work for societally important outcomes. Maier *et al.* have shown that evidence in support of nudging is subject to publishing bias (Maier *et al.*, 2022). When that bias is controlled for, there is little or no evidence of efficacy across the range of outcomes that have been studied. This indicates that academics, policymakers and governments have invested many billions of pounds in an approach that is incapable of achieving the ends to which we have a shared interest. Indeed, given the emerging evidence on nudging, it is possible that belief in it may have reduced the efficacy of pandemic responses that often depended upon it. Too often, belief in the Overton Window and belief that *sensible* can be equated with *minimal* has led researchers to endorse research, policy and practice that has had a distortionary effect on public resources and people's lives.

It sounds banal to suggest that the crises our societies face cannot be addressed by inadequate policy, but too often this position has appeared radical in ways that are historically distinctive. Human history is one of persistent change and reform in response to crises, but also by virtue of policy entrepreneurs' persuasion. The neoliberal reforms of the past four decades, many of which have contributed to our permacrisis, represented clear, radical shifts that contemporary assumptions would present as unfeasible. There is a need to remind ourselves that change is possible and to explore means of using policy to that end.

One approach to overcoming this roadblock in evidence-based policymaking lies in *adversarial co-production*. This is an approach that was first applied to welfare, but has gradually been applied to a much broader range of policy areas (Ardron *et al.*, 2025; E. Johnson, Thew, *et al.*, 2025; Hudson *et al.*, 2025). It represents an adaptation of adversarial collaboration in behavioural science (Mellers, Hertwig and Kahneman, 2001; Tetlock and Mitchell, 2009; Clark and Tetlock, 2022; Clark *et al.*, 2022; Costello, Clark and Tetlock, 2022). That approach is intended to improve research via collaboration with those who hold competing hypotheses, and partly involves each side exploring what it would take to convince them of the position they currently oppose. Daniel Kahneman, the originator of Adversarial Collaboration, and subsequent proponents, most notably those involved in the Penn Arts and Sciences Adversarial Collaboration Project (Penn Arts, 2025), conceives of the method as a means of improving the process underpinning protocol development, data collection and publication through the following principles:

> (a) understand and articulate their opponents' perspective so well that each side feels fairly characterized; (b) work together to design mutually agreed-upon studies that have potential to adjudicate competing hypotheses and that they agree, ex ante, could change their minds; and (c) jointly publish the results, regardless of the outcome. (Clark *et al.*, 2022, p. 6)

The approach is informed by the notion that scientists 'are constrained by the same cognitive biases, limitations, and trade-off calculations as mere mortals' (Clark *et al.*, 2022, p. 3). Some of its proponents contend that behavioural science is particularly prone to the problems this perpetuates as a result of a) its having comparatively low consequences, mainly confined to embarrassment, for producing 'inaccurate' findings; b) its focus on provocative, moral-political topics that may be subject to particular social desires of the researcher and/or broader society; and c) the fact that it deals with very complex, abstract and interacting variables and social/psychological constructs that can be finessed to obtain different results (Clark *et al.*, 2022, p. 4). This has produced a range of innovative pieces of research with underpinning design on which a larger proportion of colleagues agree. It is a transformative approach at a time of paradigmatic polarisation.

The methodological deficits identified by Clark and colleagues have the potential to be amplified throughout the stages of the policy development process. Policies are often presented to the public on the basis of 'objective' benefits assumed by those who design them to be salient, but which may be regarded as irrelevant or less relevant by communities. The avoidance of macro-economic harm by remaining in the EU was clearly irrelevant to many voters in left-behind communities who had witnessed long-term decline in living standards and who simply could not imagine their lives declining further. Policymakers face difficulty in disentangling their material interests from the interests of others and in grasping the bases of differences of opinion on policies. This, combined with the assumption that perceptions are fixed and grounded in value commitments with no clear relationship to material interest, has contributed to inertia and error in policymaking and created path dependencies that compound each crisis in turn. We need to remind ourselves that necessary change is possible.

9.2 Persuasion is possible

During the pandemic, evidence emerged within the UK from furlough, which granted state support for wages during the pandemic, and a range of other interventions that reducing conditionality and increasing universality within the welfare system would enable policymakers to mitigate the impacts of COVID-19. The findings we have referenced in this book on Basic Income suggest that it is an economically affordable, multipurpose policy instrument capable of improving public health, preventing or delaying, for example, 200,000 to 550,000 cases of anxiety and depression between 2010–2030 within the fourteen- to twenty-four-year-old cohort – enough to pay for 750 mental health hospital nurses annually (Chen *et al.*, 2023). Even though the policy is an economic instrument, exploration of public opinion has generally been driven by consideration of fit with people's values, rather than understanding of its material impacts (Hamilton, Yorgun and Wright, 2022). This focus on presenting Basic Income in terms of values and the notion that people's values are fixed parts of people's identities meant that there was widespread belief among policymakers concerned with political legitimacy that Basic Income as a transformative policy sat outside the 'Overton Window' (Cowan, 2020; Gopal and Issa, 2021) and was not feasible for implementation due to public opposition (Berry, 2021).

As we have mentioned, the notion of a policy being permanently outside of that window is odd. Once outlying policies have been implemented over the past few decades, most of which have made societies worse. As such, there is reason to examine means of persuasion. Fisher contrasts two paradigms: rational choice, in which actors develop preferences by evaluating arguments according to the quality of evidence presented; and narrative, in which human beings are storytellers with pre-existing beliefs who identify what they see as good reasons for preferences from historically and culturally contingent stories (Fisher, 1987). While Hornikx and others have asserted the value of the former (2007, 2018), Morgan *et al.* contend that narrative is more persuasive than statistics (2002). We decided to explore the impact of narrative by adopting adversarial collaboration from behavioural science and adapting it as 'adversarial co-production' for policy development.

Our approach builds on and inverts Greve's evaluation of evidence of impact from narratives on perceptions of welfare policy via 'myths' that link people's often genuine concerns for their material interests to self-defeating policy appraisals (Greve, 2020). This phenomenon is apparent in the opposition of many of the poorest in society to taxing the richest (Shapiro, 2002) or in their support for inequalities justified through skill and opportunity in the 'American Dream' (Hochschild, 1995). We noted evidence of narratives being deployed successfully to highlight people's genuine material interests, with impact on lower-SES groups increasing support for redistributive policies that enhance resources (Piff *et al.*, 2020).

Successful narratives 'help each other see from different perspectives' (Stone, 2011, p. x), invoking interests that align with policy content. They require the following components:

- A protagonist likely to share interests with the reader;
- An antagonist, whether implied or explicit with interests opposed to those of the reader;
- A description of the salient material context and interests of the reader;
- Culturally and/or historically particular examples of the way in which the policy at hand enhances the interests of the reader.

Traditionally, scholars imagined that the function of reasoning was *intra*-personal: a capacity that allows individual minds to work through complex questions and reach true conclusions. A more modern view is that the function of reasoning is primarily *inter*-personal or argumentative (Mercier and Sperber, 2011): reasoning works dialogically, through persuasion, to allow multiple individuals, whose interests may differ, to coordinate on joint action.

In accordance with the inter-personal view, people tend to produce very weak arguments for beliefs they already hold, until they are challenged through dialogue by others who hold different positions (Trouche *et al.*, 2016). When challenged, they either produce better arguments, to persuade their interlocuters, or change their minds when it becomes clear that there are grounds for the network to settle on a different course. This research demonstrates the strengths and weaknesses of human rationality. When individuals have comfortable or intuitive positions to hand, their reasoning is often me-sided and superficial. Through argumentative processes, lay people can create jointly deep and nuanced rationales for courses of action (Trouche, Sander and Mercier, 2014). Experts and non-experts alike grossly underestimate the extent to which discussion in groups can improve the quality of reasoning (Mercier *et al.*, 2015). This psychological research provides the foundations for contemporary experiments with deliberative democracy (Mercier and Landemore, 2012).

It makes sense, then, that those most able to understand the salient aspects of narratives capable of persuasion are those who most oppose the policy, not those who support it. As such, adversarial co-production of narratives uses an underpinning theory of reason to identify relevant actors on specific policy issues in electorally critical areas to develop arguments most likely to persuade opponents to support the policy.

9.3 The method in practice

There are three stages to adversarial co-production of narratives. While it is possible to conduct these stages via paper survey or the second stage via interview, cost and efficiency mean that it is easier to complete via online survey using a participant provider, such as Prolific. Participants are paid according to the time taken to complete surveys.

9.3.1 Stage 1: screener to assess initial level of support for policies

It is necessary first to screen the target population to identify opponents. In our *Act Now* surveys, we conducted a fifteen-minute screening survey with 693 participants with Red Wall constituency postcodes or, due to platform limitations, area postcodes with a large proportion of Red Wall constituencies on Prolific. Red Wall constituencies are seen to be particularly prone to electoral concern about the viability of progressive policies and contain a disproportionate amount of communities targeted for Levelling Up (Johnson, Johnson and Nettle, 2022; M. T. Johnson *et al.*, 2023). Within a survey presenting and assessing ten different policy areas, we presented brief, bullet-point outlines of proposals for reform. This is a description of education reform:

Reforms to education would improve educational outcomes by:

- Increasing educational spending by at least 9 per cent to pre-austerity levels.
- Removing private school charitable status.
- Prohibiting profit-making schools.
- Removing further and higher education tuition fees.

Evidence suggests that some impacts of the policies include:

- Ensuring that all children and young people have access to high-quality schools, colleges and university education.

- Improving the ability of children and young people from families on low to medium incomes to achieve good outcomes by removing the ability of wealthy individuals to buy advantage through private education.
- Securing children from the effects of student loan debt.
- Controlling our education system democratically through local authorities.

Participants are then to rate policies on a 100-point sliding scale via a horizontal slider anchored with 0 = strongly disagree and 100 = strongly agree. This elicits very basic popularity data to enable identification of firm opponents of each policy area for adversarial co-production of narratives. This is an essential first stage.

9.3.2 Stage 2: adversarial co-production of narratives

It is then necessary to identify a sufficient number of opponents of the relevant policy by their rating the policy less than 20/100. We identify ten per policy. These opponents are then invited to develop narratives that elicit features of the policies to persuade voters like them of its merits. Participants produce written narratives of a minimum of 150 words. The text produced is then standardised for language, style and length at 150 words +/- 10 per cent max. At least four narratives are produced around the most cohesive ideas expressed, using the text provided by participants to organise prose around four specific justificatory elements.

The following four themes for education narratives were identified:

> Narrative 1 – absolute gains: At first glance you may think these policies are too radical and expensive, but we are simply reversing some of the many years of cuts. Education is a basic human right and every child should have the same opportunity to access excellent schools, progress to high quality technical and higher education, get good jobs and succeed in life. By increasing funding to pre-austerity levels, these policies give state schools, colleges and universities the resources they need to provide every child with the best start in life and to equip them with the skills that will help them flourish. By removing all state education fees, we would break down the social class barriers and ensure that we can all stay in education regardless of background. Because we all benefit when those talented, well-educated graduates go out into the workforce, we have good reasons to stop them leaving universities with huge debts that prevent many people from even trying in the first place.
>
> Narrative 2 – relative gains: Our nepotistic education system is rigged against normal people. In education, ability is evenly spread, but opportunity is not. Currently, too many people's chances of getting on in life are adversely affected by where they live. Rich people are subsidised by taxpayers to buy

advantages for their children by paying for tax free private education, often leapfrogging over more talented working class children. These reforms would mean that rich parents are no longer able to buy advantages and that more working class children would be able to attend university and succeed in life without worrying about high levels of student debt. Attendance at university would be more based on grades and abilities as opposed to ability to pay. Tuition fees can be covered by taxation on the wealthy, as they were for many of us in the past. These policies end the postcode lottery of life and bring our communities up to the level of more prosperous areas.

Narrative 3 – security: The UK education system is insecure. There are practical issues like defective concrete in schools, falling attendance levels since COVID-19 and low staffing levels, particularly for those who need additional support, such as those with special educational needs. When education spending was at pre-austerity levels, there was more stability within the state education system. We had smaller class sizes and funding for resources. Teachers are now leaving the profession in their droves due to demands of the job. Cost cutting hits those at the chalk face hardest. Local authorities should have more control, removing destructive competition between schools in the new academy system that forces some schools into closure. These reforms return spending to pre-austerity levels to allow schools to pay for increased salaries, food and energy costs and to remove the normalising effect of students starting their working life with a huge debt to repay. This creates security throughout the whole system, stabilising young people's lives as they enter adulthood.

Narrative 4 – economic benefit: These reforms would put the UK ahead of other countries in terms of having a highly educated population. Children are the workforce of the future and the country as a whole depends on keeping ahead of technological advancements by training suitable candidates and graduates to fill the jobs we need. These policies would benefit the country as a whole, stimulating economic growth. If more people earn more because they are in higher-paying jobs, then it is natural that they will then pay higher taxes. Higher taxes means that more money is available to be spent on the NHS, roads and welfare. This will increase opportunities even further, increasing social mobility, improving the skills and learning of the workforce and ultimately increasing productivity in the economy. The country as a whole will benefit from having the best professional people and we may be able to attract more talent to the country, rather than the best people moving away and paying taxes in other countries.

9.3.3 Stage 3: narrative treatment

A final, public opinion survey is then conducted. The sample needs to be large enough to explore relationships between demographic, socioeconomic and other variables, such as health or exposure to crime, levels of support for the policy and impact of narratives on post-treatment levels of support. In the Act Now survey, we ensured effective representation among Red Wall constituents by first opening the survey to 916 residents with Red Wall postcodes or area postcodes with a large proportion of Red Wall constituencies and then opened the survey to a further 1,305 participants across Britain.

In this final stage, participants are presented with the same brief, often bullet-point, description of the policy or policies and their prospective, evidenced impacts. Participants are asked to rate their opposition or support for those policies on a scale of 0–100. They are then shown a randomised adversarially co-produced narrative and asked to rate its persuasiveness on a scale of 0–100 and then to rate their opposition or support for the policy again on a scale of 0–100. Each participant is assigned to one of the narrative groups on the basis of which group had the fewest responses at the time of their viewing the question. This ensures an equal chance of each participant being assigned to each group, though no specific quotas on the basis of initial, pre-treatment support are necessarily used. Participants are then asked to rate the policy again. This enables measurement of the impact of the narrative.

Participants are then asked to provide basic demographic data and socioeconomic data. There is evidence that subjective rating of socioeconomic status is important in determining people's preferences, insofar as people with higher levels of objective income may also have higher levels of expenditure on things like mortgages that render their levels of non-committed income low. As such, self-rating status on the MacArthur ladder of subjective socioeconomic status (Adler *et al.*, 2000), and perceived risk of destitution on a 100-point sliding scale are useful measures (Nettle *et al.*, 2024; Villadsen *et al.*, 2024). For health status, PHQ-8 (Kroenke, Spitzer and Williams, 2001) is an effective measure of depression, GAD7 (Spitzer *et al.*, 2006) is an effective measure of anxiety and it is possible to use a single item life satisfaction as a proxy for health status (Guney, Kalafat and Boysan, 2010; Mamani-Benito *et al.*, 2022). Political affiliation and voting intention are easy to identify, while faith in politicians can be established by a six item list of the following statements, measured ordinally from strongly disagree to strongly agree: 'Politicians are all the same' (higher scores, lower faith); 'Politics can be a force for good' (higher scores, higher faith); 'It doesn't matter which party is in government' (higher scores, lower faith); 'Politicians don't care about people like me' (higher scores, lower faith); 'Politicians want to make things better' (higher scores, higher faith); 'We shouldn't rely on government to make things better' (higher scores, lower faith) (M. T. Johnson *et al.*, 2023).

This permits analysis of pre- and post-treatment levels of support, levels of rating association between demographic, socioeconomic, health and political affiliation characteristics. The first data to report are basic demographic data on sex, ethnicity and age and also a description of any weighting to be applied. Next, political preferences are required as weighting may also be needed. Tables are generally important in making reporting accessible. Tables 9.1–9.3 illustrate this.

Analysis of raw levels of support, breakdown in levels of strength or opposition, average change in score and significance of any change in particular benefits from table presentation.

While there was a linear impact of each narrative, there was no evidence of a statistically significant narrative treatment effect on support for education reform on participants overall, which increased by 0.72 points (p = 0.2693) on average across all narratives. However, as 18.11 per cent chose 100 at the pre stage, there was little room on the scale for improvement among a large proportion of respondents. However, there was a large and significant increase in support among pre-treatment haters of 4.04 points (p = 0.0092).

Regression analysis can then be used to analyse associations between demographic, socioeconomic, health and political affiliation characteristics and levels of support. In this case, low socioeconomic status and poor health predict higher levels of support, and male gender, older age and higher socioeconomic status predict lower levels of support. Similar associations were found with regard to the amount of pre-post change in score. There are at least plausible reasons to believe that these findings are reliable. The policy aims to redistribute opportunity to those with fewer resources; older people are less able directly to benefit as parents or students, and men may be less directly engaged with schools or feel that boys are less likely to benefit, given gender trends in educational attainment (Roberts, Bolton and Wilson, 2025).

Table 9.1 Socioeconomic and health statistics

Variable	*Mean*	*Median*	*Standard deviation*
Age	47.96	48	16.74
Left–Right preferences	45.97	50	21.01
Household net income per annum	40,156.70	34,000	39,420.12
Perceived risk of destitution	26.85	19	26.86
MacArthur ladder	5.3	5	1.61
Perceived control of life	61.41	65.17	22.69
Life satisfaction score	61.64	68	24.15
GAD-7	5.14	4	5.2
PHQ-8	4.45	3	4.96

Table 9.2 Level and change in support pre-post treatment

Sample	*% before*	*% after*	*Mean (before)*	*Median (before)*	*Standard deviation (before)*	*Mean (after)*	*Median (after)*	*Average change in score*	*(p)*
All	100	100	70.73	77	26.5	71.46	78	0.72	–.269
Lovers (≥70)	58.54	60.92	88.79			87.51		–1.29	–.052
Haters (≤30)	9.44	9.3	11.82			15.87		4.05	–< .001
0 scores	1.79	1.19							
100 scores	18.11	17.70							

Table 9.3 Rating of narratives

Subname	*Relative gains mean*	*Relative gains median*	*Security mean*	*Security median*	*Absolute gains mean*	*Absolute gains median*	*Economic benefit mean*	*Economic benefit median*
All	68.76	75	70.51	75	69.05	75	65.44	70
Lovers	83.15	88	82.26	85	83.55	84	80.3	84
Haters	20.67	10	27.1	15.17	24.89	22.67	17.11	9.88

While gender and ethnicity are less commonly significant predictors of the policies we have examined, socioeconomic status, health status and voting intention have always been significant. Using adversarial co-production demonstrates that levels of support among firm opponents can be increased effectively and that voters can be persuaded to support progressive policy.

9.4 Explaining preferences

A body of evidence now indicates an association between higher levels of inequality and lower health, of wellbeing and social outcomes. Indeed, a recent study of twenty-two countries has concluded that rising inequality is directly linked to declining levels of happiness (Bartram, 2022). This is true even when there have been absolute gains by virtue of economic growth. The impacts are profound. The pandemic has highlighted the enormous cost of health inequalities that track socioeconomic inequalities. Indeed, we have found that nearly half of all sixteen- to twenty-four-year-olds meet clinical threshold levels of anxiety and depression on the SF-12 measure, with morbidity driven by subjective socioeconomic markers such as perception of status and financial distress (Chen *et al.*, 2023; Villadsen *et al.*, 2024). However, progressive policymakers currently face a challenge in countries with rising inequality of wealth: there appears to be a trend of lower-income voters rejecting traditional parties of the centre and centre-left and supporting centre-right and right-wing parties (Polacko, 2022). In part this may reflect declining faith in the ability of left and centre-left parties – and the government in general – to make things better. Given that parties of the right and centre-right are associated with the very policies that promote inequality in the first place, there is a hypothetical downward spiral in which support for parties committed to reducing inequality falls as inequality rises, preventing the economic source of dissatisfaction being addressed.

The electorally critical 'left-behind', 'Red Wall' constituencies in Wales and the North and Midlands of England (MacKinnon, 2020) (see Mackinnon 2020) are archetypal examples of areas that stand to benefit from redistribution, but have recently begun to support right-wing parties. The loss of many of these constituencies in the 2019 UK General Election has led the Labour leadership to tactically eschew redistributive policy in favour of mimicking the English identity politics of the Conservative and Reform Parties (M. T. Johnson *et al.*, 2023). Not only has Labour's popularity receded in government, it also means that the very policies that might stop the downward spiral are being abandoned. This may be tactically naive, since evidence suggests that voters' support for policies associated with right-wing politicians is grounded in perception of material benefit, whether through mitigating zero-sum competition for low-paid employment via Brexit or 'pork barrel' infrastructural investment (Huber and Ting, 2013).

Our findings suggest that people's perception of socioeconomic status, financial distress and exposure to risk of destitution significantly increase redistributive preferences: those who stand to benefit most from redistribution are indeed aware of their material interests. The strong correlations between anxiety and depression and between both conditions and income are supportive of income as a social determinant of mental health. While anxiety and depression are treated as distinct conditions, our findings suggest substantive overlap both in socioeconomic causation and attitudinal impact.

This is apparent in levels of support for three different Basic Income schemes of differing degrees of generosity. Support is lowest for Scheme 1, which retains the complexity of the present welfare system but offers partial supplements through a small universal payment. Support is higher for Scheme 3, a full MIS scheme, which offers full protection for individuals and eliminates most conditional benefits. The most popular scheme was the intermediate Scheme 2. Were individuals concerned solely with fiscal and monetary restraint, there would have been a linear appraisal in reverse numerical order. In our results, Scheme 1 is unique insofar as support was consistent across age groups. Older participants are fairly consistent in their rating of the schemes. This may be because they are already in receipt or close to receipt of age-conditional Basic Income of comparable size to the payments. Scheme 2 and Scheme 3 differ insofar as support is much higher among younger participants. This may be because the schemes benefit a much broader body of the population much more clearly, granting more generous support to those dependent upon work for satisfaction of their needs.

As Figure 9.1 shows, the least generous Scheme 1 was about equally supported across the socioeconomic position spectrum, while Schemes 2 and 3 had markedly higher support amongst respondents of lower socioeconomic position. All schemes were more highly supported by younger respondents, but this was particularly true for the intermediate Scheme 2.

We have highlighted the importance of relative gains previously. There is more evidence of that impact here. Scheme 1 may be regarded solely as supporting the least well-off – externalised 'others' with whom there is little expectation of reciprocity. This is a particular deficit in the scheme, since the large number of conditions attached to payment renders it much less appealing to those in work, who may view the payment as inadequate.

Vitally, this externalisation leaves the scheme open to precisely the same objections as Universal Credit and other needs- and means-based payments: as something for 'others' to progressively diminish as those in work experience greater financial distress. Fiscal responsibility may not be the salient consideration for voters in this regard. In contrast, Schemes 2 and 3 may

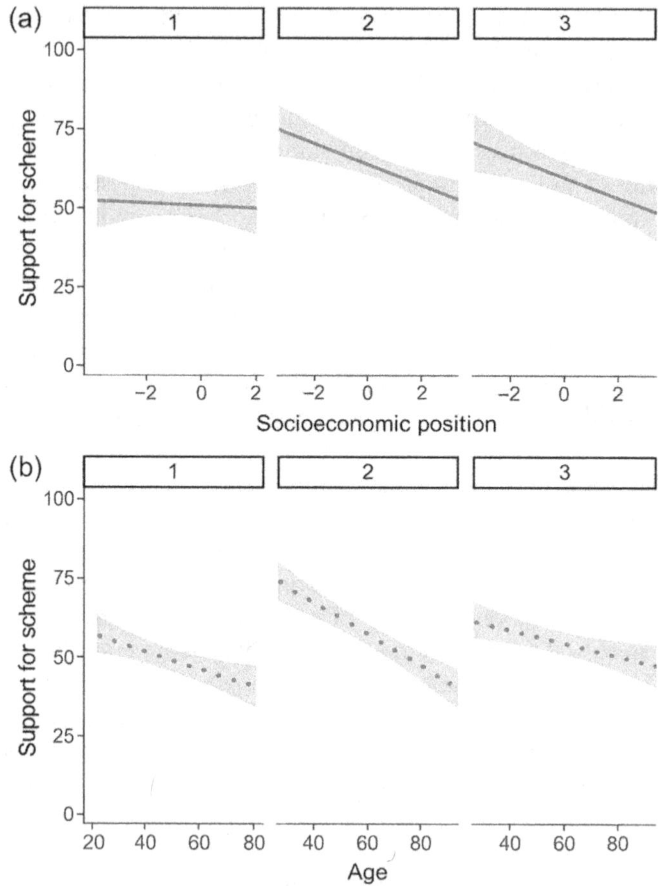

Figure 9.1 Levels of support by treatment, SES, sense of control and faith in government

be perceived as benefitting participants specifically as an in-group. Again, this supports the notion that progressive politicians have good reason for adopting schemes that are grand in their formulation, specifically because they benefit those more likely to vote. Scheme 2 may be more popular than Scheme 3 because it is the intermediate scheme and was perceived as a reasonable compromise.

9.5 The political challenge

Despite policymaker misgivings, mean levels of support for Basic Income remain historically high, especially in comparison to other welfare or health policies (Health Foundation, 2022, p. 56). This finding, which has been repeated in several similar studies, emphasises the extent to which voters are aware of the need for upstream interventions to mitigate risk. Even if individuals do not immediately regard themselves as personal beneficiaries, they broadly regard the policy as being of value. This is significant for progressive politicians seeking support in 'left-behind' communities.

People with low levels of control have higher levels of support for our example redistributive policy. This is at odds with claims of insurmountable social conservatism in 'Red Wall' constituencies. People want more control over their lives and recognise that redistribution in the form of secure, predictable income can increase it. However, those who perceive low levels of control also have less faith in the government. Having more faith in the government is associated with increased support for our redistributive measure. As such, it may be that even though individuals recognise the need for the policy, they may not be persuaded to vote by virtue of lack of faith in the government's capacity to improve their interests. Moreover, the literature on the desire of those with anxiety and depression to avoid upheaval and uncertainty presents opponents of progressive change with the capacity to suppress support. This is a common and effective tactic among centre-right and right-wing politicians, with claims of 'chaos with Ed Miliband' in 2015 and a 'Coalition of chaos' between Labour and the SNP in 2017, both deployed to some success, even though the outcome was upheaval through the Brexit referendum in 2016 and the subsequent internal conflict within Government during the Conservative minority administration of 2017–19. Progressive politicians therefore face the dual challenges of having to present policies capable of increasing control while resisting claims from opponents that such measures will lead to uncertainty and unpredictability.

This is particularly problematic in the UK, in which the main progressive party, Labour, oversaw the Global Financial Crisis of 2007/2008 in government, underplayed the scale and impact of migration – both of which have significant impacts in Red Wall constituencies – and then decided not to enact change once elected back into office in 2024. There is little reason to suppose that not offering change on the basis that voters seek continuity and technocratic competence is not feasible: progressive politicians' views of their historical records may not be the same as those of voters. As such, politicians need to both emphasise that the present system is chaotic and that redistribution is the means of reducing uncertainty.

This leaves the question of funding and a return to some of the core concerns of TriplePC. At a time of a cost-of-living crisis, any increase in income tax for the vast majority of workers is likely to be unpopular. As such, there are tactical options that require examination: firstly, externalising costs through land and wealth taxes in ways that a majority of voters view as beneficially redistributive; secondly, by being less concerned with fiscal neutrality. A decade of rising public debt and historically significant investments to pay for COVID-19 mitigation measures has been associated with few clear consequences in day-to-day lives. The public may be less concerned about abstract debt considerations and achieving static fiscal neutrality than they were in 2010. There is scope for narratives of investment and growth out of crisis.

9.6 The relationship between delivery and reason

This topic highlights pathways through to delivery of progressive public policy. Politicians need to both recognise voters' need for greater control and for a belief in the ability of policies to reduce uncertainty and unpredictability. The current balance pursued by progressive politicians between attractiveness and plausibility may require rethinking. Those on the right have successfully promoted 'grand schemes' that are sufficiently attractive in their promising improvement in material conditions as to override voters' concerns about uncertainty and unpredictability. Progressive politicians have, in redistributive policies such as Basic Income, access to schemes that can attract voters *and* deliver greater control, certainty and predictability. The evidence presented here and elsewhere suggests that redistributive policies, properly framed and narrated, have the capacity to persuade voters. The outstanding question is whether politicians can be persuaded to change direction on that basis.

Adversarial co-production offers a potential impact in a number of policy areas. Pilot work on Basic Income ought to serve as encouragement for colleagues committed to EBPs currently regarded as lying outside the Overton Window, but for which there is a fundamental need. There is an urgent need within policymaking circles in particular to grasp the reality that transformative policy, though expensive up-front, is considerably cheaper than the alternative: mass social disintegration and climate-based extinction. Given Labour's express belief that essential EBP, such as wealth tax and an adequate Green New Deal, are not feasible due to the need to appeal to older, wealthy voters, there is a genuine need to understand a truism and make the case for transformative policy through persuasion. As Labour's forebears in 1945 recognised, sometimes the most expensive policies, such as the creation of the NHS, are so essential that society cannot afford not to implement them; the cost of pursuing policies that seem sensible by virtue of their being minimal and uncontroversial, but which are ineffective, is far greater. Adversarial co-production gives policymakers the ability to engage with firm opponents to come up with means of making policy capable of addressing our permacrisis; taking people's opinions at face value and treating the Overton Window as fixed does not.

9.7 What is needed? Experimental engagement with all?

There is, though, a real need to consider the risks of the approach. There is at least the possibility that those with extreme and outlying views who oppose EBP might produce distorting or deliberately damaging narratives capable of undermining support overall. Indeed, there are various extremist groups who have an interest in advancing policy that actively discriminates against others and exacerbates crisis. There is a real reason to question whether climate change sceptics or eugenicists should have a voice in policy presentation. It is precisely this phenomenon that motivates our interest in adversarial co-production. There is a recognised need to overcome 'echo chambers' that provide potentially misleading understandings of people's positions. It is not that adversarial co-production advances policies supported by climate change deniers or eugenicists, but that engagement with those who oppose EBP enables identification of salient elements of evidence and prospective impact to persuade others who hold similar positions. This is a crucial means of engaging citizens who are currently alienated from the technocratic approach criticised by Bandola-Gill, Grek and Tichenor (2023) and who need persuading that the policies are not elite abstractions or impositions. This is crucially important for left-behind communities, whose voices are silent or go unacknowledged and unheard, and who are most in need of intervention, and demonstrates the genuine reflexivity advanced by Bandola-Gill, Grek and Tichenor.

Indeed, the risks of adversaries distorting policies can be mitigated during the research process outlined above by virtue of qualitative feedback among the broader population, as well as among fellow opponents. The greater risk, at present, is that those with such positions continue to be alienated from policies that have the potential to benefit them as members of society. With the growth in echo chambers and polarisation, the need for controlled co-production of narratives offers a means of addressing much broader social pathologies. This may be consistent with addressing epistemic injustice (Mouffe, 2000; Chambers *et al.*, 2022), but is driven primarily by instrumental concern for finding means of persuading on policies with transformative impact.

9.8 Conclusion

This chapter has demonstrated how adversarial co-production represents a paradigm shift in evidence-based policymaking, moving beyond static assumptions about public opinion towards active engagement with policy opponents to develop persuasive narratives. Drawing on adversarial collaboration from behavioural science, this methodology recognises that reasoning functions primarily through dialogue and persuasion, allowing individuals with differing perspectives to coordinate on beneficial collective action.

The three-stage process – screening for opponents, co-producing narratives with them and testing persuasive effects – has proven remarkably effective across multiple policy domains. Our findings on Basic Income and education reform challenge the widespread belief that transformative policies lie permanently outside the Overton Window. Firm opponents, when exposed to adversarially co-produced narratives emphasising material interests through relatable protagonists and concrete examples, show statistically significant increases in support. Crucially, those with lower socioeconomic status and poorer health – precisely those who would benefit most from redistribution – demonstrate awareness of their material interests and responsiveness to well-constructed arguments.

The methodology addresses a critical failure in contemporary politics: the tendency of policymakers to treat public preferences as fixed, leading them to abandon necessary transformative policies in favour of minimal, ineffective interventions. History demonstrates that radical policy shifts are possible when properly advocated – the neoliberal transformation itself proves this. Progressive politicians must recognise that voters seek greater control and predictability, which redistributive policies can provide when framed appropriately.

However, these challenges remain: rebuilding faith in government's capacity to deliver, resisting opponents' claims of chaos and also developing funding narratives around wealth taxation and productive investment rather than fiscal neutrality. Adversarial co-production offers policymakers essential tools for persuading alienated electorates to support the transformative measures our permacrisis demands.

The point of this chapter is that the basic elements of economic and health evidence produced via microsimulation need to clearly be connected to public opinion evidence and, most importantly, narration, in order to ever make an impact on policy. The activities of this chapter enable you to identify paths towards the development of that evidence on popularity that is so keenly needed in order to persuade elected officials of the value of doing the right and sensible thing.

10

Conclusion

10.1 The implications and applications of this book

The 2024 General Election was marked by repeated criticism of Labour's modest tax reform plans. Then Prime Minister, Rishi Sunak, tweeted, 'You name it, Labour will tax it'. Britain desperately needs the 'decade of national renewal' Keir Starmer promised, but the biggest obstacle to that is what Labour is promising not to do: comprehensively reform the tax system to fund a whole-of-government programme to secure and rebuild Britain.

The Government desperately needs to raise more revenue. We have public health, crime and housing crises that can be attributed squarely to the unprecedented increase in poverty and inequality since the Global Finance Crisis. School ceilings are literally crumbling, our transport system is both expensive and unreliable and private water companies are *de facto* bankrupt. The vast majority of local authorities will need bailing out over the next parliament. Fundamentally, the failure to invest imposes enormous costs on services and the country as a whole.

Labour's rejection of tax and spend may seem sensible. In the face of the cost-of-living crisis as well as decades of attacks on Labour for supporting ever-so-slightly higher rates of income tax than the Tories, it is understandable for older Labour policymakers to fear headlines regarding tax increases. However, Britain is now totally different from the country it was in 1992 and, indeed, in 2019. Tax on those who can afford it is now popular in ways that are important.

The attempt by private schools and private school parents to use Conservatives and an increasingly desperate Conservative-supporting press to advocate against the removal of charitable status has been soundly rejected, with 57 per cent of the population supporting the policy and only 16 per cent opposed (IPSOS, 2023). In the past, voters could imagine having sufficient resources at some point in a hypothetical future to pay for their children to go to private school. But now, it just looks like voters are paying for an ever-smaller group of people to gain an unfair advantage over their own kids.

The 2024 UK General Election was the first since baby boomers reached adulthood in which a clear majority of them did not see their preferred party in government. For those under fifty, a statement like 'Labour will take us back to the 1970s' sounds like a good thing. Frankly, things are very much worse now than they were then in a number of ways, and raising tax in order to fund the very things we have lost over the past four decades – nationalised infrastructure and functioning health, welfare and industrial sectors – is attractive. As well as manufacturing, we need production, including green energy, and services, including social care.

From around 1979 to 2007, the policies built on Hayek's ideas seemed to be working sufficiently well for a sufficient number of Britons to keep voting for them. There was a massive growth of wealth for a significant number of Britons, mainly in the form of housing. The Global Financial Crisis of 2007/2008 posed a challenge for this consensus. For Friedman, events such as this create opportunities for policymakers:

> Only a crisis – actual or perceived – produces real change. When that crisis occurs, the actions that are taken depend on the ideas that are lying around. That, I believe, is our basic function: to develop alternatives to existing policies, to keep them alive and available until the politically impossible becomes the politically inevitable. (Friedman, 1982, pp. xiii–xiv)

It was the Conservative Party, through the leadership of David Cameron and George Osborne, that took advantage of this opportunity to enact the ever-intensifying policy trajectory of neoliberal reform that the current Labour Government has adopted wholeheartedly. We have examined elements of this approach above: a much smaller government with reduced public spending and markets liberated from even more of the regulation that might have prevented or mitigated the source of the crisis in public budgets in the first place. The success of these governments in advancing these policies has lain in narrative. Cameron and Osborne's notion of 'fixing the roof while the sun is shining' – the fallacy of comparing national economies to household ones – was so effective that opposition parties either bought into it or felt that there was no reasonable alternative.

But these policies have continued to fail, and with the legacy of the pandemic, the cost-of-living crisis and now the US influence in Europe changing, things are starting to shift. Among those crises, it is important to create ideas that are lying around, even if politicians have rejected them as impossible. Friedman successfully overturned decades of Keynesian, social democratic/democratic socialist policies in the UK, in much of the rest of Europe and even in the US. It is sometimes very difficult to appreciate how much the United States changed from the Keynesian New Deal of President Franklin D. Roosevelt in the 1930s and 1940s, which directly saved Friedman from destitution, to the post-Ronald Reagan era shaped by Friedman's ideas from the 1980s onwards.

There is often a presumption within research that the success of knowledge production for policy depends on providing good evidence to the right people. This is the premise of knowledge partnership schemes, policy engagement programmes and other Higher Education Institution endeavours on which significant public funds are expended without evidence of impact on actual policymaking (Mäkelä, Boaz and Oliver, 2025). The problem is that evidence only ever underpins policy when it demonstrably advances the interests of policymakers.

The policies enacted in Hayek's and Friedman's names have demonstrably failed in practice, with declining living conditions for the vast majority in developed countries in the last fifteen to twenty years. The free market they held to be both more efficient and morally justifiable does not operate effectively or efficiently for essentials such as housing, medicine and water. Someone with few resources growing up has a severe and often insurmountable disadvantage to overcome in accessing those markets. We now have an economy where luxuries can be far cheaper than they ever were, but essentials are completely out of reach.

It is in that context that highly dubious research methods have thrived in producing policy-based evidence. Methods can be shaped to provide the results that the researchers want based on their bias, ideology or desire for personal advancement. The Behavioural Insights Team or 'Nudge Unit' (Institute for Government, 2020) became incredibly influential after it was established by David Cameron to enact the 'Nudge Theory' of US behavioural economists Richard Thaler and Cass Sunstein (Thaler and Sunstein, 2008). The theory they promoted fitted perfectly with Cameron's desire for improved outcomes with no additional (or in fact reduced) public investment by just 'nudging' people into the 'right' decisions. Examples include drawing on behavioural economic assumptions regarding loss aversion to change the default option for a question in a tax return form and sending messages about impending fines to reduce evasion and benefit sanctioning to reduce welfare recipience, which the team eventually acknowledged was ineffective. Crucially, though, there is now growing evidence that not only is nudging ineffective in the majority of applications and at a statistical level overall (Maier *et al.*, 2022), but also that key studies by leading 'nudgers' were either biased or engaged in active data manipulation (Degerman *et al.*, 2024). There is some evidence that changing the default option in a form can be effective in directing people towards a particular answer, but that ought not to be the basis of a huge, funding-dominating discipline.

As such, it is not enough to just produce 'good' research. It is just as important to be able to communicate it effectively to different audiences, to persuade people to take it on and to influence the influencers. Interestingly, there are plenty of people who could have told the government that nudging or expecting corporations to act in the public interest are follies in the face of actual crises. We have gone from twenty-six thousand food parcels being distributed in 2008/2009 to more than 3.1 million food parcels being distributed in 2023/2024 by Trussell Trust centres alone (Statista, 2025). It is not possible for the Behavioural Insights Team to nudge that many people into magically discovering food.

What is actually needed is a social safety net that protects people from getting to that point. And, the point of all of this is that if you do not make the case even for the bleeding obvious, someone making the case for the patently ridiculous will.

The reality is that voters increasingly see tax as being a central means of improving our lives. Years of reducing tax rates on business or bribing the wealthy to live in Britain have failed to deal with regional inequality and poor productivity. Instead, there is scope for researchers to advance evidence for a new economy that directs investment to where it is needed most. In historical terms, UK income tax is a relative aberration, with permanent introduction only taking place in 1842 and application only to the very highest earners until the early-middle part of the twentieth century. The relative value of income from work as opposed to that from wealth has been reduced so significantly in recent decades that there is a genuine opportunity for new forms of policy development that reconfigure the tax system. This book is a means of enabling researchers to start developing evidence for this.

Alongside that evidence, it is important to consider some very general principles in advancing that evidence to policymakers.

First and foremost, evidence that matters is that which shows that enaction is in the apparent interest of policymakers. This is why Chapter 6 is such an important element of the approach advanced above. Showing that policy is popular and electorally valuable is as important, if not even more important than showing that it is affordable and feasible.

Second, it is important that evidence be communicated clearly in succinct briefings. There are myriad good guides to this (NIHR, 2025). Communicating in and on policymakers' own terms is essential but time-consuming. See time invested in sitting through tedious events as important: do work during that time, even if that work is just doing emails.

Third, it is inevitable that any evidence that does not match policymakers' underpinning assumptions will be rejected at first sight. The current government has had fifteen years of evidence that its current policies are harmful, including to its own interests. It is essential to be resilient, to accept this and to identify those policymakers who stand to gain when those obstinately adhered to failing policies fall from office. This resilience includes ignoring patronising 'nice idea, nobody would vote for it' claims from policymakers who are, actually, often the ones to be voted out of office. One senior metropolitan leader who was recently voted out of office and is currently embroiled in scandal made this claim regarding Basic Income – they sought us out for engagement immediately upon resolution of one inquiry into their behaviour. If your methods are reliable and your evidence comprehensive, be confident that, eventually, you will succeed.

Fourth, it is essential to understand that if your evidence does indicate a new and important thread of study and policy, it is likely that the vast majority of requests for funding will be rejected, precisely because it is new. Funding for research reifies and entrenches broken evidence. Nudgers continue to receive enormous sums of money, precisely because their ideas are not new and do not call for change. This is why Higher Education Institutions are important in providing the kind of employment security that the otherwise unemployed Milton Friedman received from the New Deal in order to develop his ideas. Funding will, eventually, flow from your research, but up-front investment in publishing and advancing collaborative approaches to dissemination is required.

The crucial conclusion we want to emphasise is that Friedman faced exactly these challenges. He and his fellow believers were regarded as weirdos with extremist ideological positions. History suggests those assumptions were correct, but the point of importance is that they simply ignored the hostility and ensured that their ideas were those that were lying around when Margaret Thatcher and Ronald Reagan sought out approaches to advance their interests in the wake of 1970s challenges. Your ideas could very well be the ones lying around for the policymakers of the present.

Be resilient and persist.

References

Abrahams, D. (2016) *Hansard*. Westminster: House of Commons. Available at: https://hansard.parliament.uk/Commons/2016-11-16showNoDebateMessage=True (Accessed: 12 August 2025).

Adeline, A. and Delattre, E. (2017) 'Some Microeconometric Evidence on the Relationship between Health and Income', *Health Economics Review*, 7(1), p. 27. Available at: https://doi.org/10.1186/s13561-017-0163-5

Adelle, C. *et al.* (2020) 'Making Sense Together: The Role of Scientists in the Coproduction of Knowledge for Policy Making', *Science and Public Policy*, 47(1), pp. 56–66. Available at: https://doi.org/10.1093/scipol/scz046

Adler, N. E. *et al.* (2000) 'Relationship of Subjective and Objective Social Status with Psychological and Physiological Functioning: Preliminary Data in Healthy, White Women', *Health Psychology*, 19(6), pp. 586–592. Available at: https://doi.org/10.1037/0278-6133.19.6.586

Advani, A., Chamberlain, E. and Summers, A. (2020) 'Wealth Tax Commission', *Retrieved August*, 3, p. 2023. London: Wealth Tax Commission. Available at: https://www.lse.ac.uk/International-Inequalities/Assets/Documents/WealthTaxCommission-Final-report.pdf (Accessed: 28 May 2026).

Agency for Healthcare Research and Quality (2024) *Medical Expenditure Panel Survey*. Rockville, MD: AHRQ. Available at: https://meps.ahrq.gov/ (Accessed: 12 May 2026).

Akanni, L., Lenhart, O. and Morton, A. (2022) 'Income Trajectories and Self-Rated Health Status in the UK', *SSM – Population Health*, 17, p. 101035. Available at: https://doi.org/10.1016/j.ssmph.2022.101035

Andrews, K. (2023) 'Tax Rises "Causing Brain Drain to England"', *The Times*. Available at: https://www.thetimes.co.uk/article/scotland-s-tax-policies-contribute-to-financial-talent-drain-9gfmsmch2 (Accessed: 19 May 2026).

Anyaegbu, G. (2010) 'Using the OECD Equivalence Scale in Taxes and Benefits Analysis', *Economic & Labour Market Review*, 4(1), pp. 49–54. Available at: https://link.springer.com/content/pdf/10.1057/elmr.2010.9.pdf (Accessed: 12 May 2026).

Ardron, K. *et al.* (2025) 'Climate Change Mitigation and Workers' Interests: Why Framing a Green New Deal as Redistributive and Security-Enhancing Is Key to Popularity', *F1000* [preprint].

Armingeon, K. and Bonoli, G. (eds) (2006) *The Politics of Post-Industrial Welfare States: Adapting Post-War Social Policies to New Social Risks*. London: Routledge. Available at: https://www.routledge.com/The-Politics-of-Post-Industrial-Welfare-States-Adapting-Post-War-Social-Policies-to-New-Social-Risks/Armingeon-Bonoli/p/book/9780415459754 (Accessed: 13 August 2025).

Asghar Zaidi, M., Hagenaars, A. and de Vos, K. (1994) *Poverty Statistics in the Late 1980s: Research Based on Micro-Data*. Luxembourg: Office for Official Publications of the European Communities. Available at: https://op.europa.eu/en/publication-detail/-/publication/9c787f17-acb6-4f4b-badc-49a2310e65f7 (Accessed: 12 May 2026).

Atkinson, A. (2015) *Inequality: What Can Be Done?* Cambridge, MA: Harvard University Press. Available at: https://www.hup.harvard.edu/books/9780674979789 (Accessed: 13 August 2025).

Atkinson, A. and Stiglitz, J. (2015) *Lectures on Public Economics*. Princeton, NJ: Princeton University Press. Available at: https://press.princeton.edu/books/hardcover/9780691166414/lectures-on-public-economics (Accessed: 13 August 2025).

Baker, C. and Kirk-Wade, E. (2023) *Mental Health Statistics: Prevalence, Services and Funding in England*. London: House of Commons Library. Available at: https://commonslibrary.parliament.uk/research-briefings/sn06988/ (Accessed: 5 July 2023).

Bandola-Gill, J., Grek, S. and Tichenor, M. (2023) 'The Rise of the Reflexive Expert? Epistemic, Care-Ful and Instrumental Reflexivity in Global Public Policy', *Global Social Policy*, 23(3), pp. 481–498. Available at: https://doi.org/10.1177/14680181221145382

Bansak, K. *et al.* (2023) 'Using Conjoint Experiments to Analyze Election Outcomes: The Essential Role of the Average Marginal Component Effect', *Political Analysis*, 31(4), pp. 500–518. Available at: https://doi.org/10.1017/pan.2022.16

Bardach, E. and Patashnik, E. M. (2019) *A Practical Guide for Policy Analysis: The Eightfold Path to More Effective Problem Solving*. 6th edn. Washington, DC: CQ Press.

Barnes, L., Blumenau, J. and Lauderdale, B. E. (2022) 'Measuring Attitudes toward Public Spending Using a Multivariate Tax Summary Experiment', *American Journal of Political Science*, 66(1), pp. 205–221. Available at: https://doi.org/10.1111/ajps.12643

Barton, C. (2020) 'Constituency Data: Universal Credit Rollout', *House of Commons Library*. Available at: https://commonslibrary.parliament.uk/social-policy/welfare-pensions/benefits/constituency-data-universal-credit-roll-out/ (Accessed: 30 June 2020).

Bartram, D. (2022) *Does Inequality Enhance Life Satisfaction?: A Longitudinal Investigation*. Available at: https://policycommons.net/artifacts/2324973/inequality-ls/3085501/ (Accessed: 17 June 2022).

BBC News (2019) 'Scotland's "Period Poverty" Bill Lodged', *BBC News*. Available at: https://www.bbc.com/news/uk-scotland-scotland-politics-48027903 (Accessed: 19 May 2026).

Bechtel, M. M. and Liesch, R. (2020) 'Reforms and Redistribution: Disentangling the Egoistic and Sociotropic Origins of Voter Preferences', *Public Opinion Quarterly*, 84(1), pp. 1–23. Available at: https://doi.org/10.1093/poq/nfaa006

Bell, A., Fairbrother, M. and Jones, K. (2019) 'Fixed and Random Effects Models: Making an Informed Choice', *Quality & Quantity*, 53(2), pp. 1051–1074. Available at: https://doi.org/10.1007/s11135-018-0802-x

Bell, A. and Jones, K. (2015) 'Explaining Fixed Effects: Random Effects Modeling of Time-Series Cross-Sectional and Panel Data', *Political Science Research and Methods*, 3(1), pp. 133–153. Available at: https://doi.org/10.1017/psrm.2014.7

Bernardi, L. and Johns, R. (2021) 'Depression and Attitudes to Change in Referendums: The Case of Brexit', *European Journal of Political Research*, 60(2), pp. 339–358. Available at: https://doi.org/10.1111/1475-6765.12398

Berry, C. (2021) '"A Mood in the Air ... Like 1945": Democratic Socialism and the *Post-Corbyn* Labour Party', *The Political Quarterly*, 92(2), pp. 255–263. Available at: https://doi.org/10.1111/1467-923X.12991

Blundell, R. (1992) 'Labour Supply and Taxation: A Survey', *Fiscal Studies*, 13(3), pp. 15–40. Available at: https://doi.org/10.1111/j.1475-5890.1992.tb00181.x

Blundell, R. and Preston, I. (1998) 'Consumption Inequality and Income Uncertainty', *The Quarterly Journal of Economics*, 113(2), pp. 603–640. Available at: https://doi.org/10.1162/003355398555694

Börsch-Supan, A. *et al.* (2013) 'Data Resource Profile: The Survey of Health, Ageing and Retirement in Europe (SHARE)', *International Journal of Epidemiology*, 42(4), pp. 992–1001. Available at: https://doi.org/10.1093/ije/dyt088

Bourquin, P., Brewer, M. and Wernham, T. (2024) 'Trends in Income and Wealth Inequalities', *Oxford Open Economics*, 3(Supplement 1), pp. i103–i146. Available at: https://doi.org/10.1093/ooec/odad100

Bovaird, T. (2007) 'Beyond Engagement and Participation: User and Community Coproduction of Public Services', *Public Administration Review*, 67(5), pp. 846–860. Available at: https://doi.org/10.1111/j.1540-6210.2007.00773.x

Bradshaw, J. and Keung, A. (2022) *Estimates of Fuel Poverty in January 2023*. York: Social Policy Research Unit. Available at: https://jonathanbradshaw.blogspot.com/2022/08/estimates-of-fuel-poverty-in-january.html (Accessed: 19 May 2026).

Brazier, J., Roberts, J. and Deverill, M. (2002) 'The Estimation of a Preference-Based Measure of Health From the SF-36', *Journal of Health Economics*, 21(2), pp. 271–292. Available at: https://doi.org/10.1016/S0167-6296(01)00130-8

Brazier, J. E. and Roberts, J. (2004) 'The Estimation of a Preference-Based Measure of Health From the SF-12', *Medical Care*, 42(9), pp. 851–859. Available at: https://doi.org/10.1097/01.mlr.0000135827.18610.0d

Bremer, B. and Bürgisser, R. (2022a) 'Lower Taxes At All Costs? Evidence from a Survey Experiment in Four European Countries'. *SocArXiv*. Available at: https://doi.org/10.31235/osf.io/e6ds9

Bremer, B. and Bürgisser, R. (2022b) 'Public Opinion on Welfare State Recalibration in Times of Austerity: Evidence from Survey Experiments', *Political Science Research and Methods*, 10(4), pp. 666–684. Available at: https://doi.org/10.1017/psrm.2021.78

Bremer, B. and Bürgisser, R. (2023) 'Do Citizens Care About Government Debt? Evidence from Survey Experiments on Budgetary Priorities', *European Journal of Political Research*, 62(1), pp. 239–263. Available at: https://doi.org/10.1111/1475-6765.12505

Brice, W. (2015) *Using SAS to Model the Distributional Impact of Government Policies*. Washington, DC: SAS. Available at: https://www.sas.com/content/dam/SAS/en_gb/doc/other1/events/sasforum/slides/manchester-day1/W.Bryce%20SAS%20Forum%20UK%20-%20HMT%20slides.pdf (Accessed: 12 May 2017).

British Sociological Association (2022) 'Citizens of Countries that Become More Unequal as their Economy Grows Are Less Happy, Says Research'. Available at: https://www.britsoc.co.uk/media-centre/press-releases/2022/april/citizens-of-countries-that-become-more-unequal-as-their-economy-grows-are-less-happy-says-research/ (Accessed: 21 April 2022).

Bryant, C. G. A. (1985) *Positivism in Social Theory and Research*. London: Macmillan Education UK. Available at: https://doi.org/10.1007/978-1-349-17759-2

Burkhauser, R. V. *et al.* (2017) *Survey Under-Coverage of Top Incomes and Estimation of Inequality: What Is the Role of the UK's SPI Adjustment?* National Bureau of Economic Research Working Paper. Available at: https://doi.org/10.3386/w23539

Cabinet Secretary for Communities and Local Government (2019) *Income Supplement: Ministerial Statement*. Hollyrood: Scottish Government. Available at: https://www.gov.scot/publications/statement-income-supplement/ (Accessed: 19 February 2025).

Cairney, P. (2016) *The Politics of Evidence-Based Policy Making*. London: Palgrave Macmillan UK. Available at: https://doi.org/10.1057/978-1-137-51781-4

Cairney, P. (2020) *Understanding Public Policy*. 2nd edn. London: Red Globe Press.

Case, A. and Deaton, A. (2003) *Consumption, Health, Gender, and Poverty*. Policy Research Working Paper no. 3020. Washington, DC: World Bank. Available at: http://hdl.handle.net/10986/18261 (Accessed: 19 February 2025).

Centers for Disease Control and Prevention (2024) 'Behavioral Risk Factor Surveillance System'. Available at: https://www.cdc.gov/brfss/ (Accessed: 12 May 2026).

Centre for Research in Social Policy (2025) 'The Minimum Income Standard for the United Kingdom', *Loughborough University*. Available at: https://www.lboro.ac.uk/research/crsp/minimum-income-standard/ (Accessed: 19 May 2026).

Chai, A. and Moneta, A. (2010) 'Retrospectives: Engel Curves', *Journal of Economic Perspectives*, 24(1), pp. 225–240. Available at: https://doi.org/10.1257/jep.24.1.225

Chamberlain, E. (2020) *Defining the Tax Base: Design Issues*. Wealth and Policy Working Paper no. 108. London: CAGE. Available at: https://doi.org/10.47445/108

Chambers, J. M. *et al.* (2022) 'Co-Productive Agility and Four Collaborative Pathways to Sustainability Transformations', *Global Environmental Change*, 72, p. 102422. Available at: https://doi.org/10.1016/j.gloenvcha.2021.102422

Charness, G. and Rabin, M. (2002) 'Understanding Social Preferences with Simple Tests', *The Quarterly Journal of Economics*, 117(3), pp. 817–869.

Chatfield, C. (1995) 'Model Uncertainty, Data Mining and Statistical Inference', *Journal of the Royal Statistical Society. Series A (Statistics in Society)*, 158(3), pp. 419–466. Available at: https://doi.org/10.2307/2983440

Chen, T. *et al.* (2023) 'Quantifying the Mental Health and Economic Impacts of Prospective Universal Basic Income Schemes Among Young People in the UK: A Microsimulation Modelling Study', *BMJ Open*, 13(10), p. e075831. Available at: https://doi.org/10.1136/bmjopen-2023-075831

Child Poverty Action Group (2021) *Welfare Benefits and Tax Credits Handbook 2021/22*. Available at: https://askcpag.org.uk/publications/-225624/welfare-benefits-and-tax-credits-handbook-2021/22 (Accessed: 22 February 2025).

Child Poverty Action Group (2022) *Welfare Benefits and Tax Credits Handbook, 2023/24*. Available at: https://cpag.org.uk/shop/handbook/welfare-benefits-tax-credits-handbook-202324 (Accessed: 9 December 2023).

Chong, D. and Druckman, J. N. (2007) 'Framing Theory', *Annual Review of Political Science*, 10, pp. 103–126. Available at: https://doi.org/10.1146/annurev.polisci.10.072805.103054

Clark, C. J. *et al.* (2022) 'Keep Your Enemies Close: Adversarial Collaborations Will Improve Behavioral Science', *Journal of Applied Research in Memory and Cognition*, 11(1), pp. 1–18. Available at: https://doi.org/10.1037/mac0000004

Clark, C. J. and Tetlock, P. E. (2022) 'Adversarial Collaboration: The Next Science Reform', in C. L. Frisby *et al.* (eds) *Political Bias in Psychology: Nature, Scope, and Solutions*. New York: Springer. Preprint available at: https://www.researchgate.net/publication/352101647_Adversarial_Collaboration_The_Next_Science_Reform (Accessed: 12 May 2026).

Clausing, K. A. (2012) 'Who Pays the Corporate Tax in a Global Economy?' *National Tax Journal*, 66(1). Available at: https://papers.ssrn.com/abstract=2213581 (Accessed: 22 February 2025).

Cobham, A. and Sumner, A. (2014) 'Is Inequality all about the Tails?: The Palma Measure of Income Inequality', *Significance*, 11(1), pp. 10–13. Available at: https://doi.org/10.1111/j.1740-9713.2014.00718.x

Common Sense Policy Group (2024a) *Act Now: A Vision for a Better Future and a New Social Contract*. Manchester: Manchester University Press.

Common Sense Policy Group (2024b) *Spend to Save Britain: A Common Sense Approach to the 2024 Budget*. Newcastle upon Tyne: Northumbria University.

Common Sense Policy Group (2025a) *Basic Income: The Policy That Changes Everything*. Bristol: Policy Press.

Common Sense Policy Group (2025b) *Data Science*. Newcastle: Common Sense Policy Group. Available at: https://commonsense.northumbria.ac.uk/tools-and-training/data-science/ (Accessed: 29 November 2025).

Cooper, K. and Stewart, K. (2021) 'Does Household Income Affect Children's Outcomes? A Systematic Review of the Evidence', *Child Indicators Research*, 14(3), pp. 981–1005. Available at: https://doi.org/10.1007/s12187-020-09782-0

Corbetta, P. (2003) 'Sampling', in Piergiorgio Corbetta (ed.) *Social Research: Theory, Methods and Techniques*. London: SAGE Publications, pp. 210–231. Available at: https://doi.org/10.4135/9781849209922

Costello, T. H., Clark, C. J. and Tetlock, P. E. (2022) 'Shoring Up the Shaky Psychological Foundations of a Micro-Economic Model of Ideology: Adversarial Collaboration Solutions', *Psychological Inquiry*, 33(2), pp. 88–94. Available at: https://doi.org/10.1080/1047840X.2022.2065130

Cowan, R. (2020) *Universal Basic Income*. 13, 682, c.74WH. Westminster: House of Commons Library. Available at: https://hansard.parliament.uk/commons /2020-10-13showNoDebateMessage=True (Accessed: 6 May 2025).

Crawford, I., Keen, M. and Smith, S. (2010) *Dimensions of Tax Design: Value Added Tax and Excises, Institute for Fiscal Studies*. Oxford: Oxford University Press. Available at: https://ifs.org.uk/books/value-added-tax-and-excises (Accessed: 18 October 2023).

Creedy, J. (2003) *Survey Reweighting for Tax Microsimulation Modelling*. Treasury Working Paper Series [preprint]. Available at: https://ideas.repec.org//p/nzt/nztwps/03-17.html (Accessed: 22 February 2025).

Crerar, P. (2023) 'Rachel Reeves Rules Out Wealth Tax If Labour Wins Next Election', *The Guardian*. Available at: https://www.theguardian.com/politics /2023/aug/27/rachel-reeves-rules-out-wealth-tax-if-labour-wins-next-election (Accessed: 19 May 2026).

Crewe, I. and King, A. (1995a) 'Of Merger and a Dead Parrot', in I. Crewe and A. King (eds) *SDP: The Birth, Life and Death of the Social Democratic Party*. Oxford: Oxford University Press, pp. 411–440. Available at: https://doi.org/10 .1093/oso/9780198280507.003.0021

Crewe, I. and King, A. (1995b) 'Who Was to Blame?', in I. Crewe and A. King (eds) *SDP: The Birth, Life and Death of the Social Democratic Party*. Oxford: Oxford University Press, pp. 441–452. Available at: https://doi.org/10.1093/oso /9780198280507.003.0022

Davillas, A., Jones, A. M. and Benzeval, M. (2019) 'The Income-Health Gradient: Evidence From Self-Reported Health and Biomarkers in Understanding Society', in Mike Tsionas (ed.) *Panel Data Econometrics*. London: Elsevier, pp. 709–741. Available at: https://doi.org/10.1016/B978-0-12-815859-3.00022-6

Davis, A. *et al.* (2022) *A Minimum Income Standard for the United Kingdom in 2022*. York: JRF. Available at: https://www.jrf.org.uk/report/minimum-income -standard-uk-2022 (Accessed: 23 June 2023).

De Agostini, P. and Hudson, N. (2019) *Child Poverty in Scotland: Forecasting the Impact of Policy Options*. Hollyrood: Scottish Government. Available at: https://sp-bpr-en-prod-cdnep.azureedge.net/published/2019/4/9/Child-poverty-in -Scotland--forecasting-the-impact-of-policy-options/SB%2019-18.pdf.

Deaton, A. (2019) *The Analysis of Household Surveys : A Microeconometric Approach to Development Policy*. Washington, DC: World Bank. Available at: https://documents.worldbank.org/en/publication/documents-reports/documentdetail/en/593871468777303124 (Accessed: 19 February 2025).

Degerman, D. *et al.* (2024) 'After Nudging: the Ethical Challenge of Post-Pandemic Policymaking in the UK', *Humanities and Social Sciences Communications*, 11(1), pp. 1–9. Available at: https://doi.org/10.1057/s41599-024-02980-z

Department for Business, Energy & Industrial Strategy (2019) *Fuel Poverty Trends 2019*. London: Department for Business, Energy & Industrial Strategy. Available at: https://www.gov.uk/government/statistics/fuel-poverty-trends-2019 (Accessed: 12 May 2026).

Department for Business, Innovation and Skills (2016) 'New National Living Wage to Give Living Standards Boost to Over a Million Workers', *GOV.UK*. Available at: https://www.gov.uk/government/news/new-national-living-wage-to-give-living-standards-boost-to-over-a-million-workers (Accessed: 19 August 2025).

Department for Levelling Up, Housing and Communities (2022) *Levelling Up the United Kingdom: White Paper*. London: HMSO. Available at: https://www.gov.uk/government/publications/levelling-up-the-united-kingdom (Accessed: 24 April 2023).

Department for Work and Pensions (2014) *Uncertainty in Family Resources Survey-Based Analysis*. London: Department for Work and Pensions. Available at: https://www.gov.uk/government/publications/uncertainty-in-family-resources-survey-based-analysis (Accessed: 22 February 2025).

Department for Work and Pensions (2015) *Households Below Average Income Series: Quality and Methodology Information Report*. Available at: https://assets.publishing.service.gov.uk/government/uploads/system/uploads/attachment_data/file/200775/appendix_2_hbai12.pdf (Accessed: 12 May 2026).

Department for Work and Pensions (2019) *The Family Resources Survey*. Available at: http://research.dwp.gov.uk/asd/frs/ (Accessed: 16 November 2012).

Department for Work and Pensions (2024) *Households Below Average Income: An Analysis of the UK Income Distribution: FYE 1995 to FYE 2023*. London: Department for Work and Pensions. Available at: https://www.gov.uk/government/statistics/households-below-average-income-for-financial-years-ending-1995-to-2023/households-below-average-income-an-analysis-of-the-uk-income-distribution-fye-1995-to-fye-2023 (Accessed: 11 August 2024).

Department for Work and Pensions (2024a) *Family Resources Survey*. London: Department for Work and Pensions. Available at: https://www.gov.uk/government/collections/family-resources-survey--2 (Accessed: 1 January 2025).

Department for Work and Pensions (2024b) *Family Resources Survey 2022/23: Disability Data Tables*. London: GOV.UK. Available at: https://assets.publishing.service.gov.uk/media/65f0363a981227001af612bc/c4-disability.xlsx (Accessed: 22 May 2024).

Department for Work and Pensions (2025) 'Householdsbelow Average Income (HBAI) Statistics'. Available at: https://www.gov.uk/government/collections/households-below-average-income-hbai--2 (Accessed: 28 May 2026).

Department of Education (2025) *National Pupil Projections: Methodology*. Available at: https://explore-education-statistics.service.gov.uk/methodology/national-pupil-projections-methodology (Accessed: 29 October 2025).

Department of Health and Social Care (2018) *Prevention Is Better Than Cure*. Available at: https://assets.publishing.service.gov.uk/government/uploads/system/uploads/attachment_data/file/753688/Prevention_is_better_than_cure_5-11.pdf (Accessed: 10 January 2019).

Dickins, T. E. (2023) 'Inequality and Existential Threat: A Reply to "Fairness, Generosity and Conditionality in the Welfare System: The Case of UK Disability Benefits" by Elliot Johnson and Daniel Nettle', *Global Discourse: An Interdisciplinary Journal of Current Affairs*, 13(2), pp. 221–224. Available at: https://doi.org/10.1332/204378920X16067940365026

Dilnot, A. W. and Stark, G. K. (1986) 'The Poverty Trap, Tax Cuts, and the Reform of Social Security', *Fiscal Studies*, 7(1), pp. 1–10. Available at: https://doi.org/10.1111/j.1475-5890.1986.tb00410.x

Dowding, K. (2020) *It's the Government, Stupid: How Governments Blame Citizens for Their Own Policies*. Bristol: Bristol University Press.

Druckman, J. N. (2001) 'The Implications of Framing Effects for Citizen Competence', *Political Behavior*, 23(3), pp. 225–256. Available at: https://doi.org/10.1023/A:1015006907312

Drummond, M. F. *et al.* (2015) *Methods for the Economic Evaluation of Health Care Programmes*. 4th edn. Oxford: Oxford University Press.

Duclos, J.-Y. (1995) 'Modelling the Take-Up of State Support', *Journal of Public Economics*, 58(3), pp. 391–415. Available at: https://doi.org/10.1016/0047-2727(94)01484-6

Dunn, W. N. (2018) *Public Policy Analysis: An Integrated Approach*. 6th edn. New York: Routledge.

Dustmann, C., Rajah, N. and van Soest, A. (2003) 'Class Size Education and Wages', *Economic Journal*, 113(485), pp. 99–120.

Dwyer, P. *et al.* (2020) 'Work, Welfare, and Wellbeing: The Impacts of Welfare Conditionality on People with Mental Health Impairments in the UK', *Social Policy & Administration*, 54(2), pp. 311–326. Available at: https://doi.org/10.1111/spol.12560

Edelman, A., Sanders, D. and Leiserson, C. (2024) *Interactive Computational Thinking*. Cambridge, MA: MIT. Available at: https://computationalthinking.mit.edu/Fall24/ (Accessed: 21 October 2025).

ELSA (2019) *The English Longitudinal Study of Ageing (ELSA)*. ELSA. Available at: https://www.elsa-project.ac.uk.

European Commission (2011) *Questions and Answers: Value Added Tax (VAT), European Commission*.Brussels: European Commission. Available at: https://ec.europa.eu/commission/presscorner/detail/en/memo_11_874 (Accessed: 22 February 2025).

European Social Survey (2024) 'About the European Social Survey'. Available at: https://www.europeansocialsurvey.org/ (Accessed: 19 May 2026).

EuroSPRIG (2019) *Spreadsheet Mistakes: News Stories*. Brussels: EuroSPRIG. Available at: https://eusprig.org/research-info/horror-stories/ (Accessed: 28 May 2026).

Eurostat (2023) 'EU Statistics on Income and Living Conditions (EU-SILC)'. Luxembourg: Eurostat. Available at: https://ec.europa.eu/eurostat/web/microdata/european-union-statistics-on-income-and-living-conditions (Accessed: 19 May 2026).

Eurostat (2024) 'European Health Interview Survey (EHIS)'. Luxembourg: Eurostat. Available at: https://ec.europa.eu/eurostat/web/microdata/european-health-interview-survey (Accessed: 19 May 2026).

Feenberg, D. and Coutts, E. (1993) 'An Introduction to the TAXSIM Model', *Journal of Policy Analysis and Management*, 12(1), pp. 189–194. Available at: https://doi.org/10.2307/3325474

Financial Times (2024) 'Thames Water Warns Ageing Assets Pose "Risk to Public Safety"', *Financial Times*. Available at: https://www.ft.com/content/a3a68af3-3b3b-419e-a1cf-931ddd2652d9 (Accessed: 19 May 2026).

Fishburn, P. C. and Willig, R. D. (1984) 'Transfer Principles in Income Redistribution', *Journal of Public Economics*, 25(3), pp. 323–328. Available at: https://doi.org/10.1016/0047-2727(84)90059-8

Fisher, W. R. (1987) *Human Communication as Narration: Toward a Philosophy of Reason, Value, and Action*. Columbia, SC: University of South Carolina Press.

Forget, E. L. (2013) 'New Questions, New Data, Old Interventions: The Health Effects of a Guaranteed Annual Income', *Preventive Medicine*, 57(6), pp. 925–928. Available at: https://doi.org/10.1016/j.ypmed.2013.05.029

Forget, E. L. and Frankel, S. (2024) 'Flirting with a Basic Income in Canada: Were the Lessons Worth the Risk of Popular Backlash?', *International Social Security Review*, 77(1–2), pp. 67–83. Available at: https://doi.org/10.1111/issr.12354

Francis-Devine, B. (2025) 'Poverty in the UK: Statistics', *House of Commons Library*. Available at: https://commonslibrary.parliament.uk/research-briefings/sn07096/ (Accessed: 19 August 2025).

Friedman, M. (1982) *Capitalism and Freedom*. New York: Phoenix.

Fry, V. and Stark, G. (1993) *The Take-Up of Means-Tested Benefits, 1984–90*. R41. London: IFS. Available at: https://www.econstor.eu/bitstream/10419/64604/1/72044232X_ocr.pdf (Accessed: 19 May 2026).

Gibson, M., Hearty, W. and Craig, P. (2020) 'The Public Health Effects of Interventions Similar to Basic Income: A Scoping Review', *The Lancet Public Health*, 5(3), pp. e165–e176. Available at: https://doi.org/10.1016/S2468-2667(20)30005-0

Giles, C. and McCrae, J. (1995) *TAXBEN: The IFS Microsimulation Tax and Benefit Model*. Working Paper Series. London: Institute for Fiscal Studies. Available at: https://ifs.org.uk/publications/taxben-ifs-microsimulation-tax-and-benefit-model (Accessed: 11 January 2025).

Goebel, J. *et al.* (2019) 'The German Socio-Economic Panel (SOEP)', *Jahrbücher für Nationalökonomie und Statistik*, 239(2), pp. 345–360. Available at: https://doi.org/10.1515/jbnst-2018-0022

Goodman, A. and Webb, S. (1994) *For Richer, for Poorer: The Changing Distribution of Income in the United Kingdom, 1961–91*. London: IFS. Available at: https://doi.org/10.1920/co.ifs.1994.0042

Gopal, D. P. and Issa, R. (2021) 'What is Needed for Universal Basic Income?', *British Journal of General Practice*, 71(710), pp. 398–398. Available at: https://doi.org/10.3399/bjgp21X716861

Government Finance Function and HM Treasury (2022) *The Green Book (2022)*. London: TSO. Available at: https://www.gov.uk/government/publications/the-green-book-appraisal-and-evaluation-in-central-governent/the-green-book-2020 (Accessed: 5 July 2023).

Green, C. *et al.* (2014) 'Cost-Effectiveness of Collaborative Care for Depression in UK Primary Care: Economic Evaluation of a Randomised Controlled Trial (CADET)', *PLoS ONE*, 9(8), p. e104225. Available at: https://doi.org/10.1371/journal.pone.0104225

Greve, B. (2020) *Myths, Narratives and Welfare States*. New York: Edward Elgar Publishing. Available at: https://www.e-elgar.com/shop/gbp/myths-narratives-and-welfare-states-9781839107917.html (Accessed: 13 August 2025).

Guney, S., Kalafat, T. and Boysan, M. (2010) 'Dimensions of Mental Health: Life Satisfaction, Anxiety and Depression: A Preventive Mental Health Study in Ankara University Students Population', *Procedia – Social and Behavioral Sciences*, 2(2), pp. 1210–1213. Available at: https://doi.org/10.1016/j.sbspro.2010.03.174

Hainmueller, J., Hopkins, D. J. and Yamamoto, T. (2014) 'Causal Inference in Conjoint Analysis: Understanding Multidimensional Choices via Stated Preference Experiments', *Political Analysis*, 22(1), pp. 1–30. Available at: https://doi.org/10.1093/pan/mpt024

Hamilton, L. (2023) 'Amartya Sen and His Understanding of Inequality', in S. S. Jodhka and B. Rehbein (eds) *Global Handbook of Inequality*. Cham: Springer International Publishing, pp. 1–15. Available at: https://doi.org/10.1007/978-3-030-97417-6_81-2

Hamilton, L., Yorgun, M. and Wright, A. (2022) '"People Nowadays Will Take Everything They Can Get": American Perceptions of Basic Income Usage', *Journal of Policy Practice and Research*, 3(2), pp. 77–95. Available at: https://doi.org/10.1007/s42972-021-00035-0

Hardill, I., Johnson, E. A. and Johnson, M. T. (2025) 'Why Britain Needs a New Beveridge and Why Politicians Need to Defer to the Evidence', *Contemporary Social Science*, 20(5), pp. 1–14. Available at: https://doi.org/10.1080/21582041.2025.2481867

Harrop, A. and Reed, H. (2015) *Inequality 2030: Britain's Choice for Living Standards and Poverty*. London: Fabian Society. Available at: https://fabians.org.uk/wp-content/uploads/2015/02/Inequality2030-2.pdf (Accessed: 8 July 2024).

Haughton, J. and Khandker, S. R. (2009) *Handbook on Poverty and Inequality*. Washington, DC: World Bank. Available at: https://documents.worldbank.org/en/publication/documents-reports/documentdetail/488081468157174849/Handbook-on-poverty-and-inequality (Accessed: 29 January 2025).

Häusermann, S., Kurer, T. and Traber, D. (2019) 'The Politics of Trade-Offs: Studying the Dynamics of Welfare State Reform With Conjoint Experiments',

Comparative Political Studies, 52(7), pp. 1059–1095. Available at: https://doi.org/10.1177/0010414018797943

Hayek, F. (1944) *The Road to Serfdom*. London: Palgrave.

Hayek, F. (1979) *Law, Legislation and Liberty*. Chicago, IL: University of Chicago Press.

Hayek, F. (2012) *Freedom and the Economic System*. Mansfield Centre, CT: Martino Fine Books.

Head, B. W. and Alford, J. (2015) 'Wicked Problems: Implications for Public Policy and Management', *Administration & Society*, 47(6), pp. 711–739.

Health Foundation (2022) *Public Perceptions of Health and Social Care Polling*. London: Health Foundation.

Hernan, M. A. and Robins, J. M. (2024) 'Causal Inference: What If', *CRC Press Taylor & Francis Group* [preprint].

Hill, K. Q. and Leighley, J. E. (1992) 'The Policy Consequences of Class Bias in State Electorates', *American Journal of Political Science*, 36(2), p. 351. Available at: https://doi.org/10.2307/2111481

Hill, M. and Hupe, P. (2014) *Implementing Public Policy*. 3rd edn. London: Sage.

Hills, J. (2004) *Inequality and the State*. Oxford: Oxford University Press.

Hirsch, D. (2019) *A Minimum Income Standard for the United Kingdom in 2019*. York: Joseph Rowntree Foundation. Available at: https://www.jrf.org.uk/report/minimum-income-standard-uk-2019 (Accessed: 19 February 2020).

HM Revenue & Customs (HMRC) (2022) *VAT Rates on Different Goods and Services, GOV.UK*. Available at: https://www.gov.uk/guidance/rates-of-vat-on-different-goods-and-services (Accessed: 19 October 2023).

HM Treasury (2024a) *HMT Public Expenditure Statistical Analyses (PESA), GOV.UK*. Available at: https://www.gov.uk/government/collections/public-expenditure-statistical-analyses-pesa (Accessed: 1 January 2025).

HM Treasury (2024b) *Impact on Households: Distributional Analysis to Accompany Spring Budget 2024*. London: HM Treasury. Available at: https://assets.publishing.service.gov.uk/media/65e83ed008eef600115a5660/Impact_on_households_-_SB24_FINAL.pdf (Accessed: 19 May 2026).

Hochschild, J. L. (1995) *Facing Up to the American Dream*. Princeton, NJ: Princeton University Press.

Holland, S. *et al.* (2024) *Basic Income for Care Leavers in Wales Pilot Evaluation: Annual Report, 2023 to 2024*. Cardiff: Welsh Government. Available at: https://www.gov.wales/sites/default/files/statistics-and-research/2024-02/basic-income-care-leavers-wales-pilot-evaluation-annual-report-2023-2024.pdf (Accessed: 19 May 2026).

Hornikx, J. (2007) 'Is Anecdotal Evidence More Persuasive than Statistical Evidence?: A Comment on Classic Cognitive Psychological Studies', *Studies in Communication Sciences: Journal of the Swiss Association of Communication and Media Research*, 7(2), p. 151. Available at: https://doi.org/10.5169/seals-791083

Hornikx, J. (2018) 'Combining Anecdotal and Statistical Evidence in Real-Life Discourse: Comprehension and Persuasiveness', *Discourse Processes*, 55(3), pp. 324–336. Available at: https://doi.org/10.1080/0163853X.2017.1312195

Horsfield, G. (2016) *Methodology – Office for National Statistics*. London: Office for National Statistics. Available at: https://cy.ons.gov.uk/peoplepopulationandcommunity/personalandhouseholdfinances/incomeandwealth/compendium/familyspending/2015/methodology#description-of-the-survey (Accessed: 19 February 2025).

Horton, T. and Reed, H. (2010) *Where the Money Goes: How We Benefit from Public Services*. London: Trades Union Congress. Available at: https://www.tuc.org.uk/sites/default/files/extras/wherethemoneygoes.pdf (Accessed: 19 May 2026).

Howard, N. *et al.* (2024) 'Prospective Health Impacts of a Universal Basic Income: Evidence from Community Engagement in South Tyneside, United Kingdom', *International Journal of Social Determinants of Health and Health Services*, 54(4), pp. 396–404. Available at: https://doi.org/10.1177/27551938241265928.

Howell, K. (2013) 'Empiricism, Positivism and Post-Positivism', in K. E. Howell (ed.) *An Introduction to the Philosophy of Methodology*. SAGE Publications, pp. 32–54. Available at: https://doi.org/10.4135/9781473957633

Howlett, M. (2011) *Designing Public Policies: Principles and Instruments*. London: Routledge.

Howlett, M., Ramesh, M. and Perl, A. (2009) *Studying Public Policy: Policy Cycles and Policy Subsystems*. 3rd edn. Toronto: Oxford University Press.

Huber, J. D. and Ting, M. M. (2013) 'Redistribution, Pork, and Elections', *Journal of the European Economic Association*, 11(6), pp. 1382–1403. Available at: https://doi.org/10.1111/jeea.12063

Hudson, K. *et al.* (2025) 'Exploring UK Residents' Views on Substantive Education Reform: Adversarially Co-Produced Narratives Indicate Fluidity in Support', *Political Research Exchange* [preprint]. Available at: https://doi.org/10.1080/2474736X.2025.2564696

Immervoll, H. and O'Donoghue, C. (2008) 'Towards A Multi-Purpose Framework Microsimulation: Lessons From EUROMOD', *International Journal of Microsimulation*, 2(2), pp. 43–54. Available at: https://doi.org/10.34196/ijm.00016

Immervoll, H., O'Donoghue, C. and Sutherland, H. (1999) *An Introduction to Euromod*. Working Paper Series EM0/99. Colchester: University of Essex. Available at: https://www.iser.essex.ac.uk/wp-content/uploads/files/working-papers/euromod/em0-99.pdf (Accessed: 19 May 2026).

International Social Survey Programme (2024) 'International Social Survey Programme'. Available at: https://issp.org/ (Accessed: 19 May 2026).

Institute for Government (2020) *'Nudge Unit', Institute for Government*. Available at: https://www.instituteforgovernment.org.uk/article/explainer/nudge-unit (Accessed: 29 August 2025).

Institute for Social and Economic Research (2022) *UK Household Longitudinal Study Mainstage Questionnaire Wave 12, v05*. Colchester: University of Essex.

Available at: https://www.understandingsociety.ac.uk/documentation/mainstage/questionnaires (Accessed: 23 May 2023).

Institute for Social and Economic Research (2023) 'Survey Timeline', *Understanding Society*. Available at: https://www.understandingsociety.ac.uk/documentation/mainstage/survey-timeline (Accessed: 15 May 2023).

Institute for Social Research (2024) *Panel Study of Income Dynamics*. Ann Arbor, MI: University of Michigan. Available at: https://psidonline.isr.umich.edu/ (Accessed: 13 February 2026).

Institute on Taxation and Economic Policy (2024) 'ITEP Tax Microsimulation Model Overview'. Washington, DC: ITEP. Available at: https://itep.org/itep-tax-model/ (Accessed: 19 May 2026).

IPSOS (2023) *Private School Polling*. London: Ipsos. Available at: https://www.ipsos.com/sites/default/files/ct/news/documents/2023-11/ipsos-polling-private-schools-charts-2023.pdf (Accessed: 19 May 2026).

Islam, F. (2025) 'What's Behind Rachel Reeves's "Hokey Cokey" on Income Tax Rises?' Available at: https://www.bbc.co.uk/news/articles/cx2yzj6619wo (Accessed: 19 May 2026).

Jacoby, W. G. (2000) 'Issue Framing and Public Opinion on Government Spending', *American Journal of Political Science*, 44(4), pp. 750–767. Available at: https://doi.org/10.2307/2669279

Jensen, C. and Petersen, M. B. (2017) 'The Deservingness Heuristic and the Politics of Health Care', *American Journal of Political Science*, 61(1), pp. 68–83.

Johnson, E., Johnson, S. B., *et al.* (2025) 'What Support Is There in the UK for Renationalisation of Public Utilities? Evidence on Drivers and Fluidity of Support via Adversarial Narrative Co-Production', *Next Research*, p. 100615. Available at: https://doi.org/10.1016/j.nexres.2025.100615

Johnson, E., Thew, A., *et al.* (2025) 'Welfare System Is a Key Public Health Measure', *BMJ*. Available at: https://doi.org/10.1136/bmj.r1822

Johnson, E. A. *et al.* (2023a) 'Designing a Generic, Adaptive Protocol Resource for the Measurement of Health Impact in Cash Transfer Pilot and Feasibility Studies and Trials in Hgh-Income Countries', *Pilot and Feasibility Studies*, 9(1), p. 51. Available at: https://doi.org/10.1186/s40814-023-01276-4

Johnson, E. A. *et al.* (2023b) 'SP2.1 Conjoint Experiment on Welfare Scheme Preferences and Predictive Tool'. *OSF*. Available at: https://doi.org/10.17605/OSF.IO/HTSQC

Johnson, E. A. *et al.* (2024) 'Breaking the Overton Window: On the Need for Adversarial Co-Production', *Evidence & Policy*, 20(3), pp. 393–405. Available at: https://doi.org/10.1332/17442648Y2023D000000005

Johnson, E. A., Johnson, M. T. and Webber, L. (2022) 'Measuring the Health Impact of Universal Basic Income as an Upstream Intervention: Holistic Trial Design that Captures Stress Reduction is Essential', *Evidence & Policy*, 18(3), pp. 583–594. Available at: https://doi.org/10.1332/174426420X15820274674068

Johnson, E. A., Reed, H. R. and Johnson, M. T. (2023) 'Can Universal Basic Income Work for Disabled People? An Examination of Existing UK Organisational and

Academic Positions', *Disability & Society* [preprint]. Available at: https://doi.org/10.1080/09687599.2023.2233688

Johnson, M., Johnson, E. and Nettle, D. (2022) 'Are "Red Wall" Constituencies Really Opposed to Progressive Policy? Examining the Impact of Materialist Narratives for Universal Basic Income', *British Politics*, 18, pp. 104–127. Available at: https://doi.org/10.1057/s41293-022-00220-z

Johnson, M. T. (2013) *Evaluating Culture: Well-Being, Institutions and Circumstance*. London: Palgrave Macmillan. Available at: https://doi.org/10.1057/9781137313799

Johnson, M. T. *et al.* (2020) 'Mitigating Social and Economic Sources of Trauma: The Need for Universal Basic Income during the Coronavirus Pandemic', *Psychological Trauma: Theory, Research, Practice, and Policy*, 12(S1), pp. S191–S192. Available at: https://doi.org/10.1037/tra0000739

Johnson, M. T. *et al.* (2022a) 'Designing Trials of Universal Basic Income for Health Impact: Identifying Interdisciplinary Questions to Address', *Journal of Public Health*, 44(2), pp. 408–416. Available at: https://doi.org/10.1093/pubmed/fdaa255

Johnson, M. T. *et al.* (2022b) *Winning the Vote with a Universal Basic Income: Evidence from the 'Red Wall'*. London: Compass. Available at: https://www.compassonline.org.uk/publications/winning-the-vote-with-a-universal-basic-income-evidence-from-the-red-wall/ (Accessed: 26 February 2023).

Johnson, M. T. *et al.* (2023) 'Can the "Downward Spiral" of Material Conditions, Mental hHealth and Faith in Government be Stopped? Evidence from Surveys in "Red Wall" Constituencies', *The British Journal of Politics and International Relations* [preprint]. Available at: https://doi.org/10.1177/13691481221146886

Johnson, M. T. *et al.* (2025) 'Rapid Response: Welfare System is a Key Public Health Measure'. Available at: https://doi.org/10.1136/bmj.r1822

Johnson, M. T., Johnson, E. A. and Winlow, S. (2025) 'Rethinking Englishness: Deep Historical Analysis of Working-Class Forms Emphasises the Importance of Redistribution for the Left', *Routledge Open Research*, 4(6). Available at: https://doi.org/10.12688/routledgeopenres.19188.1

Johnson, P. and Stark, G. (1989) 'Ten Years of Mrs Thatcher: The Distributional Consequences', *Fiscal Studies*, 10(2), pp. 29–37. Available at: https://doi.org/10.1111/j.1475-5890.1989.tb00107.x

Johnson, P., Stark, G. and Webb, S. (1990) *Taxben2: The New IFS Tax Benefit Model*. London: Institute for Fiscal Studies.

Jones, K. C. and Burns, A. (2021) *Unit Costs of Health and Social Care 2021*. Kent: Personal Social Services Research Unit. Available at: https://doi.org/10.22024/UNIKENT/01.02.92342

Kameda, T. *et al.* (2016) 'Rawlsian Maximin Rule Operates as a Common Cognitive Anchor in Distributive Justice and Risky Decisions', *Proceedings of the National Academy of Sciences*, 113(42), pp. 11817–11822. Available at: https://doi.org/10.1073/pnas.1602641113

Kang, H. (2013) 'Appropriate Design of Research and Statistical Analyses: Observational versus Experimental Studies', *Korean Journal of Anesthesiology*, 65(2), pp. 105–107. Available at: https://doi.org/10.4097/kjae.2013.65.2.105

Kaplan, R. M. and Hays, R. D. (2022) 'Health-Related Quality of Life Measurement in Public Health', *Annual Review of Public Health*, 43(1), pp. 355–373. Available at: https://doi.org/10.1146/annurev-publhealth-052120-012811

Kay, J. (2005) 'Talk of Raising the Corporate Burden Taxes Logic', *John Kay*. Available at: https://www.johnkay.com/2005/10/25/talk-of-raising-the-corporate-burden-taxes-logic/

Kay, J. (2012) 'Fewer Ingredients Will Best Serve the VAT on Food', *John Kay*. Available at: https://www.johnkay.com/2012/04/25/fewer-ingredients-will-best-serve-the-vat-on-food/

Kay, J. A., Keen, M. J. and Morris, C. N. (1984) 'Estimating Consumption from Expenditure Data', *Journal of Public Economics*, 23(1), pp. 169–181. Available at: https://doi.org/10.1016/0047-2727(84)90071-9

Keung, A. and Bradshaw, J. (2023) *Who Are the Fuel Poor? – Post-Budget Update*. York: Social Policy Research Unit, University of York. Available at: https://cpag.org.uk/policy-and-campaigns/briefing/who-are-fuel-poor-post-budget-update (Accessed: 29 June 2023).

Kingdon, J. W. (2011) *Agendas, Alternatives, and Public Policies*. 2nd edn. (updated). Boston, MA: Longman.

Knotz, C. M. (2018) 'A Rising Workfare State? Unemployment Benefit Conditionality in 21 OECD Countries, 1980–2012', *Journal of International and Comparative Social Policy*, 34(2), pp. 91–108. Available at: https://doi.org/10.1080/21699763.2018.1472136

Kondo, N. *et al.* (2009) 'Income Inequality, Mortality, and Self-Rated Health: Meta-Analysis of Multilevel Studies', *BMJ*, 339, p. b4471. Available at: https://doi.org/10.1136/bmj.b4471

Kroenke, K., Spitzer, R. L. and Williams, J. B. W. (2001) 'The PHQ-9', *Journal of General Internal Medicine*, 16(9), pp. 606–613. Available at: https://doi.org/10.1046/j.1525-1497.2001.016009606.x

Kukathas, C. (2003) *The Liberal Archepelago*. Oxford: Oxford University Press.

Laenan, T. (2023) *The Popularity of Basic Income: Evidence from the Polls*. Cham: Palgrave Macmillan.

Lansley, S. and Reed, H. (2019) *Basic Income for All: From Desirability to Feasibility*. London: Compass. Available at: https://www.compassonline.org.uk/publications/basic-income-for-all-from-desirability-to-feasibility/ (Accessed: 4 May 2023).

Lecrubier, Y. (2001) 'The burden of depression and anxiety in general medicine', *The Journal of Clinical Psychiatry*, 62 Suppl 8, pp. 4–9; discussion 10–11.

Leeper, T. J. (2020) 'Simple Conjoint Tidying, Analysis, and Visualization', *thomasleeper.com*. Available at: https://thomasleeper.com/cregg/ (Accessed: 5 September 2024).

Leulescu, A. and Agafitei, M. (2013) *Statistical Matching: A Model-Based Approach for Data Integration*. Luxembourg: Eurostat. Available at: https://ec.europa.eu/eurostat/documents/3888793/5855821/KS-RA-13-020-EN.PDF/477dd541-92ee-4259-95d4-1c42fcf2ef34?version=1.0 (Accessed: 19 May 2026).

Lindblom, C. E. (1959) 'The Science of "Muddling Through"', *Public Administration Review*, 19(2), pp. 79–88.

Living Wage Foundation (2025) 'What Is the Real Living Wage?', *Living Wage Foundation*. Available at: https://www.livingwage.org.uk/what-real-living-wage (Accessed: 19 August 2025).

Machlup, F. (1959) 'Statics and Dynamics: Kaleidoscopic Words', *Southern Economic Journal*, 26(2), pp. 91–110. Available at: https://doi.org/10.2307/1055009

Mackinac Center (2025) 'The Overton Window', *Mackinac Center*. Available at: https://www.mackinac.org/OvertonWindow (Accessed: 17 May 2024).

MacKinnon, D. (2020) 'Regional Inequalities and the Collapse of Labour's "Red Wall"', *Soundings*, 76(76), pp. 12–25. Available at: https://doi.org/10.3898/SOUN.76.01.2020

Mackley, A. *et al.* (2025) 'Managed Migration: Completing Universal Credit Rollout'. Available at: https://commonslibrary.parliament.uk/research-briefings/cbp-9984/ (Accessed: 19 August 2025).

Maier, M. *et al.* (2022) 'No Evidence for Nudging After Adjusting for Publication Bias', *Proceedings of the National Academy of Sciences*, 119(31), p. e2200300119. Available at: https://doi.org/10.1073/pnas.2200300119

Mäkelä, P., Boaz, A. and Oliver, K. (2025) 'The Capabilities in Academic Policy Engagement (CAPE) Programme in England: A Mixed Methods Evaluation'. Available at: https://doi.org/10.1332/17442648Y2025D000000050

Mamani-Benito, O. *et al.* (2022) 'Anxiety and Depression as Predictors of Life Satisfaction during Pre-Professional Health Internships in COVID-19 Times: The Mediating Role of Psychological Well-Being', *Heliyon*, 8(10). Available at: https://doi.org/10.1016/j.heliyon.2022.e11025

Marmot, M. *et al.* (2010) *Fair Society, Healthy Lives: The Marmot Review*. London: The Marmot Review. Available at: https://www.instituteofhealthequity.org/resources-reports/fair-society-healthy-lives-the-marmot-review (Accessed: 25 August 2021).

Marmot, M. *et al.* (2020) *Health Equity in England: The Marmot Review 10 Years On*. London: Institute of Health Equity. Available at: https://www.instituteofhealthequity.org/resources-reports/marmot-review-10-years-on (Accessed: 10 September 2021).

Martinelli, L. (2017) *Exploring the Distributional and Work Incentive Effects of Plausible Illustrative Basic Income Schemes*. Bath: IPR. Available at: https://www.bath.ac.uk/publications/exploring-the-distributional-work-incentive-effects-of-plausible-illustrative-basic-income-schemes/attachments/ipr-exploring-distributional-work-incentive-effects-plausible-illustrative-basic-income-schemes.pdf (Accessed: 19 May 2026).

Martinelli, L. (2020) 'A Basic Income Trilemma: Affordability, Adequacy, and the Advantages of Radically Simplified Welfare', *Journal of Social Policy*, 49(3), pp. 461–482. Available at: https://doi.org/10.1017/S0047279419000424

Matheson, C. (2018) *Hansard*. Westminster: House of Commons. Available at: https://hansard.parliament.uk/Commons/2018-06-05showNoDebateMessage=True (Accessed: 12 August 2025).

Mathur, V. *et al.* (2025) *Basic Income for Care Leavers in Wales Pilot Evaluation: Annual Report 2024 to 2025*. 20/2025. Cardiff: Welsh Government. Available at:

https://www.gov.wales/basic-income-care-leavers-wales-pilot-evaluation-annual-report-2024-2025 (Accessed: 24 March 2025).

Mayer, S. E. (1997) *What Money Can't Buy: Family Income and Children's Life Chances*. Cambridge, MA: Harvard University Press.

McCartney, G. *et al.* (2019) 'Impact of Political Economy on Population Health: A Systematic Review of Reviews', *American Journal of Public Health*, 109(6), pp. e1–e12. Available at: https://doi.org/10.2105/AJPH.2019.305001

McGann, M. and Murphy, M. P. (2023) 'Income Support in an Eco-Social State: The Case for Participation Income', *Social Policy and Society*, 22(1), pp. 16–30. Available at: https://doi.org/10.1017/S1474746421000397

McManus, S. *et al.* (2016) *Mental Health and Wellbeing in England: Adult Psychiatric Morbidity Survey 2014*. Leeds: NHS Digital.

McNamara, S. *et al.* (2023) 'Quality-Adjusted Life Expectancy Norms for the English Population', *Value in Health*, 26(2), pp. 163–169. Available at: https://doi.org/10.1016/j.jval.2022.07.005

Meade, J. (1978) *The Structure and Reform of Direct Taxation (The Meade Report)*. London: Allen & Unwin. Available at: https://ifs.org.uk/sites/default/files/output_url_files/meade.pdf. (Accessed: 28 May 2026)

Mellers, B., Hertwig, R. and Kahneman, D. (2001) 'Do Frequency Representations Eliminate Conjunction Effects? An Exercise in Adversarial Collaboration', *Psychological Science*, 12(4), pp. 269–275. Available at: https://doi.org/10.1111/1467-9280.00350

Meltzer, A. H. and Richard, S. F. (1981) 'A Rational Theory of the Size of Government', *Journal of Political Economy*, 89(5), pp. 914–927.

Mercier, H. and Landemore, H. (2012) 'Reasoning Is for Arguing: Understanding the Successes and Failures of Deliberation', *Political Psychology*, 33(2), pp. 243–258. Available at: https://doi.org/10.1111/j.1467-9221.2012.00873.x

Mercier, H. and Sperber, D. (2011) 'Why Do Humans Reason? Arguments for an Argumentative Theory', *Behavioral and Brain Sciences*, 34(2), pp. 57–74. Available at: https://doi.org/10.1017/S0140525X10000968

Mercier, H. *et al.* (2015) 'Experts and Laymen grossly Underestimate the Benefits of Argumentation for Reasoning', *Thinking & Reasoning*, 21(3), pp. 341–355. Available at: https://doi.org/10.1080/13546783.2014.961505

Meyer, B. D., Mok, W. K. C. and Sullivan, J. X. (2015) 'Household Surveys in Crisis', *Journal of Economic Perspectives*, 29(4), pp. 199–226. Available at: https://doi.org/10.1257/jep.29.4.199

Miller, A. (2017) *A Basic Income Handbook: Universal, Unconditional, Affordable*. Edinburgh: Luath.

Morgan, S. E. *et al.* (2002) 'Stories or Statistics? Farmers' Attitudes toward Messages in an Agricultural Safety Campaign', *Journal of Agricultural Safety and Health*, 8(2), pp. 225–239. Available at: https://doi.org/10.13031/2013.8427

Morgan, S. L. and Winship, C. (2015) 'Counterfacturals and Causal Inference', *Counterfactuals and Causal Inference: Methods and Principles for Social Research*. 2nd edn. Cambridge: Cambridge University Press.

Mouffe, C. (2000) *Deliberative Democracy or Agonistic Pluralism*. Wien: Institut für Höhere Studien (IHS), Wien (Reihe Politikwissenschaft / Institut für Höhere Studien, Abt. Politikwissenschaft).

Nelson, T. E. and Kinder, D. R. (1996) 'Issue Frames and Group-Centrism in American Public Opinion', *The Journal of Politics*, 58(4), pp. 1055–1078. Available at: https://doi.org/10.2307/2960149

Nettle, A. D. (2024) 'The Changing Cost of Living Study, Part Two: The Dynamics of Poverty, Anxiety and Depression', *Daniel Nettle*. Available at: https://www.danielnettle.eu/2024/02/15/the-changing-cost-of-living-study-part-two-the-dynamics-of-poverty-anxiety-and-depression/ (Accessed: 22 November 2025).

Nettle, D. *et al.* (2021) 'Why Has the COVID-19 Pandemic Increased Support for Universal Basic Income?', *Humanities and Social Sciences Communications*, 8(1), p. 79. Available at: https://doi.org/10.1057/s41599-021-00760-7

Nettle, D., Chevallier, C., *et al.* (2023) 'Short-Term Changes in Financial Situation Have Immediate Mental Health Consequences: The Changing Cost of Living Study', *OSF*. Available at: https://doi.org/10.31234/osf.io/ntsvp

Nettle, D., Chrisp, J., *et al.* (2023) 'What do British People Want from a Welfare System? Conjoint Survey Evidence on Generosity, Conditionality, Funding, and Outcomes', *SocArXiv*. Available at: https://doi.org/10.31235/osf.io/zfnuh

Nettle, D. *et al.* (2024) 'Short-Term Changes in Financial Situation Have Immediate Mental Health Consequences: Implications for Social Policy', *Social Policy & Administration*, 59(2). Available at: https://doi.org/10.1111/spol.13065

Nettle, D. *et al.* (2025a) 'What Do British People Want From a Welfare System? Conjoint Survey Evidence on Generosity, Conditionality, Funding, and Outcomes', *Poverty and Public Policy* [preprint]. Available at: https://osf.io/zfnuh (Accessed: 17 May 2024).

Nettle, D. *et al.* (2025b) 'What Do People Want From a Welfare System? Conjoint Survey Evidence From UK Adults', *Poverty & Public Policy*, 17(2), p. e70018. Available at: https://doi.org/10.1002/pop4.70018

Nettle, D., Chevallier, C., *et al.* (2025) 'Why Is Income Volatility Associated with Poor Health? Longitudinal Evidence from the UK and France', *SSM – Population Health*, 32, p. 101869. Available at: https://doi.org/10.1016/j.ssmph.2025.101869

NHS England (2019) *The NHS Long Term Plan*. London: NHS England. Available at: https://www.longtermplan.nhs.uk/publication/nhs-long-term-plan/ (Accessed: 29 June 2023).

NICE (2012) *The Guidelines Manual: Process and Methods*. London: NICE.

NICE (2022) *NICE Health Technology Evaluations: The Manual*. London: NICE. Available at: https://www.nice.org.uk/process/pmg36/chapter/economic-evaluation-2 (Accessed: 22 October 2024).

NIHR (2025) 'Guide to Writing Policy Briefs', *NIHR PRU Behavioural and Social Sciences*. Available at: https://behscipru.nihr.ac.uk/outputs/guide-to-writing-policy-briefs/ (Accessed: 21 October 2025).

Nowok, B. G. (2016) 'Synthpop: Bespoke Creation of Synthetic Data in R', *Journal of Statistical Software* [preprint]. Available at: https://doi.org/10.18637/jss.v074.i11

Obschonka, M. *et al.* (2018) 'Fear, Populism, and the Geopolitical Landscape: The "Sleeper Effect" of Neurotic Personality Traits on Regional Voting Behavior in the 2016 Brexit and Trump Elections', *Social Psychological and Personality Science*, 9(3), pp. 285–298. Available at: https://doi.org/10.1177/1948550618755874

Office for Budget Responsibility (2025) 'Public Finances Databank 2024–25'. Available at: https://obr.uk/public-finances-databank-2024-25/ (Accessed: 19 August 2025).

Office for National Statistics (2015) 'Family Spending in the UK: Calendar Year 2014 – Chapter 3: Equivalised Income', *ONS.GOV.UK*. Available at: ncome andwealth/compendium/familyspending/2015/chapter3equivalisedincome#equ ivalisation-methodology (Accessed: 23 May 2023).

Office for National Statistics (2018) *Wealth in Great Britain Wave 5*. London: Office for National Statistics. Available at: https://www.ons.gov.uk/peoplepopulatio nandcommunity/personalandhouseholdfinances/incomeandwealth/bulletins/wea lthingreatbritainwave5/2014to2016 (Accessed: 22 February 2025).

Office for National Statistics (2019a) *Living Costs and Food Survey, 2017–2018*. UK Data Service.

Office for National Statistics (2019b) 'Wealth and Assets Survey'. *UK Data Service*. Available at: http://doi.org/10.5255/UKDA-Series-2000056

Office for National Statistics (2023) *Effects of taxes and benefits on UKhousehold income – Office for National Statistics*, *Office for National Statistics*. Available at: https://www.ons.gov.uk/peoplepopulationandcommunity/personalandhous eholdfinances/incomeandwealth/bulletins/theeffectsoftaxesandbenefitsonhouse holdincome/financialyearending2022 (Accessed: 6 August 2024).

Office for National Statistics (2025a) 'Consumer Price Inflation Time Series'. *Office for National Statistics*. Available at: https://www.ons.gov.uk/economy/inflationan dpriceindices/datasets/consumerpriceindices (Accessed: 19 August 2025).

Office for National Statistics (2025b) 'Population Estimates for the UK, England, Wales, Scotland and Northern Ireland: mid-2024'. Available at: https:// www.ons.gov.uk/peoplepopulationandcommunity/populationandmigration /populationestimates/bulletins/annualmidyearpopulationestimates/mid2024 (Accessed: 19 May 2026).

Office for National Statistics (no date) 'Uncertainty and How We Measure It for Our Surveys', *Office for National Statistics*. Available at: https://www.ons.gov.uk /methodology/methodologytopicsandstatisticalconcepts/uncertaintyandhowwe measureit (Accessed: 28 November 2025).

Office For National Statistics and Department For Environment, F. (2020) 'LCF; LCFS Living Costs and Food Survey, 2001 – Living Costs and Food Survey, 2017–2018'. *UK Data Service*. Available at: https://doi.org/10.5255/UKDA-SN -8459-3

Office for Statistics Regulation (2024) 'The Use of Official Statistics in UK Public Policy: Facilitators and Barriers', *Office for Statistics Regulation*, 21 May. Available at: https://osr.statisticsauthority.gov.uk/publication/the-use-of-official -statistics-in-uk-public-policy-facilitators-and-barriers/ (Accessed: 10 November 2025).

Ojeda, C. (2015) 'Depression and Political Participation: Depression and Political Participation', *Social Science Quarterly*, 96(5), pp. 1226–1243. Available at: https://doi.org/10.1111/ssqu.12173

Ojeda, C. and Pacheco, J. (2019) 'Health and Voting in Young Adulthood', *British Journal of Political Science*, 49(3), pp. 1163–1186. Available at: https://doi.org/10.1017/S0007123417000151

Panko, R. R. (1998) 'What We Know About Spreadsheet Errors', *Journal of Organizational and End User Computing (JOEUC)*, 10(2), pp. 15–21. Available at: https://doi.org/10.4018/joeuc.1998040102

Parker, G. (2025) 'Rachel Reeves Prepares to Lift Two-Child Benefit Cap at Budget', *Financial Times*. Available at: https://www.ft.com/content/694e641d-8637-4abb-8d9e-312dd4b7a3e4 (Accessed: 28 May 2026).

Parra-Mujica, F. *et al.* (2023) 'Understanding the Relationship between Income and Mental Health among 16- to 24-year-olds: Analysis of 10 Waves (2009–2020) of Understanding Society to Enable Modelling of Income Interventions', *PLOS ONE*, 18(2), p. e0279845. Available at: https://doi.org/10.1371/journal.pone.0279845

Penn Arts (2025) *'Adversarial Collaboration Project', Penn Arts & Sciences Adversarial Collaboration Project*. Available at: https://web.sas.upenn.edu/adcollabproject/ (Accessed: 6 May 2025).

Peters, B. G. (2019) *Institutional Theory in Political Science: The New Institutionalism*. 4th edn. Cheltenham: Edward Elgar.

Picardi, C. A. and Masick, K. D. (2014) 'Variables, Measures, and Hypotheses', in C. A. Picardi and K. D. Masick (eds) *Research Methods: Designing and Conducting Research With a Real-World Focus*. SAGE Publications, Inc, pp. 11–26. Available at: https://doi.org/10.4135/9781071984314

Pickett, K. E. and Wilkinson, R. G. (2015) 'Income Inequality and Health: A Causal Review', *Social Science & Medicine*, 128, pp. 316–326. Available at: https://doi.org/10.1016/j.socscimed.2014.12.031

Piff, P. K. *et al.* (2020) 'Shifting Attributions for Poverty Motivates Opposition to Inequality and Enhances Egalitarianism', *Nature Human Behaviour*, 4(5), pp. 496–505. Available at: https://doi.org/10.1038/s41562-020-0835-8

Piketty, T. and Saez, E. (2014) 'Inequality in the Long Run', *Science*, 344(6186), pp. 838–843. Available at: https://doi.org/10.1126/science.1251936

Polacko, M. (2022) 'The Rightward Shift and Electoral Decline of Social Democratic Parties under Increasing Inequality', *West European Politics*, 45(4), pp. 665–692. Available at: https://doi.org/10.1080/01402382.2021.1916294

Portes, J. (2018) 'Austerity Really Has Hit Poor People Hardest – The Figures Prove It', *The Guardian*. Available at: https://www.theguardian.com/commentisfree/2018/mar/14/austerity-poor-disability- george-osborne-tories?CMP=share_btn_url (Accessed: 19 May 2026).

Portes, J. and Reed, H. (2018a) *The Cumulative Impact of Tax and Welfare Reforms*. London: Equality and Human Rights Commission. Available at: https://www.equalityhumanrights.com/sites/default/files/cumulative-impact-assessment-report.pdf (Accessed: 19 May 2026).

Portes, J. and Reed, H. (2018b) *The Cumulative Impact on Living Standards of Public Spending Changes*. Research Report 120. Manchester: Equality and Human Rights Commission. Available at: https://www.equalityhumanrights.com/sites/default/files/cumulative-impact-on-living-standards-of-public-spending-changes.pdf (Accessed: 9 November 2023).

Public Health Scotland (2024) *PHS Welcomes Increase in MUP to Maintain Effectiveness*. Edinburgh: Public Health Scotland. Available at: https://publichealthscotland.scot/news/2024/september/phs-welcomes-increase-in-mup-to-maintain-effectiveness/ (Accessed: 28 November 2025).

Pudney, S. and Sutherland, H. (1994) 'How Reliable Are Microsimulation Results?: An Analysis of the Role of Sampling Error in a U.K. Tax-Benefit Model', *Journal of Public Economics*, 53(3), pp. 327–365. Available at: https://doi.org/10.1016/0047-2727(94)90030-2

Pugh, K. (2023) 'Living Costs and Food Survey QMI', *ONS.GOV.UK*. Available at: https://www.ons.gov.uk/peoplepopulationandcommunity/personalandhouseholdfinances/incomeandwealth/methodologies/livingcostsandfoodsurveyqmi

QualityMetric (2022) *SF-6D® Health Utility, Quality Metric | We Measure Health*. Available at: https://www.qualitymetric.com/health-surveys/sf-6d-health-utility/ (Accessed: 29 July 2022).

Rasinski, K. (1989) 'The Effect of Question Wording on Public Support for Government Spending', *Public Opinion Quarterly*, 53(3), pp. 388–394. Available at: https://doi.org/10.1086/269158

Rawls, J. (1971) *A Theory of Justice*. Cambridge, MA: Harvard University Press.

Reche, E., König, H.-H. and Hajek, A. (2019) 'Income, Self-Rated Health, and Morbidity. A Systematic Review of Longitudinal Studies', *International Journal of Environmental Research and Public Health*, 16(16), p. 2884. Available at: https://doi.org/10.3390/ijerph16162884

Redson, A. (2019) *Tolley's Yellow Tax Handbook 2019–20*. London: Tolley.

Reed, H. (2017) 'The Gender Impact of Austerity in the UK under the Conservative-Liberal Democrat Coalition Government, 2010–15', in BargawiH. , G. Cozzi and S. Himmelweit (eds) *Economics and Austerity in Europe*. London: Routledge, pp. 113–134. Available at: https://www.book2look.com/book/B8MS1NrmrH (Accessed: 19 August 2025).

Reed, H. (2020) 'The Distributional Impact of Tax and Social Security Reforms in the UK from 2010 to 2017', *Social Policy and Society*, 19(3), pp. 470–486. Available at: https://doi.org/10.1017/S1474746420000093

Reed, H. and Portes, J. (2014) *Understanding the Parental Employment Scenarios Necessary to Meet the 2020 Child Poverty Targets*. London: Social Mobility and Child Poverty Commission. Available at: https://assets.publishing.service.gov.uk/media/5a7eeb5940f0b62305b84015/3b_Poverty_Research_-_Final.pdf (Accessed: 8 July 2024).

Reed, H. and Portes, J. (2021) *The Impact of Public Spending Changes in Northern Ireland*. Belfast: Northern Ireland Human Rights Commission. Available at: https://nihrc.org/assets/uploads/publications/Northern-Ireland-Public-Spending-report_FULL.pdf (Accessed: 19 May 2026).

Reed, H. R. *et al.* (2023) 'Universal Basic Income is Affordable and Feasible: Evidence from UK Economic Microsimulation Modelling', *Journal of Poverty and Social Justice*, 31(1), pp. 146–162. Available at: https://doi.org/10.1332/175982721X16702368352393

Reed, H. R., Johnson, E. A., *et al.* (2024) 'Estimating the Effects of Basic Income Schemes on Mental and Physical Health among Adults Aged 18 and Above in the UK: A Microsimulation Study', *PLOS Mental Health*, 1(7), p. e0000206. Available at: https://doi.org/10.1371/journal.pmen.0000206

Reed, H. R., Nettle, D., *et al.* (2024) 'Examining the Relationship between Income and both Mental and Physical Health among Adults in the UK: Analysis of 12 Waves (2009–2022) of Understanding Society', *OSF* [preprint]. Available at: https://doi.org/10.17605/OSF.IO/SKPYB

Rincon, L. (2023) 'A Robin Hood for All: A Conjoint Experiment on Support for Basic Income', *Journal of European Public Policy*, 30(2), pp. 375–399. Available at: https://doi.org/10.1080/13501763.2021.2007983

Rincón, L., Vlandas, T. and Hiilamo, H. (2022) 'What's Not to Like? Benefit Design, Funding Structure and Support for Universal Basic Income', *Journal of European Social Policy*, 32(4), pp. 467–483. Available at: https://doi.org/10.1177/09589287211072638

Roberts, N., Bolton, P. and Wilson, S. (2025) 'Educational Attainment of Boys'. Available at: https://commonslibrary.parliament.uk/research-briefings/cdp-2024-0043/ (Accessed: 21 October 2025).

Rogers, N. T. *et al.* (2024) 'Estimated Changes in Free Sugar Consumption One Year after the UK Soft Drinks Industry Levy Came into Force: Controlled Interrupted Time Series Analysis of the National Diet and Nutrition Survey (2011–2019)', *J Epidemiol Community Health*, 78(9), pp. 578–584. Available at: https://doi.org/10.1136/jech-2023-221051

Rohaly, J., Carasso, A. and Saleem, M. (2005) *The Urban-Brookings Tax Policy Center Microsimulation Model: Documentation and Methodology for Version 0304*. Washington, DC: Urban Institute. Available at: https://www.urban.org/research/publication/urban-brookings-tax-policy-center-microsimulation-model (Accessed: 19 May 2026).

Roosma, F. and van Oorschot, W. (2019) 'Public Opinion on Basic Income: Mapping European Support for a Radical Alternative for Welfare Provision', *Journal of European Social Policy*, p. 0958928719882827. Available at: https://doi.org/10.1177/0958928719882827

Rowlingson, K., Sood, A. and Tu, T. (2021) 'Public Attitudes to a Wealth Tax: The Importance of "Capacity to Pay"', *Fiscal Studies*, 42(3–4), pp. 431–455. Available at: https://doi.org/10.1111/1475-5890.12282

Rubin, D. B. (2025) 'Estimating Causal Effects of Treatments in Randomized and Nonrandomized Studies', *ResearchGate* [preprint]. Available at: https://doi.org/10.1037/h0037350

Rudin, C. (2019) 'Stop Explaining Black Box Machine Learning Models for High Stakes Decisions and Use Interpretable Models Instead', *arXiv*. Available at: https://doi.org/10.48550/arXiv.1811.10154

Sabatier, P. A. and Jenkins-Smith, H. C. (1993) *Policy Change and Learning: An Advocacy Coalition Approach*. Boulder, CO: Westview Press.

Sabatier, P. A. and Weible, C. M. (2014) *Theories of the Policy Process*. 3rd edn. Boulder, CO: Westview Press.

Saez, E. and Zucman, G. (2019) *The Triumph of Injustice*. New York: W. W. Norton & Company. Available at: https://wwnorton.com/books/9781324002727 (Accessed: 22 February 2025).

Savage, M., Callan, T. and Walsh, J. R. (2015) 'A Profile of Financial Incentives to Work in Ireland'. Available at: https://www.tara.tcd.ie/handle/2262/75035 (Accessed: 29 July 2024).

Scheuer, F. and Slemrod, J. (2021) 'Taxing Our Wealth', *Journal of Economic Perspectives*, 35(1), pp. 207–230. Available at: https://doi.org/10.1257/jep.35.1.207

Schofield, D. J. *et al.* (2017) 'A Brief, Global History of Microsimulation Models in Health: Past Applications, Lessons Learned and Future Directions', *International Journal of Microsimulation*, 11(1), pp. 97–142. Available at: https://doi.org/10.34196/ijm.00175

Scottish Government (2021) *Food Insecurity and Poverty: Response to UN Special Rapporteur Communication*. Hollyrood: Scottish Government. Available at: https://www.gov.scot/binaries/content/documents/govscot/publications/progress-report/2021/02/scottish-government-response-un-food-insecurity-poverty/documents/food-insecurity-poverty/food-insecurity-poverty/govscot%3Adocument/food-insecurity-poverty.pdf (Accessed: 19 May 2026).

Sefton, T. (2002) *Recent Changes in the Distribution of the Social Wage*. London: Centre for Analysis of Social Exclusion, London School of Economics.

Sen, A. (1999) *Commodities and Capabilities*. New Delhi: Oxford University Press.

Shahidi, F. V. *et al.* (2019) 'The Impact of Social Assistance Programs on Population Health: A Systematic Review of Research in High-Income Countries', *BMC Public Health*, 19(1), p. 2. Available at: https://doi.org/10.1186/s12889-018-6337-1

Shapiro, I. (2002) 'Why the Poor Don't Soak the Rich', *Daedalus*, 131(1), pp. 118–128.

Shimonovich, M. *et al.* (2024) 'Causal Assessment of Income Inequality on Self-Rated Health and All-Cause Mortality: A Systematic Review and Meta-Analysis', *The Milbank Quarterly*, 102(1), pp. 141–182. Available at: https://doi.org/10.1111/1468-0009.12689

Shove, E. (2010) 'Beyond the ABC: Climate Change Policy and Theories of Social Change', *Environment and Planning A: Economy and Space*, 42(6), pp. 1273–1285. Available at: https://doi.org/10.1068/a42282

Simon, H. A. (1957) *Models of Man: Social and Rational*. New York: Wiley.

Smith, A. (1776) *An Inquiry into the Nature and Causes of the Wealth of Nations*. Online: Project Gutenberg. Available at: https://www.gutenberg.org/files/3300/3300-h/3300-h.htm (Accessed: 19 May 2026).

Smith, K. B. and Larimer, C. W. (2017) *The Public Policy Theory Primer*. 3rd edn. Boulder, CO: Westview Press.

Smith, T. W. *et al.* (2024) 'General Social Surveys, 1972–2024'. Chicago, IL: NORC at the University of Chicago. Available at: https://gss.norc.org/ (Accessed: 19 May 2026).

Soh, S.-E. *et al.* (2021) 'Measurement Properties of the 12-Item Short Form Health Survey Version 2 in Australians with Lung Cancer: A Rasch Analysis', *Health and Quality of Life Outcomes*, 19(1), p. 157. Available at: https://doi.org/10.1186/s12955-021-01794-w

Sohil, F., Sohali, M. U. and Shabbir, J. (2022) 'An Introduction to Statistical Learning with Applications in R', *Statistical Theory and Related Fields*, 6(1), p. 8. Available at: https://doi.org/10.1080/24754269.2021.1980261

Sonnega, A. *et al.* (2014) 'Cohort Profile: The Health and Retirement Study (HRS)', *International Journal of Epidemiology*, 43(2), pp. 576–585. Available at: https://doi.org/10.1093/ije/dyu067

Spitzer, R. L. *et al.* (2006) 'A Brief Measure for Assessing Generalized Anxiety Disorder: The GAD-7', *Archives of Internal Medicine*, 166(10), pp. 1092–1097. Available at: https://doi.org/10.1001/archinte.166.10.1092

Stadelmann-Steffen, I. and Dermont, C. (2020) 'Citizens' Opinions About Basic Income Proposals Compared – A Conjoint Analysis of Finland and Switzerland', *Journal of Social Policy*, 49(2), pp. 383–403. Available at: https://doi.org/10.1017/S0047279419000412

Standing, G. (2011) *The Precariat: The New Dangerous Class*. London: Bloomsbury.

Standing, G. (2020) *Battling Eight Giants: Basic Income Now*. London: I.B. Tauris.

Standing, G. (2021) *The Corruption of Capitalism: Why Rentiers Thrive and Work Does Not Pay*. Hull: Biteback.

Stark, G. (2014) 'STB2 – Web Interfaces for Scotben Using Genie', *Github*. Available at: https://github.com/grahamstark/STB2 (Accessed: 19 May 2026).

Stark, G. (2017) 'Were Indyref and Brexit Driven by the Same Factors?', *Source News*. Available at: https://sourcenews.scot/graham-stark-were-indyref-and-brexit-driven-by-the-same-factors/ (Accessed: 19 May 2026).

Stark, G. (2023a) 'Conjoint'. *Github*. Available at: https://github.com/grahamstark/ScottishTaxBenefitModel.jl/blob/master/matching/lcf_frs_matching.jl (Accessed: 19 May 2026).

Stark, G. (2023b) 'ScottishTaxBenefitModel.jl / matching / lcf_frs_matching.jl at master grahamstark/ScottishTaxBenefitModel.jl'. *Github*. Available at: https://github.com/grahamstark/ScottishTaxBenefitModel.jl/blob/master/matching/lcf_frs_matching.jl (Accessed: 29 November 2025).Stark, G. *et al.* (2025) 'The Public PolicyPreference Calculator (TriplePC): Developing a comprehensive welfare policymicrosimulation', *International Journal of Microsimulation*, 18(2), pp.79–93. Available at: https://doi.org/10.34196/ijm.00323.

Stark, G. (2024) 'Scotben – A Tax Benefit Model For Scotland', *Github*. Available at: https://github.com/grahamstark/ScottishTaxBenefitModel.jl/ (Accessed: 19 May 2026).

StataCorp (2017) 'Stata Statistical Software': College Station, TX: StataCorp LLC. Available at: https://www.stata.com/stata15/ (Accessed: 8 July 2024).

Statham, R., Parkes, H. and Gunson, R. (2021) *Securing a Living Income in Scotland: Towards a Minimum Income Guarantee*. Edinburgh: IPPR Scotland. Available at: https://www.ippr.org/articles/securing-a-living-income-in-scotland (Accessed: 29 July 2024).

Statista (2025) 'UK Food Bank Usage 2025'. *Statista*. Available at: https://www.statista.com/statistics/382695/uk-foodbank-users/ (Accessed: 22 August 2025).

Stiglitz, J. (2016) *The Revolution of Information Economics: The Past and the Future*. Washington, DC: World Bank. Available at: https://business.columbia.edu/sites/default/files-efs/imce-uploads/Joseph_Stiglitz/The%20Revolution%20of%20Information%20Economics_The%20Past%20and%20the%20Future.pdf (Accessed: 28 May 2026).

Stone, D. (2011) *The Policy Paradox*. New York: W. W. Norton & Company.

Sund, R. *et al.* (2017) 'How Voter Turnout Varies between Different Chronic Conditions? A Population-Based Register Study', *Journal of Epidemiology and Community Health*, 71(5), pp. 475–479. Available at: https://doi.org/10.1136/jech-2016-208314

Sutherland, H. and Figari, F. (2013) 'EUROMOD: The European Union Tax-Benefit Microsimulation Model', *International Journal of Microsimulation*, 6(1), pp. 4–26.

Svallfors, S. (2010) 'Public Attitudes', in F. G. Castles et al. (eds) *The Oxford Handbook of the Welfare State*. Oxford: Oxford University Press, pp. 241–251. Available at: https://doi.org/10.1093/oxfordhb/9780199579396.003.0016

Synthetic Data Vault (2022) 'Synthetic Data Vault'. *Human Data Interaction Project*. Available at: https://hdi-dai.lids.mit.edu/projects/synthetic-data-vault/ (Accessed: 19 May 2026).

Taylor-Gooby, P., Leruth, B. and Chung, (eds) (2017) *After Austerity: Welfare State Transformation in Europe after the Great Recession*. Oxford: Oxford University Press.

Tetlock, P. E. and Mitchell, G. (2009) 'Implicit Bias and Accountability Systems: What Must Organizations Do to Prevent Discrimination?', *Research in Organizational Behavior*, 29, pp. 3–38. Available at: https://doi.org/10.1016/j.riob.2009.10.002

Thaler, R. H. and Sunstein, C. R. (2008) *Nudge*. New Haven, CT: Yale University Press. Available at: https://yalebooks.yale.edu/book/9780300262285/nudge/ (Accessed: 13 August 2025).

Thatcher, M. (1975) *Let Our Children Grow Tall: Speech to the Institute of SocioEconomic Studies*. London: Institute of SocioEconomic Studies. Available at: https://www.margaretthatcher.org/document/102769 (Accessed: 16 May 2024).

The Atlantic (2016) 'Donald Trump and the Politics of Fear', *The Atlantic*. Available at: https://www.theatlantic.com/politics/archive/2016/09/donald-trump-and-the-politics-of-fear/498116/ (Accessed: 19 May 2026).

The Green Party (2025) 'Creating a Fairer, Greener Economy'. Available at: https://greenparty.org.uk/about/our-manifesto/creating-a-fairer-greener-economy/ (Accessed: 19 May 2026).

The Guardian (2023) 'Industry Backlash at Sunak's Damaging U-Turn on Northern Leg of HS2', *The Guardian*. Available at: https://www.theguardian.com/uk-news/2023/oct/04/industry-backlash-at-sunaks-damaging-u-turn-on-northern-leg-of-hs2

The Social Metrics Commission (2024) *The Social Metrics Commission – A New Measure for Poverty in the UK*. London: Social Metrics Commission. Available at: https://socialmetricscommission.org.uk/ (Accessed: 22 February 2025).

Thomson, R. M. *et al.* (2021) 'How Income Changes Affect Mental Health for Working-Age Adults: A Systematic Review and Meta-Analysis', *The Lancet*, 398, p. S4. Available at: https://doi.org/10.1016/S0140-6736(21)02547-2

Thomson, R. M. *et al.* (2022) 'How Do Income Changes Impact on Mental Health and Wellbeing for Working-Age Adults? A Systematic Review and Meta-Analysis', *The Lancet Public Health*, 7(6), pp. e515–e528. Available at: https://doi.org/10.1016/S2468-2667(22)00058-5

Thomson, R. M. *et al.* (2024) 'Short-Term Impacts of Universal Basic Income on Population Mental Health Inequalities in the UK: A Microsimulation Modelling Study', *PLOS Medicine*, 21(3), p. e1004358. Available at: https://doi.org/10.1371/journal.pmed.1004358

Tibber, M. S. *et al.* (2021) 'The Association between Income Inequality and Adult Mental Health at the Subnational Level – A Systematic Review', *Social Psychiatry and Psychiatric Epidemiology* [preprint]. Available at: https://doi.org/10.1007/s00127-021-02159-w

Torry, M. (2019) *Static Microsimulation Research on Citizen's Basic Income for the UK: A Personal Summary and Further Reflections*. EM13/19. University of Essex. Available at: https://www.iser.essex.ac.uk/wp-content/uploads/files/working-papers/euromod/em13-19.pdf (Accessed: 29 May 2026).

Trouche, E. *et al.* (2016) 'The Selective Laziness of Reasoning', *Cognitive Science*, 40(8), pp. 2122–2136. Available at: https://doi.org/10.1111/cogs.12303

Trouche, E., Sander, E. and Mercier, H. (2014) 'Arguments, More Than Confidence, Explain the Good Performance of Reasoning Groups', *Journal of Experimental Psychology: General*, 143(5), pp. 1958–1971. Available at: https://doi.org/10.1037/a0037099

Uberoi, E. and Johnston, N. (2022) *Political Disengagement in the UK: Who is Disengaged?* Westminster: House of Commons Library. Available at: https://commonslibrary.parliament.uk/research-briefings/cbp-7501/ (Accessed: 2 November 2024).

UK Government (2018) 'Data Protection', *GOV.UK*. Available at: https://www.gov.uk/data-protection (Accessed: 22 November 2025).

Centre for Microsimulation and Policy Analysis (2024) 'UKMOD'. Available at: https://www.microsimulation.ac.uk/ukmod/ (Accessed: 19 August 2025).

Understanding Society (2024) *Understanding Society: The UK Household Longitudinal Study*, *Understanding Society*. Available at: https://www.understandingsociety.ac.uk/ (Accessed: 1 January 2025).

United Nations (2000) *Classification of the Functions of Government (COFOG)*. New York: United Nations. Available at: https://unstats.un.org/unsd/classifications/Family/Detail/4 (Accessed: 19 August 2025).

United Nations Development Programme (2019) *The 2019 Global Multidimensional Poverty Index (MPI) Human Development Reports*. Geneva: United Nations Development Programme. Available at: http://hdr.undp.org/en/2019-MPI (Accessed: 19 May 2026).

University of Essex (2024) *UK Data Archive, UK Data Archive*. Available at: https://www.data-archive.ac.uk/ (Accessed: 19 August 2025).

University of Sheffield (2024a) *SF-6D & SF-6Dv2 – Calculating QALYs from the SF-36, SF-12 and the Standalone SF-6Dv2, University of Sheffield Licensing*. Available at: https://licensing.sheffield.ac.uk/product/SF-6D (Accessed: 5 September 2024).

University of Sheffield (2024b) *The SF-6D: An Internationally Adopted Measure for Valuing Health and Assessing the Cost Effectiveness of Health Care Interventions*. Available at: https://www.sheffield.ac.uk/economics/research/impact-and-knowledge-exchange/sf6d (Accessed: 16 July 2024).

US Census Bureau (2023) *Survey of Income and Program Participation (SIPP)*. Washington, DC: US Census Bureau. Available at: https://www.census.gov/sipp/ (Accessed: 19 May 2026).

US Census Bureau (2024) *Current Population Survey*. Washington, DC: US Census Bureau. Available at: https://www.census.gov/programs-surveys/cps.html (Accessed: 19 May 2026).

Vedung, E. (2017) *Public Policy and Program Evaluation*. 2nd edn. New York: Routledge.

Vilagut, G. *et al.* (2013) 'The Mental Component of the Short-Form 12 Health Survey (SF-12) as a Measure of Depressive Disorders in the General Population: Results with Three Alternative Scoring Methods', *Value in Health*, 16(4), pp. 564–573. Available at: https://doi.org/10.1016/j.jval.2013.01.006

Villadsen, A. *et al.* (2024) 'How Far Can Interventions to Increase Income Improve Adolescent Mental Health? Evidence From the UK Millennium Cohort Study and Next Steps', *Journal of Prevention and Health Promotion*, 5(1), pp. 153–181. Available at: https://doi.org/10.1177/26320770231204993

Vincent, A. G. (2025) 'Do Reform UK's Tax and Spending Plans Add Up?' *Financial Times*. Available at: https://www.ft.com/content/8b5fe097-413b-4c7e-958c-61fadae91608 (Accessed: 19 May 2026).

Walker, P. (2025) 'Keir Starmer Should Be Bold and Consider a Wealth Tax, Neil Kinnock Says', *The Guardian*. Available at: https://www.theguardian.com/politics/2025/jul/06/neil-kinnock-keir-starmer-wealth-tax (Accessed: 19 May 2026).

Ware, J. E. (2002) *How to Score Version 2 of the SF-12 Health Survey (with a Supplement Documenting Version 1)*. QualityMetric Incorporated. Available at: https://books.google.co.uk/books?id=Ft4lvgAACAAJ (Accessed: 19 May 2026).

Weimer, D. L. and Vining, A. R. (2017) *Policy Analysis: Concepts and Practice*. 6th edn. New York: Routledge.

Welsh Government (2022) 'Basic Income for Care Leavers in Wales, Pilot Announced', *GOV.WALES*. Available at: https://gov.wales/basic-income-care-leavers-wales-pilot-announced (Accessed: 22 March 2022).

Whiteford, P. (2022) 'How Generous Is the British Welfare State? Part 3: Comparing Assistance for Households', *IPR blog*, 17 November. Available at: https://blogs.bath.ac.uk/iprblog/2022/11/17/how-generous-is-the-british-welfare-state-part-3-comparing-assistance-for-households/ (Accessed: 28 May 2026).

Wickham, S. *et al.* (2020) 'Effects on Mental Health of a UK Welfare Reform, Universal Credit: A Longitudinal Controlled Study', *The Lancet Public Health*, 5(3), pp. e157–e164. Available at: https://doi.org/10.1016/S2468-2667(20)30026-8

Widerquist, K. (2017) 'The Basic Income Guarantee Experiments of the 1970s: A Quick Summary of Results – Karl Widerquist', *Widerquist.com*. Available at: https://widerquist.com/basic-income-guarantee-experiments-1970s-quick-summary-results/ (Accessed: 20 August 2025).

Wilkinson, R. G. and Pickett, K. (2010) *The Spirit Level: Why Equality Is Better for Everyone; [With a New Chapter Responding to their Critics]*. Publ. with a new postscript. London: Penguin Books.

William Lawrence, N. (2014) *Social Research Methods: Qualitative and Quantitative Approaches*. 7th edn. London: Pearson.

Wilson, H. and Finch, D. (2021) *Unemployment and Mental Health*. London: The Health Foundation. Available at: https://www.health.org.uk/publications/long-reads/unemployment-and-mental-health (Accessed: 23 May 2023).

Wispelaere, J. D. and Morales, L. (2016) 'The Stability of Basic Income: A Constitutional Solution for a Political Problem?', *Journal of Public Policy*, 36(4), pp. 521–545. Available at: https://doi.org/10.1017/S0143814X15000264

Women's Budget Group *et al.* (2017) *Intersecting Inequalities: The Impact of Austerity on Black and Minority Ethnic Women in the UK*. London: Runnymede Trust. Available at: https://wbg.org.uk/wp-content/uploads/2018/08/Intersecting-Inequalities-October-2017-Full-Report.pdf (Accessed: 8 July 2024).

Working Group on Inequalities in Health (1980) *Black Report*. London: Department of Health and Social Security. Available at: https://www.sochealth.co.uk/national-health-service/public-health-and-wellbeing/poverty-and-inequality/the-black-report-1980/black-report-foreword/ (Accessed: 2 August 2020).

World Bank (2025) *World Development Indicators*. Washington, DC: World Bank. Available at: https://databank.worldbank.org/reports.aspx?source=2&series=SI.POV.GINI&country= (Accessed: 22 February 2025).

Wren-Lewis, S. (2016) *A General Theory of Austerity*. Oxford: Oxford University. Available at: http://pinguet.free.fr/wrenlewis516.pdf (Accessed: 19 May 2026).

YouGov (2025a) *Should Private Schools Be Banned?* London: YouGov. Available at: https://yougov.co.uk/topics/politics/trackers/should-private-schools-be-banned (Accessed: 19 May 2026).

YouGov (2025b) 'Would You Support or Oppose the Government Nationalising British Steel?', *YouGov*. Available at: https://yougov.co.uk/topics/politics/survey-results/daily/2025/04/11/e7dec/1 (Accessed: 12 April 2025).

Index

EU authorised representative for GPSR:
Easy Access System Europe, Mustamäe tee 50,
10621 Tallinn, Estonia
gpsr.requests@easproject.com

www.ingramcontent.com/pod-product-compliance
Lightning Source LLC
LaVergne TN
LVHW010109050926
847404LV00029BA/317
9781807075125